The Beginning of Tomorrow

*Call to the North
Churches Working Together in Mission*

— JOHN GAUNT HUNTER —

Sacristy Press

Sacristy Press
PO Box 612, Durham, DH1 9HT

www.sacristy.co.uk

First published in 2019 by Sacristy Press, Durham

Copyright © John Gaunt Hunter 2019
The moral rights of the author have been asserted

All rights reserved, no part of this publication may be reproduced or transmitted in any form or by any means, electronic, mechanical photocopying, documentary, film or in any other format without prior written permission of the publisher.

Scripture quotations taken from the *Revised English Bible*, copyright © Cambridge University Press and Oxford University Press 1989. All rights reserved.

Every reasonable effort has been made to trace the copyright holders of material reproduced in this book, but if any have been inadvertently overlooked the publisher would be glad to hear from them.

Sacristy Limited, registered in England & Wales, number 7565667

British Library Cataloguing-in-Publication Data
A catalogue record for the book is available from the British Library

ISBN 978-1-78959-029-6

*This is to Isaac, my grandson,
Isabelle, Jessica and Arabella, my granddaughters,
and Sheila, my wife, whose patient love has
enabled this account to reach completion.*

Foreword

"The further north, the more intransigent." This pungent remark of George Andrew Beck, Roman Catholic Archbishop of Liverpool, to the author of this book sums up many of the obstacles faced by the movement they were guiding in the 1970s to bring together Christians of different traditions in order to spread the Christian gospel in the north of England. Northerners were strong-minded, sometimes priding themselves on their obstinacy, and some had their own ecclesiastical corners to defend. Yet the movement went forward under the title "Call to the North", promoting a variety of events in many localities that were designed to challenge the unchurched. In Doncaster, for example, a Postal Mission, a Town Planning Conference, and an Ecumenical Rally were sandwiched between a Bible Week and a Bible Exhibition. The whole venture was strikingly interdenominational, uniting church and chapel, Protestant and Catholic, and even attracting some Pentecostal support for a while. Its aim was not simply to hold a single mission but to change the religious culture of the North by making continuous united missionary activity a priority. The degree of success in combining Christian forces was remarkable. The co-operation between David Sheppard, Anglican Bishop of Liverpool, and Derek Worlock, Roman Catholic Archbishop of the same city, has become a celebrated episode in twentieth-century church history, but here was a similar effort to overcome the divisive legacy of the past that preceded the collaboration on Merseyside. It also took place over a much wider area than what happened in Liverpool. Call to the North broke the inherited ecclesiastical mould.

There has been no previous account of this large-scale ecumenical undertaking. Nobody is better qualified to chronicle it than John Gaunt Hunter, because he was the organizing secretary from start to finish. He expresses warm appreciation of many of the prime movers such as Donald Coggan, then Archbishop of York, but he does not hide the difficulties which they encountered – regional tensions, theological differences, institutional delays, and supremely the departure of those who, like Coggan, gave leadership to the movement. Here is a full narrative of a sustained attempt to reverse the decline in churchgoing of the previous decade. Church historians of the future may still want to stress the religious crisis of the 1960s, but they will also need to take account of enterprises such as this which resisted the decay of the faith. It may well be that other developments such as the contemporary rise of charismatic renewal were more important in stemming the tide of secularization, but Call to the North showed that churches with a traditional ethos were also capable of fresh missionary schemes. There were people of vision in the Anglican, Roman Catholic and Free Churches of the north of England. By no means all of them were intransigent.

David Bebbington
Professor of History, University of Stirling
28 February 2019

Preface

For everything its season, and for everything under heaven, its time.

Ecclesiastes 3:1 (REB)

In May 1971 the Research and Development Officer of the Archbishops' Council on Evangelism wrote from London to the Archbishop of York's office concerning an ecumenical mission in the Northern Province that had come to the notice of Lambeth. John Poulton suggested it was:

> an experiment which could then be analysed and used for a basis for further action on a national scale . . . copies of all documents could be kept so that as careful an assessment as possible becomes possible.

The Archbishop of York took this request seriously. As a result, letters and documents were kept and later, authors were commissioned to write up this project—unique in the life of the national Church, indeed of Christendom. The proposed book, however, failed to appear. "There is a time and tide for everything," Stuart Blanch commented, when he was Archbishop of York himself and asked that the story of Call to the North be told.

In 2012 David Bebbington, Professor of History at the University of Stirling, came to Cambridge to deliver the Moule Memorial Lecture on the history of evangelicalism. During the course of the lecture he spoke about the remarkable evangelistic project, Call to the North. Afterwards, discovering that I, the one-time secretary to Call to the North, was in his audience, he urged me to write about what had been an important project of ecumenical evangelism, "before all trace was lost". "The result," he said, "should be a real boon to future historians and might help our understanding of Christian mission in the past—and in the future."

I had access to some of the papers that had been stored, as well as an intimate knowledge of the movement; so perhaps that "time and tide" had now arrived, and this book is the result. It is an account of a twentieth-century visionary exercise in mission which was and remains unique. Never before nor since has there been a project of Christian mission which has encompassed not only a whole Province, but also one that has united all the traditional Christian denominations in its execution.

In presenting this picture of Call to the North (CTN) I have not avoided the tensions and struggles involved in bringing to birth an attempt to change the religious culture of a whole Province.[1] The nature of that struggle, however, has meant that no similar endeavour in mission has been attempted elsewhere in the Anglican Communion or, for that matter, in any other part of the Christian Church. This account has been written in the hope, however, that it may provide inspiration for further endeavours in this field, and material evidence for bringing future projects to birth.

The book has three parts. Part 1, "The Time is Ripe", deals with the apparent impossibility of bringing together the multitude of differing church traditions, interests, theologies, and loyalties, and describes how this was overcome. Part 2, "Thinking It Through", relates the remarkable success of the enterprise as it achieved a common endeavour in Christian witness right across the North during Holy Week and Easter 1973. Part 3, "The New Brooms", describes how attempts were finally made to try and convert this common experience into a movement of continuous united mission to the North of England. The ultimate failure of this vision as the new brooms swept it away is not avoided.

The account seeks to give credit to the vision, holiness, and sheer strength of character of those who led this remarkable mid-twentieth-century movement, described by Bishop John Howe, Executive Officer for the Anglican Communion (1969–71), as "an assembly that was unique".[2] In speaking of a proposed Northern Initiative in Evangelism in 1970, the then Bishop of Middleton, Ted Wickham, described it as "The Beginning of Tomorrow". The appositeness of the phrase is underlined by the possibility that a nadir of religious practice in England may have been reached today.[3] Thus CTN may perhaps represent the beginnings of a return to faith in England, and a return that assists our churches in their quest for unity.

The account, as presented, has been written from a mid-twentieth-century viewpoint. The 1960s were a decade regarded by many historians and missiologists as highly significant.[4] Therefore it recounts the thinking and relationships which, although obvious today, appeared impossible fifty years ago. The original flavour of the times in which this exercise in ecumenical mission took place has been maintained, and the reader is invited (as far as possible) to look at the exercise through mid-twentieth-century eyes. Endnotes, however, take account of subsequent developments.

I am grateful to the Revd Dr David Goodhew for reading the manuscript and for his comments, for the help of the Revd Dr Dick Williams of Liverpool and Dr Michael Clark of Ingleton, to the Revd Kevin Logan for proofreading and for his insights, and to my wife Dr Sheila Hunter for her unremitting encouragement.

Finally, I confess to suffering from the shortcomings associated with our common humanity. Although this account has been meticulously researched from the original documents, it remains a personal reminiscence of a vast and complicated exercise of mission. It is my hope that the account, at best, may prove an inspiration to other Christians, or at least a resource for future endeavours in this field.

John Gaunt Hunter
October 2015

Contents

Foreword iv
Preface vi

Part 1: The Time is Ripe 1
Soundings 3
How It All Started. 5
Testing for Reality. 17
The Gathering of the Clans 20
Reflection. 27
The Time is Ripe. 32
Taking Stock 43
Whether or Not to Go Forward: A Second Gathering at
    Bishopthorpe. 55
After Bishopthorpe II. 64
Where Now? 73
Preparing for Bishopthorpe III. 80
Final Decision Time: Bishopthorpe III 91

Part 2: Thinking It Through 99
Taking Things Forward 101
The Context. 106
The Think Tank. 118
Motivating and Informing the Clergy: Bishopthorpe IV 126
Articulating the Vision 132
The Trumpet Sounds 151
Clearing the Decks: Bishopthorpe V 171
All Stations Go 180

Part 3: The New Brooms **191**
Looking Forward 193
The Way Ahead... 197
Vision, Impasse, and Decline: Bishopthorpe VI & VII............ 212
Structures.. 219
The New Brooms 224

Postscript...**237**

Glossary of Names **238**
Bibliography **245**
Notes **249**

PART 1

The Time is Ripe

CHAPTER 1

Soundings

A child of its time or a child of the future?

This question is bound to be asked about a "movement" which, against all expectations either within the churches or without them, actually happened. The pioneering nature of this event, together with a sense of unpredictability, gave to those associated with its conception a sense of incredulity and apprehension. However, below this and driving it forward was also a note of Christian hope and commitment in the lives of a small group of able Christian leaders.

The apprehension sprang from the fact that such a visionary endeavour had never been attempted before. Indeed, those concerned with the movement came from traditions which for centuries had represented opposing, even competing, points of view. The commitment and hope came from the Christian faith which now united lives in a common vision. The new and unique fact about Call to the North was that those who until now had been divided in history and religion, sometimes bitterly, were proposing to join forces. This was at a time when Britain itself was engaged in combating terrorism in Northern Ireland and when property, indeed life, in England and also in Ireland was being destroyed daily before our eyes.

In Northern Ireland, Republican and Loyalist, Catholic and Protestant were locked in a savage religious and political conflict which was taking lives and destroying communities. This was a conflict that spilt over into Britain itself, wracking London with savage destruction, violence, and death, and spreading to the Midlands and the North.[5] Television coverage brought this terrorism and conflict into the living rooms of everyone, not only in the British Isles but across the world.

Surprisingly then, this was the very time that the North Country church leaders, Protestant and Catholic, chose to call their people to engage together in mission. They asked their members to study together, to walk together through the streets of their towns and villages, and to witness together to the gospel which, as they reminded their flocks, was their common heritage.

The pace of church relationships suddenly quickened. Evangelistic action in the face of a doubting world came to the fore as a focus of union, rather than doctrinal debate or social concern which had hitherto been the main, somewhat tentative, points of contact between the churches. For the first time ever in modern times, leaders and people of a historic Province were preparing to enter the front line of Christian mission together. Among many in leadership positions across the North this prospect caused unease. There were many who counselled caution. None lacked apprehension, yet few, when faced with the challenge of this opportunity, were prepared to be actively hostile. Together, despite uncertainties and doubts, this is how positive, clear-headed, and faithful leadership by a godly and prayerful ecumenical group of church leaders won the day.

This was true for all the churches. However, an example might be drawn from the Roman Catholic Church. Bishop Joseph Gray, then Auxiliary Bishop of Liverpool, an Irishman, was both conservative and very proper. He was a canon lawyer, trained at Maynooth, normally dressed in clerical black, solidly built, his pectoral cross gleaming with Catholic authority.[6] Unexpectedly, he found himself required by his Archbishop to join a group of Baptists, members of the Free Churches, and Anglicans to discuss mission. Then he found himself listening to Protestants considering apostolic witness and being expected to pray with them. This was quite the reverse of all his Catholic traditional upbringing, practice, and belief; he appeared stunned. Gray remained silent throughout the first meeting, but afterwards, once the spell was broken, he gave of his best, bursting with ideas and insights. This experience was completely new across the North in the late 1960s.

CHAPTER 2

How It All Started

The genesis of Call to the North could be attributed to a small group of laity and bishops meeting in 1968, in London, at the time of the tenth Lambeth Conference. The Conference had drawn Anglican Bishops from across the world to Church House, Westminster, where the Archbishop of Canterbury, Michael Ramsey, chaired the gathering. Church House is the administrative centre for the Church of England. Its Great Hall had served as the first meeting place for the United Nations after the Second World War, and is now the home of the General Synod of the Church of England.

The Lambeth Conference was meeting under the title, "The Renewal of the Church in Faith, in Mission, and in Unity". The conference also gave an opportunity for a number of fringe groups of bishops to pursue specialist concerns. Given that the title of the current Lambeth Conference focused on mission, it was at one such group that the idea that the Church of England should take the lead in world mission was mooted.

The occasion was over lunch at the English Speaking Union, where three bishops met with a Roman Catholic layman and one of their own clergy. The clergyman, author and historian John Pollock, had written to the Bishop of Liverpool to suggest that this Lambeth Conference might offer an opportunity for the Church of England to take the lead in mission.[7] In this he had been joined by John Todhunter, a distinguished Roman Catholic layman, who also wrote and appealed to the bishop to think in terms of a national mission, believing that "the wider the scope of a mission, the greater the likelihood of success".[8]

Stuart Blanch was the new Bishop of Liverpool and a known Evangelical. In responding to the invitation to lunch at Pollock's club to discuss the proposal, he suggested that he be joined by the Archbishop of York, Donald Coggan, and the Bishop of Coventry, Cuthbert Bardsley, as Blanch knew that both were committed to evangelism.[9] During lunch, John Todhunter suggested that the Southern Baptist evangelist Dr Billy Graham might be invited to head up such a national mission. He commented that Graham was "exceedingly effective as a preacher . . . like a Redemptorist preaching mission, only better than the best I have ever heard".[10] Both letter writers believed that for such an enterprise to be successful, bishops, both Anglican and Catholic, together with the Free Church Federal Council, would need to issue the invitation, organize the campaign, and commend it to their people. This, they suggested, might initiate a national campaign supported by all the churches.

The time, they urged, was ripe: the country appeared to be ready to listen. The Jesus Movement was capturing the ears of young people; others appeared to be searching for "the Guru", some indeed now turning to eastern religions. Moreover, the churches were experiencing dramatic change, and none more so than the Roman Catholic Church. In England and Wales, Roman Catholic membership had experienced vigorous expansion during this century. Prominent conversions together with immigration from Europe had led to strong growth and a heady optimism, when suddenly and quite unexpectedly, towards the end of the 1950s, this growth slowed and then reversed into a sharp decline. The decline now matched continental Catholicism where decline had been, as it had with English Protestantism, long-term.[11] Even overseas traditional bastions of Catholicism such as South America had, by the rise of the new Charismatic Movement, seen a falling away from the practice of the Catholic faith.

In 1962 a new Pope, John XXIII (1958–63), quite unexpectedly called an assembly of Roman Catholic bishops from across the world, the Second Vatican Council. He sought to address the alarming decline with the aim of making Catholicism fit for purpose in the twentieth century. Under his benign leadership, a door in the high and inflexible wall that had thus far surrounded the Roman Catholic Church was opened towards the Protestant churches. They were now no longer to be regarded as schismatic bodies, rejected for their heresy, but as "separated brethren".

The Church of England's position in the nation was still strong, but perilous. From the publication in 1962 of *Facts and Figures about the Church of England*,[12] it was apparent that the national church had been losing ground since the late nineteenth century, although most of the Anglican leadership appeared to overlook—or at least not publically acknowledge—this uncomfortable truth. Other statistics showed that Free Church membership had also moved into decline since the end of the First World War.

Despite this evidence of a national decline in Christian practice, the concept of all Christian people engaging in an ecumenical movement of mission was novel. Indeed, in the mid-twentieth century the suggestion of a united endeavour in mission by the Christian churches appeared to many to be both impractical and unreal; its failure, they believed, would be inevitable. Thus, once the idea from the meeting at the English Speaking Union was dropped into the episcopal pool of the Lambeth Conference, despite the bishops now discussing "The Renewal of the Church in Mission", it floated but briefly before sinking from sight. It was helped on its way by the suggestion—which acted like a lead balloon—that an American evangelist be invited to take on the campaign leadership. Although the waters closed swiftly over the suggestion, it was not before one of the younger English diocesan bishops caught a glimpse of how the idea might be developed.

How about the North?

The Bishop of Liverpool, Stuart Blanch, wondered if this vision might become a practical proposition if concentrated in a smaller area. Although hailing from the South of the country himself, he was now in Liverpool; with great sensitivity he caught the atmosphere of the ancient Province of York, united as it was by history and culture. Might such an ecumenical mission inspire the whole Northern Province, he asked himself.

Stuart Blanch came to his See in 1966 on the retirement of the much-loved Clifford Martin. Blanch was tall, gentle, and retiring, with modesty, charm, and a reputation for biblical scholarship. The new bishop demonstrated his leadership by giving vision to his people. His brilliant speaking gifts (never the same sermon twice) always offered a new insight, they were biblically based and grounded in the contemporary world, and thus he won people's hearts and minds. He had no need to direct or command; people appeared anxious to understand and to follow. Such were his voice and mastery of the English language that it was said he could read from a telephone directory and his listeners would be agog. When this was allied to an incisive idea, the experience proved convincing for many who heard.

Stuart Blanch, however, was concerned not only for the people of his Diocese of Liverpool, but also with the importance of mission for the Church of England, the national church. The Church, as he saw it, had been created for mission. Not a flash-in-the-pan campaign, which left a parish hopeful, its incumbent overwhelmed, and the world unmoved. Rather he looked to the mission of the Church's Lord, which would transform that world and make all things new. The task of the Church was not the maintenance of its structures but the proclamation of the truth of Jesus Christ.

Now it was not a commonplace for Bishops of Liverpool to receive letters about mission from Roman Catholic laypeople. Indeed, given the ecclesiastical colour of the Liverpool Diocese, John Todhunter's letter was something of a wonder. Liverpool was reputed to be one of the most evangelical, if not Protestant or Low Church, of the dioceses of the Church of England. This was a product of history and perhaps of sociology. The great Irish famine of the mid-nineteenth century led to the flight from Ireland of vast numbers of Roman Catholics, with the resulting establishment of a large Catholic settlement in the north of Liverpool. In turn, this produced its low-church mirror image in the existing local churches. This was a fact church leadership could not afford to ignore.

Liverpool, moreover, was a community with a recent history of economic deprivation and suffering. Its greyness, nevertheless, was tinged with a remarkable sense of spontaneous humour,[13] together with a love of football. Its magnificent commercial Victorian architecture, moreover, had brought it world fame.[14]

At the dawn of the twentieth century, a combination of piety and Protestant defiance had produced the largest of all English cathedrals, set on the splendid eminence of St James—a mount above the heart of the city. The great table (high altar) of the cathedral, set below a reredos of the Last Supper with its stone chair for the clergy at the north end of the table, was a visible and defiant rejection of the Roman Catholic sacrifice of the mass where the priest stood with his back to the congregation, offering the sacrifice on behalf of the faithful. It was here that Stuart Blanch was enthroned, following the Liverpool diocese's Reformed tradition, without a mitre.[15]

The nineteenth century had dealt harshly with the Church of England on Merseyside. Up to the end of the eighteenth century the church had been well placed, with a Tory Town Council, which had allowed Liverpool, perhaps better than many, to cope with the population explosion associated with the Industrial Revolution. Parish church building expanded with the growth of population. However, when the Whigs, as pillars of Dissent, gained political control and sold off the advowsons,[16] a slow decline set in as the church then failed to keep pace with the continuing swift growth of population.

Clergy, therefore, found the numbers of people in their parishes growing to levels quite beyond their capacity to serve effectively. The Revd Dr Abraham Hume, vicar of a slum parish in Vauxhall of some 13,000 people, wrote in the 1840s of a visitation he had made, house to house and court by court, as was customary in those days of Victorian piety.

> Fewer than one hundred families come to church regularly, yet these people are neither Dissenters nor Papists they are all lost sheep of the Church of England, who call themselves Protestants but should rather be called pagans.[17]

The Liverpool diocese had been created in 1880, by the detachment of the northern part of the Diocese of Chester. Since then, under a line of distinguished evangelical bishops, it had displayed immense energy. Churches had been built to serve the expanding and predominantly working-class Merseyside population. Social outreach was emphasized, but evangelism lay at the heart of many parishes. Under its first and vigorous new bishop (J. C. Ryle) the Church of England's membership on Merseyside recovered and its role in the community was revived.

However, the low-church Protestant nature of the diocese in the nineteenth century had the effect of limiting the bishop's relationships with the new Anglo-Catholic Movement. As the swift growth of Church of England membership developed, a series of Tractarian parishes were planted by wealthy supporters of the movement, to bear witness to the Catholic tradition. These, in this field of militant Protestantism, were greeted with open hostility. As a result, the early years of the diocese were not without tension. Slowly, over the years, the leadership was able to be more accommodating to the new thinking. Thus by the time Stuart Blanch arrived, it was possible for real relationships to be developed at all levels, not only within the diocese but between the separated denominations. The fires of controversy had died down and there was a new awareness between the churches of the contribution each could make to their common witness in the face of increasing secularism.[18]

A further factor making for inter-church harmony in the post-war world had been the effect of the intensive bombing during the Second World War. Whole areas of poor terraced housing towards the centre of the city of Liverpool had been destroyed. Although devastating, it had the benign effect of breaking up Catholic and Protestant ghettos, centres of traditional loyalty and mutual hostility. Their membership had now been distributed indiscriminately to the outer suburbs and to new towns. After the war the effect was further enhanced by the slum clearance programmes which moved the remains of these communities to the new towns, so producing a communal mix where ancient animosities could no longer be sustained. The old, vicious, internecine strife of the pre-war days thus became a thing of the past, but it was a memory slowly forgotten as pockets of prejudice and sectarian housing remained. This was the background against which Stuart Blanch was to prepare his initiative.

Would the bishops agree?

Following the 1968 Lambeth Conference, Stuart Blanch had to represent his diocese at the Northern Convocation of the Church of England. This body met in York and was the traditional governing institution of the Northern Province. Chaired by Archbishop Donald Coggan, this venerable gathering, dating back to AD 784, was the nearest thing the North of England has ever had to its own parliament. The Convocation meeting on 9 October 1968 now presented the Bishop of Liverpool with a useful occasion for flying an ecumenical missionary kite, one where the winds might not prove too unkindly, if indeed there was any wind at all.[19]

So with the experience of Lambeth and the enthusiasm of Todhunter and Pollock in mind, Stuart Blanch mooted the idea of "doing something together for the North". The Archbishop was encouraging as the Upper House of Bishops listened in silence. However, the general opinion was that the concept was unlikely to work. The House therefore recommended the Bishop of Liverpool should go back to his new diocese and try out the idea there. At least Merseyside was thought to provide a useful laboratory for any ecumenical experiment, however bizarre. The reputation of Liverpool as a hotbed of religious strife seemed to guarantee that the concept would be severely tested.

The Free Churches

On Merseyside relationships between the Free Churches and the Church of England in the twentieth century had generally been good, and so it was unlikely that the Bishop would find any resistance to co-operation in mission. The Free Churches had their distinctive witness, both evangelical and social, which had been demonstrated during the nineteenth century when the Dissenting Interest had flourished. Prosperous chapels had been built in the centre of the town, and later they had followed the movement of the middle classes out to the suburbs. Names like Rathbone and Roscoe became famous for Free Church benevolence, enterprise, and social concern. Quakers and Unitarians contributed to the fame of Liverpool as a city in the forefront of social research and experiment. It was a centre far ahead of its peers in this field and its pre-eminence was backed by the benefaction and generosity of the "Free Church conscience".

The evangelical side of the Free Church witness was influenced by a heavy immigration from Wales. Welsh chapels, with their fine preaching and evangelical zeal, became a feature of Liverpool. Perhaps even more important was the influence of the Irish Protestant immigrants established in the non-denominational chapels and Orange Halls which studded the Everton Heights and proclaimed, by both public demonstration and graffiti, their sturdy attachment to the Protestant Faith. It was a faith that viewed with deep suspicion anything that might smack of compromise with "the other side of the house"—Rome. Orange and Green riots in Liverpool dated back at least as far as 1819 and "The Twelfth" (12 July, the anniversary of the Battle of the Boyne) was notorious for its internecine strife.[20] This was celebrated in pre-war days with both excitement and the ferocity of sectarian warfare. The event may have been all but forgotten by the rest of England, but in Liverpool—even in post-war days—it was a boisterous occasion. "The Twelfth" drew thousands onto the streets to watch the Orange procession, a mile or more in length, with fine horses, fife bands, and open Bibles, marching through town.

However, in the 1960s the real influence and power of the Free Churches on Merseyside lay rather in the courts of the traditional churches, and in particular the Methodist Church. At this time Liverpool was blessed in having as its Methodist Chair Rex Kissack, a man of thoughtful disposition and ecumenical stature. For many years he had lived in Rome as the Representative General of the Methodist Missionary Society. Thus he came to be one of the "separated brethren" to be invited to attend Vatican II. Moreover, his position as liaison officer with the Methodist Church in Italy gave him a wide understanding of Protestant thinking in that country. His own church was within sight and sound of the papal apartments, which led John XXIII to comment, when Rex was introduced in 1962 by Cardinal Willebrands, "*Siamo prossimi*"—"So we are neighbours".

Now, as head of a busy and lively Methodist District spanning both sides of the Mersey, Rex was an ideal ally for Stuart Blanch. Moreover, his reputation and weight were felt far beyond Liverpool in Free Church circles. His faintly Manx tones and sparse white hair were well known, not only in Methodism but in Anglican and—to a lesser extent—in English Catholic circles. It was natural for the Bishop to turn to him in seeking to exploit the cautious initiative of Convocation. Rex was quietly enthusiastic, uncertain what would come of the idea but ready to lend his weight to its support in any exploratory talks that might take place. Much, he believed, would depend on the attitude of the Roman Catholic Church.

The Roman Catholics

In Archbishop George Andrew Beck, the Roman Catholic Church had placed one of its finest servants on Merseyside. Liverpool was the most populous and powerful of the Catholic provinces in England and Wales.[21] However, it was also one of the most conservative, thus not the most propitious choice for ecumenism. One hundred and twenty years earlier some 250,000 Irish, at the height of the Potato Famine, had landed in Liverpool, then a community of some 300,000 Lancashire people living along the banks of the Mersey. These were men and women of a different culture, language, and religion who had been driven from their homes by hunger and who were burdened with a dislike of England. The event polarized the city.

The Catholics occupied the inner and lower wards around Vauxhall and Scotland Road and down towards the docks. They built their chapels by stealth, and in the early nineteenth century saw them burned by "Church and King" mobs. They competed desperately for work with the English working class, being exploited by people of all faiths and none as employers searched for cheap labour. They then lived out their lives in the squalor of the courts and yards of their slum ghettoes. From this unpromising start grew up a community which was to provide the Catholic Church of England and Wales with its most splendid diocese—the new Rome, as it was nicknamed by Scousers (as Liverpudlians are often called), a diocese to be crowned by one of the most significant cathedrals of English Catholicism. By the 1960s Archbishop Downey's pre-war dream of Catholics taking a lead in local politics had resulted in a Roman Catholic occupying every mayor's parlour in the boroughs of Merseyside.[22]

George Andrew Beck had become known as one of the leading educationalists of the English Catholic Church, first as Bishop of Brentwood and later of Salford. A religious of the Augustinian Order, Beck was tall and spare. The visitor, however, was struck by his apparent personal holiness, although he had a reputation for an uncompromising spirit. It was known that in 1954 he had written to *The Times* to explain why Catholics could not say the Lord's Prayer with other Christians.[23] But of course, time had not stood still, and with the Second Vatican Council beginning in 1962, a new culture had embraced the Roman

Catholic Church. Archbishop Beck, with the sense of obedience imbued by his order, accepted the new relationship with "non-Catholics". So with some courage, well knowing the powerful local conservative backlash he might face, he swiftly agreed to meet with his Anglican and Free Church counterparts.

Launching out into the deep

This was the time when the Bishop of Liverpool asked me to act as secretary for a meeting that Blanch had arranged for the church leaders of Merseyside. "Sit in the corner, say nothing, and take notes," were his instructions. As his Diocesan Missioner my role lay in encouraging mission and ecumenism in the diocese.

The meeting took place on 2 December 1968 at Bishop's Lodge, the home of Stuart Blanch, and consisted of the Anglican Bishop, the Catholic Archbishop, and the Methodist Chair, together with David Savage, who represented the Baptist Church, and Harold Springbett of the Presbyterian Church on Merseyside. Such were the times that the Archbishop only agreed to attend the meeting providing it was regarded as strictly private, indeed secret, with no mention of it to the press. Furthermore, no minutes were to be taken.

The Bishop of Liverpool opened the meeting and set the scene. He told of the letters he had received and of the meetings at Lambeth and York. He spoke of the concern which had been expressed by our local civic authorities for the future prospects of our society. "People are puzzled," he said, "and hungry for some sense of direction. The novelists point to man's terrible sense of isolation in the universe,[24] God appears remote; materialism is a great diversion, and affluence a great soporific. This is a situation where people look to the churches for a word. Because God appears to be remote, we have to reconvert people to a consciousness of the presence and activity of God." He doubted, however, if denominational appeals were any longer a valid form of mission. "Might we" he asked, "think in terms of saying something with a united voice?"

Although the atmosphere was somewhat strained at the start, the spirit of the meeting was warm. The Bishop, in his purple stock, spoke quietly and persuasively; the Archbishop (in his purple socks) looked austere and serene on the settee, fingertips together. Rex Kissack sat alongside the Archbishop, and the rest were on chairs. It was an important occasion for Rex as a Methodist who had spent a lifetime working for evangelism and unity. When answering for the Methodists, he said that "as God had raised up the Methodists to spread scriptural holiness in the land, they could hardly miss out on something like this." To which the Archbishop murmured, "Well said." Looking back later on the meeting Rex commented, "I was giving God the glory for letting me see his salvation." Such was the significance of such a meeting to church leadership in 1968.

The group, after its first meeting, decided to meet again on 14 March, and indeed again on 6 June. Each time the area of discussion widened. There was a common recognition of differences, but also a sense of unity in presenting the claims of Christ to the people of the North.[25] The churches were as one in their common task. Honesty, however, compelled the leaders to admit to the problem of the unpreparedness of their fellow church people, clerical and lay, for such an exercise. Half their people, they felt, would resent ecumenism as a form of betrayal while the other half would be alarmed at the prospect of mission.

Despite these realities, obedience to the Spirit, concern for the people of the North, and the spiritual needs of those outside their own members drove the leaders forward, almost with a sense of urgency. If the exercise they were proposing did prove trying to their own faithful, there was a suggestion that the leadership might have to think of speaking to those uncommitted to any faith over the heads of their own members. If it had been difficult to set up meetings in Liverpool, the prospect of mounting some form of campaign right across the North was even more daunting.

Those present at the Convocation in York had heard the Bishop of Durham, Ian Ramsey, respond to the Bishop of Liverpool's enquiry by suggesting that a festival rather than a conventional mission would appeal not only to church people but to many outside the life of the churches. This would be particularly true for many in the North who had a residual sympathy for and loyalty to the Christian faith. Such a festival might speak to a wide range of men and women. Stuart Blanch now relayed this idea to the Liverpool group. Rex Kissack suggested that it might take the form of an Edinburgh Festival in various cities. This would involve a large number of fringe groups and engage local dramatic, musical, and professional skills and so make use of the wealth of local talent available. Within the festival, where every local project would have some Christian emphasis, the churches themselves might be given clear opportunities to preach the gospel, each church being responsible for its own style of presentation.

The Presbyterian representative to the meetings, Harold Springbett, was, however, deeply concerned with the social and cultural implications of the gospel, underlined by the current strike at Halewood, Ford's car plant a mile or two down the road. What had we to say to labour and management, he asked, or to the unrest of our students in our universities? To the problems of inflation, and the immorality of printing money? The disaster of unemployment exercised the Bishop of Liverpool, particularly among school leavers of Kirkby, a new town. It was clear that somehow a gospel that challenged the world in its complex conflicts was not being heard, as the Church continued to proclaim the message of personal salvation. This led someone to ask, "Does the gospel of the kingdom have anything to say to the dynamics of our culture?"[26] It was a question that was to colour the next ten years and drew from the Archbishop the comment, "We are on to something alarming here."

As the new year dawned (1969), it seemed as if the Bishop of Liverpool had explored the challenge given him by Convocation in York. The idea was germinating on Merseyside even though there was little to show for the steady series of meetings that had been quietly taking place at Bishop's Lodge.

Moreover, Rex Kissack had not been idle. A letter to the Home Missions department of the Methodist Church had brought an immediate response from Leslie Davison, the author of a significant work on evangelism, *Sender and Sent*,[27] and in 1963 the first President of the British Methodist Conference to be received by a Pope. Meanwhile Rex Kissack had also taken the opportunity to talk informally with Free Church leaders in the North and to discuss their reaction to the idea of some common exercise. This had resulted in his now having a list of those Free Church leaders he considered essential for future action.

CHAPTER 3

Testing for Reality

Enter York

The pace of ecumenical discussion on mission quickened with Lent, a season which—four years later—was to see many parts of the North alive with activity. In our thinking it had been suggested that we concentrated on Holy Week,[28] when Roman Catholics and Anglicans traditionally looked for heightened spirituality, and a time often then reflected in the media.

The Rector of Liverpool, C. Edwyn Young, had planned for a number of distinguished preachers to come to his Parish Church of Our Lady and St Nicholas at the Pier Head. These were for a series of lunch-hour services during Lent 1969. The Archbishop of York, Donald Coggan, had been invited to open the series, as the Northern Primate. Stuart Blanch took this opportunity to invite the Archbishop to his home in Woolton Park following the service. Here, Bishop Blanch planned to introduce Donald Coggan to his Roman Catholic counterpart, the Archbishop of Liverpool. Such a meeting, although a commonplace later, was, at that time in the 1960s, unprecedented; Roman Catholics officially did not meet Protestants.[29] So again, only on the understanding of complete privacy could the Archbishop of Liverpool agree to be there.

The occasion also included Rex Kissack, Chair of the Methodist District, and this allowed the Bishop to summarize the gist of the talks that had taken place between church leaders in Liverpool since the last Convocation at York. Finally, the Bishop—with the prior agreement of the Catholic leader—proposed that a meeting of all northern church leaders might now be called. This, he suggested, could take place later in the year, preferably at Bishopthorpe, the home of the Archbishop of

York. At such a meeting the idea of an ecumenical Province-wide mission might be tested.

Such a mission, Stuart Blanch suggested, would be an exercise in leadership. Unlike traditional missions which were inspired and led by a group of the like-minded, whether of Evangelicals or Catholics, often with the support of a church leader, this would be led by the church leaders themselves. "We will be active in mission," he emphasized, "united in obedience to the Divine commission." The whole idea appeared to be new and surprising to Donald Coggan.

However, the Archbishop of York was impressed by the speed at which things had moved since Convocation had met. He was also impressed at the presence of the Roman Catholic Archbishop.[30] He found the readiness of the Catholic Church to row in alongside the Church of England and the Free Churches surprising, but deeply impressive. However, he was cautious. He knew his bench of bishops; he knew that some of his fellow bishops would be delighted to meet with Roman Catholics, but less happy about the presence of Free Church leaders. Others might feel at home with the Free Churches but anxious in case we were playing into the hands of Rome.

By now the afternoon was wearing on, and the Archbishop was anxious to be away, before the light failed, back across the Pennines on the long run to York. He stood with his back to the fire as he contemplated the proposal. But Rex Kissack was not yet finished. He had sent York his list of church leaders, "all of which must be wooed and won, tribal chiefs as we might see them". This was sixteen more than all the Anglican bishops of the North. The Archbishop could see the point but felt that the numbers involved would make any real consultation impossible. The proposal, he shrewdly believed, would moreover sweep in a vast number of the lukewarm and defeat the whole object of the exercise.

Donald Coggan had come to York some eight years previously, the first Evangelical to hold that primatial see. Coggan was a scholar with steel in his fibre; his pale blue eyes behind gold-rimmed spectacles could undo a muddled thinker. The Diocese of York had received him warily. Yet he had endeared himself to the people of Yorkshire and played fair in his appointments. However, he now felt unsure of this proposal from Liverpool. Coggan's whole experience of mission and evangelism had taught him that such a project needed single-minded and like-minded leadership.³¹ What, he asked himself, lay behind this strange proposal? What had the message of Rome to do with Luther, Calvin, and the Fathers of the English Reformation? Again, how was he to understand this massive invasion of Free Church leaders?

Rex Kissack, however, was adamant. All must be invited, and to lunch. Rex knew his men and the imperative need to dissipate a "history of suspicion and a psychology of inferiority/superiority complexes". If the Free Church leaders were accepted as fellow-workers in Christ, they would be enthusiastic, and he observed—quoting Henri IV of France—that "if Paris was worth a mass, then church relations in the North were worth a couple of score of Bishopthorpe lunches". In the end Donald Coggan's concern for the proclamation of the gospel and the evangelical message of the church triumphed, and he agreed to the meeting being held at his home in May.³² All the leaders of the churches in the North of England would be invited, the North being that area covered by the Northern Provinces of the Anglican and Roman Catholic Churches. The meeting would be completely open but essentially private, and we would await the outcome.

CHAPTER 4

The Gathering of the Clans

Bishopthorpe, the seat of the Archbishop of York, is an imposing residence. On a sparkling May morning in 1969, church leaders from across the Province bore down on the venerable pile, part Tudor and part Strawberry Hill Gothic. As they passed under its medieval gatehouse, there seemed to be in the minds of many a sense of history in the making. Cars purred into Bishopthorpe from over the Pennines bearing church leaders from Cumbria, Lancashire, and Cheshire. Cars came also from the ancient northern fortress, the See of Durham together with Newcastle. They came also from the South, from the great industrial centre of Sheffield, from Nottingham, and the metropolis of Leeds. Meanwhile the Roman Catholics arrived, led by the Archbishop of Liverpool, George Andrew Beck, while the Free Churches had invited Aubrey Vine, of the Free Church Federal Council in London, to be their leader.

Not all those who had been invited were able to come to York, but eleven (out of fourteen) diocesan bishops of the Church of England were there, together with ten Methodist Chairs and five Roman Catholic diocesan bishops. Three Congregationalist Moderators, two Baptist Superintendents, and two Presbyterian Moderators, together with Lieutenant-Colonel Fenwick of the Salvation Army, also took part. The Archbishop had brought his chaplain, Michael Turnbull, and the Bishop of Liverpool brought me.[33] All the major Christian denominations were represented, apart from the Pentecostals and the Quakers. Moreover, every part of the North was represented.

For Donald Coggan as Archbishop of York, 28 May 1969 was a unique occasion. Never before, since the sixteenth century, had all the Christian leaders of the North met together. At Bishopthorpe both anticipation and apprehension were guests. Church leaders are busy people, with diaries that fill up some twelve months or two years in advance. So it was with awed wonder that those who had conceived the meeting looked around the great refectory table in the Bishopthorpe dining room and silently said a *Te Deum*. The response to their initiative had fully met their hopes; it was, indeed, an answer to prayer.

Why had they come?

Some members were present because of their deep concern for mission, others because of their belief in church unity, and some purely out of loyalty to their leadership. However, many were there also from a concern for the future of the people of the North. Moreover, it was at a time when all the churches felt under pressure from falling numbers.

The choice of venue was itself important. The Church of England bishops knew it well; they would have paid at least one significant visit to Bishopthorpe before their consecration or enthronement. Roman Catholic bishops in some way felt they were not complete strangers, even if this was the first occasion their Sees' representatives had been across the threshold in force since the days of Mary I. For the leaders of the Free Churches it was a significant occasion. Many had visited privately, but never before had Free Church leaders gathered there in such numbers, even if the occasion was now described discreetly as an "informal conference".

It was, above all, a North Country occasion, and this itself had its own attraction. The North had its sense of unity springing partly from history but also from geography. It was a natural "zone humane".[34] Its bounds, however, were formed by no line on the map from Deeside to Humberside or from Crewe to Grimsby, but rather in the hearts of people who knew themselves to be Northerners.[35] The northern Provinces of the Church of England and the Roman Catholic Churches corresponded roughly to this region. They encompassed the counties of Northumberland, Durham, Cumbria, and Yorkshire, Lancashire, Cheshire, and Nottinghamshire. These made up an area, so far as the Province of York was concerned, where some fifteen million people lived. In the Roman Catholic structures, however, Nottinghamshire was in their Westminster Province. The population involved was twice the size of Sweden; it was a heartland to which North Derbyshire and indeed North Lincolnshire looked—this was the home, in pre-Conquest days, of the Angles to whom England owed its name. Sub-nationalism, or regionalism, was one of the marks of twentieth-century life, and Call to the North responded to this psychological background. Moreover, the consciousness of the North as being a distinct entity within our national life had become ever more marked in television advertising since 1955. Lord Hailsham drew attention to this in his 1976 Dimbleby Lecture, and it was something of which the churches' leaders were aware.

Of course, not everyone was enamoured by the prospect of a northern initiative. Some complained that the North was far too big. Thomas Holland, the Roman Catholic Bishop of Salford, was heard to object, "This is Christianity without the Pope." There were others who feared that this might well turn out to be an exercise in Anglican triumphalism. In the end, however, thirty-six out of the forty-five invitations actually brought both a positive attendance and ultimately a positive response when it came to a decision.

The Archbishop's purpose

As host, the Archbishop of York (Donald Coggan) presided. He opened the conference with a short review of the situation facing the churches in the North of England and the needs of the people of the North. He then asked the question:

> Can we, at a given point in time, unitedly together, with all the means at our disposal, say a word to which the world might listen?

The room at Bishopthorpe appeared crowded. All the chairs around the great dining table were occupied by the rich variety of denominations. In the centre, George Andrew Beck sat on Archbishop Coggan's right, with Aubrey Vine opposite. There was no seating protocol; those unable to find a seat at the table were crammed into window seats. Others were on spare chairs in an outer ring about the table, all of which made for informality and genuine warmth.[36] Above the gathering, portraits of long-departed prelates of York, in lawn sleeves and black scarves, gazed down from darkening varnish and gilded frames. Outside, beyond the tall Gothic windows with their ecclesiastical glass, swept the River Ouse. The atmosphere was expectant, but cautious.

Even so, the morning went badly. Few felt able to make a positive response to the Archbishop's question. Many felt that the time was not ripe, others that the churches were not ready. Indeed, some complained that the churches varied so much in their needs that a Billy Graham campaign with coaches converging, say, on Manchester, was out of the question. Others maintained that talking was no longer acceptable; the world had had enough of being lectured by the churches.

J. A. Figures, a Manchester Congregationalist, pointed to the danger of trying to organize something without knowing what we intended to say. John Moorman, then Bishop of Ripon, said in his gentle scholarly way that he was aware not only of the lack of Christianity in the world but also of the lack of Christianity within the churches. "They will oppose a mission," he said, "even if only on the grounds that they do not have enough hymn books." Ian Ramsey, Bishop of Durham, speaking with gestures, pointed to the dangers of direction from the top. "What was needed," he declared, "was local initiatives". If it might be thought, or construed, perhaps misconstrued or even imagined" that we were all to be caught up in a centrally directed crusade, he could see great difficulty at the local level.[37] Many leaders felt that what was really needed was for church people to set an example by their lives and witness that the world would note.

Then Aubrey Vine intervened. He was an able theologian who had spent many years as Professor at the Yorkshire United Theological College in Bradford. He spoke, he said, as General Secretary of the Free Church Federal Council on behalf of the Free Churches. He expressed his deep concern that the Free Churches should be recognized for what they were—truly churches of the historic Christian tradition. "Will the Anglicans and Catholics," he demanded, "come clean as to their view of the true Church?" Despite the auspiciousness of the occasion the feelings of anxiety and uncertainty were widespread.

Lunch and prayer

Lunch came as something of a relief to the small group who had been thinking and talking about these very issues over the previous twelve months, and as the meeting broke up, the group hoped the break might help repair the ravages of the morning.

Mrs Jean Coggan and her friends had laid on a fine buffet, followed by coffee. The church leaders were then able to move away and wander together in the lovely formal gardens of the house. Lunch was followed by prayers in the simple chapel, and the afternoon proved to be a better experience. The meeting began to gain cohesion and some confidence. Wonder that the meeting had ever taken place at all began to permeate the discussions. A realization slowly became apparent that this was not a meeting of church representatives discussing church unity, but a meeting of churches discussing mission.

Stuart Blanch, Bishop of Liverpool, spoke of the widespread anxiety—not restricted to Christians—about the present condition and future prospects of our society. "The church," he said, "might be expected to have a word from God which was relevant." "Does sufficient agreement exist," he asked, "for us to work together?" If we chose a time, say Holy Week 1971 or 1972, might it provide a catalyst to release the spiritual resources of our people? At the same time, Blanch suggested, it might mobilize all people of goodwill who felt deeply about the problems society experienced today. "It is a formidable enterprise," he added, "but if God is in it we have no alternative but to go ahead."

Lincoln Minshull, Methodist Chair of the Darlington District, then spoke of the need to involve the laity, and Lt-Col Fenwick picked this up, suggesting that we should seek to work through lay groups. "The Christ-transformed life comes after prayer and fasting," he maintained. Kenneth Weights, Chair of the Newcastle Methodist District, suggested that the present church leaders gathered in conference could issue a letter to all our clergy—this might be "a call" to our people—and then see what came of it.[38]

A turning point in the day, however, came with the intervention of the Archbishop of Liverpool. He observed that, following the Decree on Ecumenism of Vatican II, Catholics would have to take very seriously any project which their separated brethren in other churches undertook in the North of England. This move by George Andrew Beck, unexpected for some but welcomed by all, signalled a new dimension in ecumenical relationships between the churches of the North. To many present, born into the Church of England and growing up in the shadow of William Temple, William Paton, and J. H. Oldham, the distant alluring vision of Christians working together in mission suddenly came into focus. With these words of the Archbishop of Liverpool, unity in mission was no longer a distant dream, but a here-and-now. If Rome were prepared to join, then exciting new possibilities presented themselves. This, perhaps, was the moment when Call to the North was born.[39]

So to the future

In the end, the conference decided that no useful purpose could be found in prolonging the discussion without members first consulting their constituencies. The two Archbishops, together with Aubrey Vine and Kenneth Weights, were asked to draw up a Bishopthorpe Statement. The church leaders could then share the Statement with their clergy and people, and so return the following year with some tangible evidence of opinion. 1972 looked sufficiently far away to be a possible year for action.

The conference agreed to meet again the following year, in May 1970. If by then, following local consultations, the church leaders were able to come to a common mind, then the Archbishop of Liverpool's contribution could provide a genuine path to united action. Meanwhile, at the suggestion of Rex Kissack, the four natural regions of the North—the North East, York, the West Riding, and the North West—were asked to co-ordinate consultations between the churches in their regions.

Further, as it was important that responsibility be fully placed in the local scene, the four regions might themselves be further divided, the Free Churches suggested, into the fourteen areas represented by the Anglican dioceses. These then might form local areas for ecumenical consultation on mission. This suggestion received general, including Roman Catholic, support and so was agreed. The decision thus meant that for the purpose of any ensuing exercise, the "North" would encompass the area covered by the Northern Provinces of the Church of England and Roman Catholic Church.

The Bishop of Liverpool was asked if I might act as secretary for the conference, as this was seen to reduce any suggestion of central direction from York.[40] Stuart Blanch gladly agreed, and the conference confirmed me as its secretary. Donald Coggan then asked me to come across to York to report to him monthly and keep him up to date.[41] With this the leaders went their separate ways from Bishopthorpe to ponder (or to forget) for another year.

Reflections

Driving home through the beautiful dry-stone-walled lanes of the Yorkshire Dales, it seemed to me that a milestone had been passed in that members had at least agreed to meet again another year. Precarious as the whole exercise appeared to be, it had taken off, as it were, into ecumenical space. Now the question the leaders at Bishopthorpe would have to answer when they returned in May 1970 would be, how could a positive response be made? Many of them would be aware of a lack of vision among their own people. The leaders all presided over flocks trained to the weekly round of churchgoing and loyalty to their local church and denomination. But this, so experience suggested, had little to say to the faith of a neighbour, let alone the culture of the nation—that was, providing that culture did not overstep too blatantly the bounds of cultural mores which church people had learnt to confuse with Christianity.

There were other constraints, one being the perceived need of each leader to preserve his own territorial independence of action, a trust he had inherited. There was also the question, a grim deterrent, of how much the world outside would be prepared to listen to the Church. Many of our contemporaries accused churches of holding the highest ideals in theory but in practice appearing to be deeply involved in the ways of our contemporary culture.[42] This meant that at times, the churches were thought to deny the teachings of their Lord. Further, the time might be ripe to exploit the vision, but would there also be the will?

After the consultation the two Archbishops, together with Dr Vine and Kenneth Weights, met to produce a Bishopthorpe Statement. This was dispatched from Bishopthorpe to all church leaders, for them to consult within their own region.

CHAPTER 5

Reflection

The church leaders of the North had gone their various ways to reflect and consult. However, before relating the consequent progress of the initiative it might be helpful to reflect on certain key factors which characterized this unique experience: Call to the North.

1. The churches acted together.

Mission is the vocation of all Christians. Generally speaking, however, in England mission or evangelism had been seen primarily as the responsibility of an individual, a group called out for the purpose, or at best a denomination. Although this emphasis on mission had not been seen primarily as competitive between churches, nevertheless each church sought to sustain or increase its own membership. In this field Catholics appeared primarily to seek to recover the lapsed;[43] the Church of England saw its responsibility as being the pastoral care of the English in general; Salvationists made their vocation the evangelization of the poor; some denominations concentrated their concerns on the spiritual needs of their own members, others on social witness. But the idea of everyone combining for mission was foreign to the conventional church culture, as each church saw its own vocation to be unique.

Uniting for mission now meant acknowledging the legitimacy of alternative ways of being church. For Roman Catholics this was an enormous step, made possible only by the leadership of John XXIII and Vatican II. Until 1962, in Catholic eyes all other Christian bodies were in error: there was only one true Church, that of Rome.[44] This difficulty persisted as Call to the North developed. One of the northern Catholic bishops confessed to being very unsure of putting his name to documents which spoke of other Christian bodies as "churches", as there was only one true Church.[45] Many in the Church of England, whilst recognizing the validity of other Christian bodies, viewed them as less than socially equal. Some Free Churchmen, on the other hand, found it difficult to concede that Anglicans could be truly Christians. Call to the North transformed these assumptions and potentially made colleagues of those who, up to 1969, could not have believed it possible to work together. Uniting for mission itself made for growth in unity.[46]

A valuable spin-off to this achievement was the public display of unity it afforded. Society generally had come to accept the Church as divided, and that churches were in competition with one another. The situation in Northern Ireland was an example of this terrible division, and such a view allowed the less sympathetic to play off one denomination against another. The antagonistic divisions of Christianity had become an offence to the gospel.[47]

2. A variety of traditions was involved.

Although mission had been nominally part of the belief system of most churches, particularly since the late eighteenth century,[48] it had been assumed that to be successful, those engaging in mission had to be of a common mind doctrinally. This was as true of Evangelicals as it was of Roman Catholics.[49] However, in Call to the North, the focus was no longer on doctrinal uniformity or denominational loyalty, but on the Lord of the Church, on Jesus and his gospel, and on commending him to the people of the North. This focus rose above the wide variety of doctrinal positions and traditions.

3. The church leadership was responsible for mission.

Mission, whether overseas or at home, had traditionally been sponsored by individuals or by large missionary societies, responding to the guidance of the Holy Spirit. Within the same church or community some members, therefore, would be involved, while others felt free to concentrate on other aspects of Christian discipleship.[50] But Call to the North was unique in that mission was now accepted to be the prime responsibility of the church leaders. The consequence was dramatic; it meant that everyone was now involved in mission, there was no opting out. However, it then fell to the leadership to convince the totality of their membership of the importance of the task of mission. Moreover, leaders had to be prepared to wait until they could carry their members with them and then to act together. This was a major departure from the past, indeed a major new concept in missiological practice.[51]

Ecumenical groups were set up, as a result, designed to involve everyone, lay and clerical. Thus those calling themselves Christian in the North of England found themselves caught up with their Christian neighbours in both ecumenism and in mission. Stuart Blanch insisted, "It was an exercise in leadership." This was a prophetic insight.

4. There was an equality of authority and responsibility between the three traditions, Anglican, Free Church, and Roman Catholic.

The Northern Initiative was clearly initiated by the Church of England, but from the start the Anglican leadership sought to share its leading and responsibility with the Free Churches on the one hand and the Roman Catholics on the other. It proved easier, however, for the Catholic Archbishop to respond than for the Free Churches, with their disparate membership and leadership. Further, with the Anglican preponderance in lay numbers and the Church of England's episcopal leadership, it was not always easy to maintain equality in representation.

5. A whole Province was engaged.

Although mission had been a factor across church life, particularly since the Evangelical Revival of the late eighteenth century, there were some churches, particularly in the Church of England, where pastoral care was felt to be more appropriate. The result was that mission as an activity of church life as a whole, despite the emphasis and the commission of Jesus (Matthew 28:19), had not been consistent.

Now a situation had been engineered where a large and distinctive section of the nation would be engaged together in mission, thus giving the churches and their gospel a much higher profile in the common consciousness. As a result, it became more difficult for the general public to ignore the churches.

6. There was an emphasis on local responsibility.

Although this was a Province-wide undertaking, the leadership focused on the local church and its ecumenical aspect. In part, this sprang from a desire to dispel any resentment by congregations at a local level, who might be wary of something being imposed from the top. More importantly, it was designed to break down inherited suspicions between denominations, many of which were felt most acutely locally. Finally, it was designed to mobilize the whole church for mission at the cutting edge, that is in local communities across the North.

7. There was a new focus on the message of Jesus.

Traditionally the focus of mission had been on the great acts of God in Christ as expounded in Paul's epistles, particularly his death for our sins and resurrection for our salvation.[52] In Call to the North, this gospel was proclaimed, but it was now set within the teaching of Jesus. The incarnate Jesus had emphasized that his gospel of God, his teaching of these kingdom values, were the reason for his incarnation. Moreover, proclaiming this gospel of the kingdom remained his command for his Church (Mark 1:14,38).

There were many Christian leaders, however (so our meetings revealed), who felt unhappy or unable to engage in mission at all. They confessed that they had lost faith in "the Church having anything to say" or believed that "people had heard it all before and we would be wasting our time". The exercise therefore required a serious attempt to change our traditional apologia so as to be relevant to modern society. This was particularly pertinent as the culture of Western Europe had ceased to take the possibility of an "afterlife" seriously, the very area on which the churches had traditionally depended for relevance.[53]

8. This was an attempt to introduce continuous mission.

Call to the North, in the vision of its founders, specifically Stuart Blanch and George Andrew Beck, was designed not only to promote mission but also to change the stance of the churches of the North from maintenance to active mission. Call to the North was not thought of as a one-off project, but "to be the beginning of tomorrow", in the hope that all the churches of the North would agree to make common purpose in a stance of continually proclaiming the gospel.[54] It was their hope that it would become a movement that would permanently transform the Church of the North from a posture of survival into a church with a continuous vocation for evangelism and mission, guided by the church leadership itself.

In this the leadership had set itself a Herculean task: that of changing the religious culture of a whole region. At Bishopthorpe an attempt was being undertaken to forge a new vision, not only of Christian unity, but of a focus on evangelism. This was the supreme task of the church, as given by her Lord and Saviour.

CHAPTER 6

The Time is Ripe

If Call to the North was "a child of the future", it was because the idea of ecumenical mission had, until the mid-twentieth century, appeared impracticable, even unimaginable. However, with Vatican II the situation changed. John XXIII had transformed the situation—what had not been possible before was now within reach. Yet, although theoretically possible, the achievement still depended on churches being able to break ancient moulds and learn to work together. The Catholic–Protestant divide was still a reality, as was indeed the more ancient Catholic–Orthodox divide. Thus, although the senior leadership of this new initiative now felt a confidence that all the traditional churches were seriously involved, their Bishopthorpe Statements had to take account of these ancient divides and be designed to assist a new unity.

The remarkable decade

The 1960s, into which Call to the North was born, was a remarkable decade. It opened with the sunshine of the Macmillan post-Suez era, the time when Britons were told that they had "never had it so good", and closed with the second Wilson administration. This was when Parliament first legalized abortion and homosexuality; it saw the assassinations of President Kennedy and Martin Luther King, and it was when the first man landed on the moon.

In ecclesiastical terms, as David Hilliard has noted, it was not only a "watershed" but also a "seedbed" in modern religious history.[55] It was the decade of John Robinson's *Honest to God* and Harvey Cox's *The Secular City*.[56] It saw the issue of the "Paul Report"[57] and witnessed the "Death of God" debate. It was also the decade of the Beatles and of the Mersey sound—four North-Country boys whose songs went round the world. But these were songs with lyrics which spoke to the hearts of people and reflected current society as it was. They had a social message. Along with their contemporaries, Simon and Garfunkel, the Beatles captivated the youthful of all ages.

It was also the decade of the Jesus Movement and anticipated the 1970s musical *Godspell* and the rock opera *Jesus Christ Superstar*.[58] These gave Christians, who had become inured to decades of ridicule and challenge from the stage and music hall, the wonder of finding the words of their Saviour the subject of packed houses—even if some were shocked by this new presentation.[59] With some astonishment, Christians heard the words of Jesus coming across to a bemused world afresh, a world where uninhibited youthfulness was rejecting the staid materialistic self-interest of its elders. The newspapers reported students revolting on the university campuses.

The 1960s also had their share of industrial troubles. The seamen's strike racked the country. The plunging Pound (with a misreading of Keynes?) led to the manipulation of the money supply. So prices were forced up, and unease and anxiety troubled society. This in turn led to ever-increasing wage demands and a greater willingness for employers to surrender for the sake of peace. Chief constables throughout the decade warned, in their annual reports, against the steadily rising rates of crime. Record levels of criminality were established year after year, despite successive Home Secretaries pumping funds into fresh police equipment and extensive prison-building programmes. The drug scene was new, corruption was emerging, the *Lady Chatterley's Lover* trial alarmed the conscience of Christians, and then Profumo scandalized the House,[60] all unique events in the lifetime of most.

Moreover, people were questioning their lack of faith: Malcolm Muggeridge was challenging thoughtless agnosticism, and Ernst Friedrich Schumacher was preparing his brilliant book, *Small Is Beautiful: A Study of Economics as if People Mattered*, which found a ready response;[61] meanwhile Trevor Huddleston was leading the attack on apartheid. These were among those who recognized their own hidden fears and anxieties in face of the destruction of the world's assets, its forests, minerals, and ecological wealth. The ravages of pollution, it was suggested, were not only an eyesore but were becoming a threat to life and to the welfare of nations.

Yet the old ways, the worship of growth and the quest for money, continued to prove alluring. The property boom made fortunes for the aggressive. Its concomitants of asset stripping and the fringe banking scene lured on the bold. At the same time it taught observant unions that self-interested power and brute force were the gateway to success and to ever higher rewards unrelated to work. The time was indeed ripe. It was a time, as Bishop Butler observed of an earlier era, "of a wonderful frugality in everything which has respect to religion and extravagance in everything else".[62]

The Bishopthorpe Statement

This was the context for the Bishopthorpe Statement, produced by the two Archbishops, together with Aubrey Vine and Kenneth Weights. The statement was sent to all Church leaders across the North calling them to engage with their people in serious discussions of five questions:

1. Is the way forward in mission to be on an ecumenical basis?
2. Is it possible to set aside short periods when the Church as a whole could speak with a united voice on a single theme, though probably using different methods according to locality and tradition?
3. If the answer to the second question is "yes", could we think in terms of Holy Week 1972 as a period when the churches could speak together a word to the North?
4. Is it possible to establish continuing groups of Christians who would seek, in deep penitence, the mind of God for the renewal of the Church and the proclamation of his Word to those scarcely touched by the gospel?
5. Have you any further suggestions to make?

There was no attempt to make this any more "ecumenical" than to provide a set of questions addressed to the individual churches across the North.

Thus much of the Church of England leadership felt, in seeking to respond to the statement, that it must concentrate on its own members. As the Bishop of Durham put it, "since there is so much uncertainty in our own church, it was not judged wise to make an approach to any other."[63] The Free Church leaders and Roman Catholics felt that they were in no position to take the initiative, so they had to let the Church of England, as the largest denomination, make the first move. "Your bishop is like Woolworths," said the Methodist Rex Kissack, "while here I am running a corner shop." Gordon Wheeler, the Roman Catholic Bishop of Leeds, smiled. "It is no use me saying anything," he said; "your man has to act, and then it will be in all the papers." Both comments astonished me, since it was the first time I realized the national responsibility that was laid on the Church of England, or the significant image that the Church of England projected in the eyes of other churches.[64]

The four groups

After the Bishopthorpe meeting, the four geographical groups suggested by Rex Kissack set to work. Their members had received the Bishopthorpe Statement which had been sent to all those invited to the May 1969 Bishopthorpe conference. It was hoped by the Archbishops that this would then be followed by a sounding of local opinion, taken in the four groups throughout the North, so that the results might be considered by the leaders when they reassembled the following year. It was not an easy exercise. Time was needed to adjust to new relationships.

At the time there were many clergy and laity who would sincerely have to reject anything that did not fully represent their school of thought. Thus once the Statement was digested, there was more than a suspicion that the phrase "saying something" was not going to say what many people felt their particular school believed, and it was essential for the world to hear. Bishop Wickham, a radical Anglican, and Bishop Holland, a conservative Roman Catholic, represented a fair cross-section of opinion in the churches of the North. Both parties were then considerably stronger and more influential than they were to be later.

Conservative Evangelicals were just as suspicious as conservative Roman Catholics; radical Baptists were just as much on guard as radical Anglicans. In this divide it wasn't that the conference faced two or three points of view that might complement each other in some common enterprise. The viewpoints held were, even if covertly, mutually irreconcilable. In all innocence, not everyone was aware of this situation when this pilgrimage in ecumenical mission began.

The conservatives of either camp were convinced of the rightness of their message, something that could not be compromised or diluted in the interests of unity. Such co-operation would be, they believed, to embark on the path of betrayal, not only of their tradition but of truth itself. Radicals, on the other hand, were deeply concerned for the freedom of individuals to be themselves. They expressed their fear of any attempt by "the Church" to impose its message or to make others into Christians in its own image. Moreover, radicals expressed their anxieties at the damage done in the past by methods used to convert souls to Christ, and their alarm at the dangers of biblical fundamentalism. In the interests of truth, therefore, they believed it was necessary to oppose, contradict, and defeat all efforts of those from whom they differed.

One of the striking lessons learned in working together was that this was not just a problem for the established Church. Conservatives, Evangelicals, and radicals were to be found in all the participating churches. Moreover, the great historical divisions between churches, which had appeared so insurmountable before we first met, in the event proved easier to overcome than the divisions which now emerged within the churches themselves. Church leaders were to discover, somewhat to their surprise, that deeper fellowship was experienced across denominational boundaries than with those of their own confession with whom they differed. "I was impressed," wrote Cecil Jarvis, the Elim representative at Bishopthorpe III, "particularly with the keenness of the Anglican Evangelicals." Anglicans were surprised to discover that Archbishop Geoffrey Fisher, a Protestant, was respected and well known by Catholic laity across the North. His visit to John XXIII in 1959 had been a milestone that was treasured and honoured by English Catholics.

The North West

Four areas making up the North had been identified by the first Bishopthorpe meeting: the North West, the North East, York, and the West Riding of Yorkshire.

The North West group was the first to meet when it gathered in September 1969 at Foxhill, once the splendid home of the Pilkington (glass) family, but now a residential centre for Chester Diocese. The Bishop of Chester, the aristocrat of the Northern Province, was the host, attended by his Suffragan of Stockport. The Archbishop of Liverpool and the Bishop of Salford represented the Catholic interest. The Free Churches were there in force, with the Methodist Chairs from Manchester, Liverpool, North Lancashire, and Carlisle together with the Baptist, Congregational, Presbyterian, and Salvation Army leaders. The Bishop of Liverpool and the Suffragan Bishop of Penrith made up the group. The Anglican Church Information Office had by now become sufficiently interested in this northern initiative to arrange a representative to report to London.

The Roman Catholic Primate George Andrew Beck was clear as to what our objective must be:

> We must aim, he said, at the uncommitted, those who have separated themselves from us. We need to be positive, neither seeking to paper over cracks nor to emphasize our differences. We need to offer them the evangelical message of Christ.

The question of how this message of Christ was going to be proclaimed emerged as the next objective. Meanwhile Stuart Blanch pointed to the context: humanity today.

> He is not interested in his sins—which do not seem to be important; he is not interested in eternal life—which seems too far away; but he is profoundly interested in this life and his place in it, in what he is as an individual and in what he is to make of it.

> Our prime point of attack must therefore be, as Christ's was, this world and the lives of men [*sic!*] in it. He too spoke to a world to which God was remote – "sheep without a shepherd".

Despite the clarity of this leadership the group was not yet emotionally ready to accept this focus on unitedly meeting the needs of those alienated from us. Members were still concerned with their differences. This concern deflected the group from grasping the message which could unite the churches.

Members found themselves trying to discover how much of their own tradition, those things to which they had been taught to be loyal, might be preserved in any united message that might emerge. The Roman Catholic Bishop of Salford, perhaps the most traditional conservative thinker among us, warned us against a message that was little more than the lowest common denominator of our faith. He was clear what the Roman Catholic Church had to say. The greatest fear, however, lay not in the field of theological differences but in the rejection by the public of any message the churches might formulate. Behind this fear lay the realization and acceptance that all, including the Roman Catholics, were shedding membership. Moreover, there was an acceptance that the traditional presentation of the Christian message had lost credibility.

The alarm which erupted at Manchester—"the Church has nothing to say"—was a truth from which many took cover. Perhaps it was better to say nothing than to have what we said publicly rejected. In place of proclamation some therefore chose social benevolence, others liturgy or other forms of activity, but all appeared to be chosen in part because preaching the traditional gospel—evangelism—was no longer felt to be acceptable, let alone effective.

Manchester's contribution

The reaction of Manchester to the Bishopthorpe Statement provided a good example of this confusion. Manchester had been represented at the meeting of the North West group, and the Bishop of Manchester had then made it clear that he would support any initiative considered advisable by the Archbishop of York. However, Bishop Greer indicated that he could not speak for the diocese as a whole and certainly not for other Manchester churches. He did promise, however, to call a meeting of Manchester church leaders to review the Statement. Bishop Greer asked me to attend in order to hear Manchester's views on the subject.

The Bishop had called the meeting in October 1969 at Bishopscourt, his fine modern home, where the leaders of all the local churches had gathered in his study to discuss the Statement. The turnout was impressive: members included two Methodist Chairs together with the leaders of the Baptist, Congregational, and Presbyterian churches, the Roman Catholic Bishop Holland of Salford, and a Canon Residentiary from the Cathedral.

The Bishop, charming, gentle, but ailing and soon to retire, appeared to feel the meeting to be something of a burden. Over the past twenty-three years he had piloted his large diocese through the hectic period of post-war demolition and the growth of vast housing estates. "So," as his successor put it, "he dragged us into the twentieth century." His tall, gracious, and frail figure immediately won sympathy; his gravitas, a respectful hearing. The Bishop told us that he had talked with the Archbishop, and we should consider the Bishopthorpe Statement together. He had meanwhile put the matter to his rural deans but had to report a cool reception. No one was keen on a Billy Graham-style crusade in the Free Trade Hall. However, he would like to know how the church leaders felt.

From the discussion that followed it was clear that those present were of the same view as the rural deans. The impossibility of reaching the outsider was generally accepted. "Whatever we say today," one leader maintained, "nobody will take any notice." It was observed that, "Manchester is such a major metro-political centre that the lessons of Liverpool, where mission may have some relevance, do not here apply."[65] Other leaders maintained that they had seen all this evangelistic activity before, and it had always come to nothing. Norman Jones, however (the Baptist Superintendent), was a man of wide vision whom the North was soon to lose to the Baptist Headquarters in London. In contrast, he believed that the Church *must* speak if ever it was to retain credibility. He pointed to the disillusionment of young people with the Church's acceptance of secularism. The Church, he believed, had connived in society's enthronement of money.

In this he was supported by J. A. Figures, the Congregationalist Moderator, who pointed out that we were not here primarily to discuss method—thus "the Free Trade Hall didn't come into it." The real question, Figures suggested, was whether the Church had anything to say to the world which we could say together. Figures was one of those unusual men whose sensitivity and quality immediately captures attention. His shrewd judgment and creative insight into the sociological changes which were affecting the churches impressed themselves on his hearers. "If we cannot go about our task with enthusiasm," he told the unenthusiastic meeting, "perhaps it is better that we do not go about it at all." "People get away with blue murder," interposed Bishop Holland, "and the Church is silent." The meeting generally agreed that the laity had nothing to say to their contemporaries, and in the light of this there was nothing to be done.

This led Canon Wright of Manchester Cathedral to question whether it was necessary for the leaders to say anything. He pointed to the importance of living the Christian life. He cited the example of the movement inspired by Charles de Foucauld called "Les petits frères de Jésus". Members did not venture to speak about their faith until others, impressed by the quality of their lives, made enquiries. Adequate lay training, he believed, would be far more effective than any number of rallies in the Free Trade Hall. It was a percipient comment as the movement was to develop along these lines. In the end nothing was decided, but the Bishop agreed to write around to see if the leaders wanted to meet again. The meeting then broke up.

It appeared to the Merseyside group that if the Manchester meeting was in any way a mirror of what was happening in the rest of the North, then the next Bishopthorpe meeting would be the last. In fact, despite this gloomy start Manchester was destined to make an important contribution to the coming "Northern Initiative".

The question of what the Church ought to be saying to society, however, had underlain the meeting at Manchester. Members were conscious that it was almost impossible to proclaim the Church's message in terms that had not been used before. On the question of apologetics it was believed that long and dedicated ministries had left able people feeling defeated.

Bishop Holland's contribution summed this up: "I am sure that we are not saying our piece as effectively as we should for the good of the country."

. . . and Salford

Following the Manchester meeting Thomas Holland, the Roman Catholic Bishop of Salford, invited me to lunch at his Tudor residence, Wardley Hall. The approaches through housing estates interspersed with railway lines spoke of someone in touch with reality. A knock at the great wooden door brought a habited nun to escort me silently and swiftly across a cobbled courtyard surrounded by timbered galleries into an inner court and a heavily beamed hall to await the arrival of the Bishop.

Thomas Holland was charm itself. A Lancashire man, he made me feel very much at home. He had had a varied career which included a period with the Navy as chaplain, leading to an award of the DSO; however, Holland had a reputation for conservatism. His period with the Catholic Missionary Society had given him valuable insights into the strengths and weaknesses of the other churches of the United Kingdom. Like others of the Roman Catholic hierarchy, Holland had seen the inside of episcopacy through the eyes of a secretaryship, having been secretary to the Apostolic Delegate. He was consecrated as Coadjutor Bishop of Portsmouth in 1960, and when George Andrew Beck was moved to Liverpool, he returned to Lancashire as Bishop of Salford.

Holland discussed the Bishopthorpe Statement. I indicated that my role was to discover what Manchester might be able to do. "Saying something" did not necessarily mean the Free Trade Hall, unless Manchester itself believed it to be appropriate. Perhaps the suggestion by Norman Jones of a small study group might be the way forward. The Bishop, however, did not think that his people would be ready for that. His belief was that the Catholic Church must declare her faith freely to the world. He thought some sort of event might be possible, to take place in parallel with any Protestant initiative, but pointed out that there had been talks on uniting the Whit Friday walks but this was not proving easy.[66] He felt that the only platform he could see himself joining would be if the churches united in defeating "that evil in our midst"—the scandal of abortion.

Strangely enough, despite what appeared to be a somewhat limited area of co-operation, the genuine warmth of the Bishop was encouraging. Also significant were his kindliness and his concern that the churches should be prepared to speak to the needs of the world. "The decree on ecumenism," Holland said, "forces us to go forward."

Early responses to the Bishopthorpe Statement, however, were dogged by the recurring question of "What could the church say that would be heard by the general public?" The people had heard the traditional gospel before. The message "Christ died for sinners" had been proclaimed from pulpit and on billboard as consistently this century as in any previous time. But today the response of our contemporaries was a shrug of the shoulders, suggesting they could not see that this message had any relevance to their lives or their future. The message no longer seemed to make sense to people; indeed, it had clearly failed to meet the felt needs of the English North Country.

If the traditional message no longer made sense, then what message was to be proclaimed by Bishopthorpe? The North West group therefore suggested to the Bishop of Liverpool that he meet with a small group to explore this issue.

CHAPTER 7

Taking Stock

The North East region of the North, perhaps the most self-conscious of its identity, looked to Ian Ramsey, Bishop of Durham. Ramsey was indeed someone who went away from Bishopthorpe to ponder. Moreover, he was indeed the natural leader of a region which manifested a strong sense of independence. Ramsey himself had astonishing energy and it was widely assumed, in Church of England circles, that he would follow his namesake to Canterbury. His powerful intellect made him a magnet to many in senior positions who needed someone of outstanding ability to undertake or to contribute to some work of significance. He was a splendid example of a prelate who never lost touch with his working-class background, and these origins made him a popular and respected figure in his mining diocese. Among all the church leaders of the North, perhaps only Walker Lee, Chair of the Leeds Methodist District, could match his empathy with the common people. Ramsey was known never to refuse a request or invitation, unless a prior commitment stood in its way. He was, in fact, all too soon to be lost to the Church—it was suggested, through overwork.

The North East

Not long after Bishopthorpe, Ian Ramsey invited me to meet him at his home in Bishop Auckland. This was a residence ancient and imposing enough to rival his brother's at York. The Bishop stood before the vast fireplace of his great library, legs akimbo, hands emphasizing every point as he outlined the particular problems of the North East. "We have a long history," he said, "the legacy of Aidan, of Cuthbert, and of Oswald." Then he pointed to the depressing history of industrial boom and bust and commented, "The Jarrow Crusade is still real in the hearts and minds of our people." He went on, "We are a community hemmed in, as it were, by the Cheviot Hills in the north, the Cleveland Hills to the south, the Pennines are at our backs, and the North Sea is at our doorstep." This makes the North East a north within the North, and because of this fierce local pride a Province-wide exercise might prove difficult to promote. The North East would want to do its own thing. For this reason Bishop Ramsey welcomed the Bishopthorpe suggestion that the regions acted as individual units. The local churches working together within the region, at the same time relating to the Province as a whole, was, he believed, a possibility for the North East to consider.

Lunch was taken in a private dining room upstairs after traversing a labyrinth of venerable passages. Mrs Ramsey presided, a charming and unpretentious hostess, who still retained the speech of her Ulster homeland. The Bishop now fell to talking about the alienation of the working class in general from the life of the churches. "The North East is different," the Bishop observed, "more like the Wigan or Leigh in Lancashire that I remember from my boyhood. Not that people flock to the churches, but there is not that fierce sense of working-class alienation that one finds elsewhere, that the church is part of 'them.'"—"Them", he believed, being the middle class, the employers, and the leadership of society.

Ramsey suggested that the way forward might lie in some sort of "Festival of Christianity for the North". This would appeal to the North East and also to those outside the churches. Ideally he felt this might take the form of something along the lines of the German *Kirchentag*,[67] but be thoroughly ecumenical. If it were possible to set it up in 1972, in parallel to what was going on elsewhere in the North, so much the better. Such an approach would allow social witness and theology to go hand in hand. If the preparations were broken down so that the real work was done in ecumenical groups—in working men's clubs as well as in churches—the North East could make a positive contribution to whatever came of the ideas concerned in the Bishopthorpe Statement.

Later the Bishop wrote to confirm his thinking, but to report that considerable caution was being expressed at the staff meetings of the bishops of two dioceses in the North East. Meanwhile he was hoping, "ecumenically if possible", to establish in every community some kind of group with theological or social concerns or both. In fact, when the next Bishopthorpe came round Ramsey was lecturing in the United States, so was unable to put this vision to his peers. It might well have changed the course of the project if he had been at the meeting.

However, by the spring Bishop Ramsey was pressing ahead, prompted by the Bishop of Newcastle, Hugh Ashdown. After consultation with Lincoln Minshull, Chair of the Darlington Methodist District, they gathered together the church leaders of the North East to discuss the Bishopthorpe Statement the following June. This was a sort of "mini Bishopthorpe group", as Ramsey called it. It was a move that was to have lasting consequences—the group was, in fact, to discuss far more than the Bishopthorpe Statement. It became a clearing house for a number of other local problems, particularly in the field of questions posed by the coming civil reorganization. Indeed it was to become, in the Bishop's words, "the recognized body responsible for major ecumenical projects and developments in the North East". However, it appeared that the weight of new social material that came before the group once again marginalized mission and evangelism.

Meanwhile the Roman Catholic hierarchy of the North East was meeting at Ushaw, the Roman Catholic seminary for the North East, to evaluate the Bishopthorpe proposal. It soon became apparent that the Archbishop of Liverpool was not having an easy time in trying to encourage his fellow diocesan bishops to back this united effort. Unlike their Anglican counterparts, Catholic bishops related not primarily to their archbishop but directly to Rome, where all decisions were made.

Archbishop George Andrew Beck, therefore, could only advise and seek to inspire. For some, including the Bishop of Middlesbrough, Bishopthorpe was a step too far; similarly Hexham and Newcastle was uncomfortable with the proposals, and Salford was cautious. For Leeds there was acute anxiety that the press had got wind of something happening. These were all bishops aware that the Vatican was a far more conservative institution than the image Pope John XXIII had projected and Archbishop Beck had embraced. Some bishops protested that press reports were premature, leading "people to think that it was certain that something was going to happen in 1972". If it did not, then there would be disillusionment, and the cause of unity and mission would be set back. However, the Decree on Ecumenism meant that the Ushaw bishops ultimately, however reluctantly, agreed to support the Primate of Liverpool's initiative.

York

In York, the second region, the Archbishop of York did not forget about Bishopthorpe either, although he did depart for a sabbatical in South Africa shortly afterwards. With the departure also of his clerical chaplain to be vicar of Heslington, the "Northern Initiative file" now fell on to the desk of the Archbishop's lay chaplain, David Blunt.[68] Blunt was destined to play a long and important role, both in what was to become CTN and in its successor, "The Northern Consultation for Mission". With the Primate out of the country, it fell to David Blunt to try and rouse some interest in the Bishopthorpe Statement within the York area. This was to prove more easily written about than achieved.

David Blunt, tall, dry, bespectacled, with a ready humour, proved invaluable to the task. He held an unusual appointment—he had moved to Bishopthorpe with his wife Dorothy at the invitation of Donald Coggan, to be his lay chaplain. This appeared to involve him in being the Archbishop's eyes and ears about the diocese, indeed his hands and voice in public relations and in dealing with the media. From time to time Blunt was the Archbishop's mouthpiece in handling the multitude of ingenious and sometimes embarrassing callers on the primatial time.

Blunt now set about writing to significant personalities concerned with evangelism in the Diocese of York. These included Stanley Linsley, Archdeacon of Cleveland, George Galliford of the Minster, and George Snow, Bishop of Whitby. Blunt felt that the best strategy for assessing York's response would probably involve the Evangelistic Committee of the diocese. He therefore called the committee together to look at the Bishopthorpe Statement. He would then make recommendations for the Archbishop to consider on his return from South Africa.

The meeting was held in March 1970 at St William's College, York. This was a Tudor establishment at the back of the Minster, a charming venue, although it offered a far from encouraging experience. Bishop Snow of Whitby was the senior dignitary present and in the chair. He was a tall, insouciant incumbent with a touch of dry humour, a mop of white hair, and a conviction that the Church had got its presentation of the gospel wrong. Experts on mission from all over the diocese were there. However, from the start the meeting was negative. In York, the heart of the enterprise on which the Archbishop set such store, speaker after speaker proved unsympathetic. "There is danger in such united statements," we were told: "they are either obvious or trite." "The Church has nothing to say to modern society," contributed a powerful lay member; "we had better keep our heads down and wait for the storm to blow over." "Thundering statements are not now effective," the meeting was informed; "the effective style is quieter, on a more personal local level."

Turning to the Bishopthorpe Statement, members then demolished Question 1, "Is the way forward in mission to be on an ecumenical basis?" Despite the ecumenical evidence of Bishopthorpe, the committee declared that such a proposal for united action in today's climate was both impracticable and unreal. This judgment by senior clerics and laity of the diocese revealed a deep and underlying measure of antipathy to mission among some who held senior positions in the Northern Province. It was an abrupt reminder of the position the Archbishop faced at home.

Furthermore, the committee "disagreed fundamentally" with Questions 2 and 3—"Could the churches speak with a united voice?" and "Could we think in terms of Holy Week 1972?" Question 4—"Could the Church establish small groups to speak to those scarcely touched by the gospel?"—aroused indignation and was declared to be unnecessary, "a duplication and complication, indicating a lack of confidence in much of the constant and ongoing work of the Church". The more voluble members of the group appeared to have made up their minds that the church leaders were thinking in terms of an *ex cathedra* style of public statement. Clearly, this is what they wanted to believe, and nothing I could say could undo that impression. Their savage attacks on this stalking horse allowed the real questions posed by the Bishopthorpe Statement, which might prove alarming and deeply challenging, to be avoided.

Bishop George Snow, as chair, had asked, "How does the Church intend to recast the presentation of its basic belief in order to be relevant to a scientific and technological age?" He was not heard; the experts in mission and evangelism appeared to be determined not to hear. The question posed too great a challenge, so Question 5 ("Have you any further suggestions to make?") remained unanswered.

York was not unique; it was a measure of what was being experienced elsewhere across the North. Now Blunt was lumbered with constructing a report with which to greet the returning Archbishop. He wrote, "I don't think the Archbishop will like our response very much." There was time, however, to work for a change of heart before the Archbishop's train drew into York, and there were others to consult in the diocese. But given the negative tone of the Anglican response, it hardly seemed wise to consult with other churches, particularly the conservative Catholic Bishop of Middlesbrough.

In fact, the return of the Archbishop did make a difference, and further work was then done on the response to the Bishopthorpe Statement. Thus the report that finally emerged from the Diocese of York was positive, despite taking into account the Evangelistic Committee's views. It contained valuable material that would prove essential to working with the media. Unfortunately Bishop Snow's own major concern, and one quite essential for the project to have any relevance to modern society— the message of the gospel and its content—did not come through at all.

The West Riding

Perhaps the most surprising aspect of this exercise was that for the first time in the experience of North-Country church people, whether positively or negatively right across the whole of the Christian North of England, mission was being discussed. Thus in the third region, the West Riding, Eric Treacy, Bishop of Wakefield, took the lead in February 1970. He invited the churches of the West Riding to meet at his home, a fine, one-time wool merchant's house on the outskirts of the town. John Taylor, Bishop of Sheffield, was present, together with representatives of the Bishops of Bradford and of Ripon. Two Methodist Chairs and the Roman Catholic Bishop of Leeds were also represented.

In contrast to the York Evangelistic Committee the Wakefield meeting was positive, endorsing the Bishopthorpe Statement and calling for an "all-out ecumenical effort in 1972". Eric Treacy wrote, "The meeting started tepid but hotted up in the course of the morning."[69] The Bishop of Bradford, meanwhile, had already written to all Councils of Churches in the diocese to encourage them to take part. Further, he suggested that his recent diocesan exercise "The Consideration" might help us involve the laity in mission. There was a suggestion that an approach be made to the heads of the media, and a demand that the emphasis of the proposed effort be prophetic rather than apologetic.

The West Riding meeting was a significant event and was followed by subsequent gatherings of West Riding church leaders, so becoming an accepted institution for the church locally.[70]

The North West

The fourth region, the North West, had agreed to set up a study panel, led by the Bishop of Liverpool, to consider how it was that the churches no longer appeared to be addressing the spiritual needs of the nation. Following the Foxhill meeting, the Bishop suggested two factors which the study panel might look at in turn: the first factor (method) had sociological connotations and the second (message) doctrinal challenges.

The first factor (method) appeared to suggest that a number of sociological issues were working against the churches. These included the economic dynamic of modern society being based on money-seeking,[71] together with secondary issues such as gentrification and the feminization of religion. Surveys revealed that despite common assumptions,[72] neither the poor nor the working class now went to church.[73] The unpopularity of the churches among working people generally meant that social sanctions were also exercised against those of their peers who were churchgoers.[74] A further sociological pressure was that of customary common practice. Communal habits, once formed, were enforced by context or environment.[75] This meant that fifty per cent of the North was estranged from religion.

Historically, the vast explosion of population which had taken place during the late eighteenth and early nineteenth centuries had led to rural churchgoers moving to factory towns. Here they found the existing ancient parish church overwhelmed, all pews being already occupied by those who could afford the pew rent.[76] There was no room for the newcomers. This situation led to Prime Minister Peel's nineteenth-century initiative which set up the Ecclesiastical Commission to provide monies for the new industrialized poor.[77] This loss of the poor and the working classes meant the loss of half the nation, as the religious census of 1851 made clear.

Again linked to contextual pressure was the impact of industrialization which resulted in low levels of churchgoing.[78] The panel noted that Catholicism and the Salvation Army did attract the poor; those belonging to the former, however, were motivated primarily by their Irish solidarity and fear of the consequences of mortal sin and hell, while the latter were but a small minority. Apparently the rich did not go to church either, many affirming a self-confident agnosticism; indeed, surveys demonstrated that well-attended churches lay almost exclusively in the middle-class suburbs of the cities, apart from some eclectic city-centre churches.

Sociologically it was also noteworthy that among all classes women formed the majority of churchgoers in England.[79] In a capitalist society working men had to compete in business where ethical behaviour, for the most part, had become nominal in favour of financial rewards. The teachings of Jesus (and thus of the Church) on love, compassion, justice, and righteousness therefore became difficult for men to practise at work. Hence the common saying, "You can't mix religion and business." Women, on the other hand, who until the early twentieth century were regarded as homemakers, found Christian imperatives fitted their role of caring for their children and their menfolk. As women began to join the wage-earning workforce, so they too found problems with the Christian ethic. The publication of Canon Boulard's *An Introduction to Religious Sociology* in its English edition in 1960 had given some understanding of these sociological factors, but the number of church leaders aware of them, let alone prepared to concede their importance, was very limited.

Such issues created within the "general mind" of the nation an inclination which, if not overtly anti-religious, was certainly inhibiting to church membership. It seemed that the churches had to identify, then understand and deal with these factors, if mission was to have any chance of success. The panel, in producing its paper on "Method", therefore considered how best the churches of the North might gain a hearing in today's world. One thing was clear; space had to be given for each area to address its local needs as it saw them to be. Thus the paper started with the assertion, "Methods will vary with the particular locality or the particular situation which is being addressed." It called finally for the Church to recover "a sense of its divinely instituted role as the guardian and exponent of a way of life which is essential to individual and communal maturity".

The aims of any united project for Holy Week 1972 would now be:

1. to associate the leadership of the Church with mission rather than maintenance;
2. to stimulate the local church to seize opportunities for effective witness;
3. to correct the prevalent impression that the Church is too divided and too preoccupied with survival for its message to be taken seriously in human affairs.

From its consideration of method the panel then turned to the question of message, or what might today be the content of the apologia or gospel. This led members to look seriously at whether their churches could agree on such a common apologetic. Norman Jones for the Baptists and the Archbishop for the Roman Catholics, however, made it very clear that they could not appear on the same platform with different gospels to proclaim. The problem was on how much could be agreed. Everyone could naturally all agree on the creeds, but no creedal formulation was likely to inspire anyone, let alone the West Riding of Yorkshire, with its demand for a prophetic touch.

The gospel message traditionally endorsed and proclaimed by all the churches had been that "Christ died for our sins according to the scriptures" based on Pauline theology (1 Corinthians 15:1–3). This gospel message had been meaningful, indeed vital, at a time when people's fear of death was only matched by their greater fear of hell or purgatory beyond the grave. But today that message had little relevance to our contemporaries, whose belief in hell had long since ceased to exist and whose concept of an afterlife was tenuous at best. Much concern and effort had been spent in the past on the communication and indeed projection of this apologia.

Now fresh attention clearly appeared to be required as to what should be an appropriate content of the Christian apologetic for the 1970s. In seeking to re-examine the gospel proclaimed by the Church, the North West panel was perhaps tackling the most important issue that faced the Church in the twentieth century. It came to believe that the answer was to be found within the teaching of Jesus himself. This was something Jesus had commissioned the Church to proclaim (Matthew 28:19). Jesus clearly felt himself impelled to proclaim that gospel of the kingdom and to declare the way of life which that kingdom encompassed. Moreover, he expected a response from men and women, and in turn he commended and trained his disciples to preach that gospel of the kingdom. The disciples knew themselves as followers of that "way" of the kingdom. Indeed, they first became known as followers of "The Way".

Thus the panel in its paper on the "Message" affirmed:

> The gospel is always the same, but the emphasis will change with the kind of society and the particular circumstances to which it is addressed.

If mission was to be seen to be relevant to the people of the North, both factors, method and message, had to be acknowledged as they were in the proclamation of Jesus.

Finally, Whalley Abbey

The venue for the second meeting of the North West group was Whalley Abbey, the Retreat House of the Diocese of Blackburn, situated in the Ribble Valley.[80] Charles Claxton, the Bishop, welcomed the group. Robust, white-haired, ruddy in complexion, and bursting with enthusiasm and energy, the Bishop spoke of the importance of what he called the traditional message of the Church, but commented that people "distrust us, because they do not see the cost of discipleship in us". This led Stuart Blanch to comment that the burden of keeping the machine going not only distracted our people from the pursuit of holiness but kept the leadership so busy that it had nothing to say.

The Bishop of Liverpool's panel had written up "the gospel message for today" in terms designed to resonate, not only with modern society, but with the gospel vision of the churches concerned. It had drawn attention to the importance of the gospel of the kingdom, as proclaimed by Jesus, being presented with an emphasis to match the needs of today's society. It suggested a "critical appraisal of the social forces which play upon the individual" and called for "an attempt to apply the teaching of the Bible to our national and economic structures". The paper concluded with an assertion that "the inalienable basis of our message is belief in Jesus of Nazareth as himself the presence of God in the world".

Once again, despite the positive, confident, and contemporary nature of the paper, conservative religious thought among members made it hard for some to accept. Bishop Holland of Salford personified this position: "The time is not ripe," he declared. Although he had listened to the debate with great interest, "it has had a numbing effect on my mental processes." If this was to be the style of the exercise, then he could not join. "Unless it means my getting up and proclaiming the teaching of my church, I want no part in it."

The reports from members of the North West region who had looked at the Bishopthorpe Statement were scarcely less discouraging. Leslie Fisher, Archdeacon of Chester, doubted if the Chester laity were ready, or indeed "if they felt they had anything to say". The Liverpool Baptist David Savage confessed that he was disappointed with "the reports from Merseyside". Herbert Raynor, the Methodist Chair of Preston, added that many Methodists would find the greatest difficulty in working across denominational barriers. "If this thing goes off half-cock," he added, "then it will be worse than nothing at all." At the same time, Bishop Richard Watson of Burnley clearly felt challenged by this interpretation of the gospel message, commenting, "We are mesmerized by our structures, structures that are about as meaningful to outsiders as those of the Boilermakers' Union are to us."

So the group went off to lunch with mixed feelings, and some with heavy hearts. After lunch, members descended to a stone-flagged passageway running beneath the old building to a chapel whose modern furnishings and design contrasted strangely with its surroundings. Here the group prayed, trying to express to God their need to fulfil the vision they had been given at Bishopthorpe: praying for—indeed demanding—the Spirit's guidance. Here members sought to express their needs as a group. Once prayers were over, the warmth of the conference room with its blazing log fire proved welcome and a sense of unity began to steal over the company. Perhaps it had been the prayers together, perhaps the realization that after centuries of division, churches were now beginning to have a chance of speaking with a united voice, based on the voice of Jesus. Maybe it was an understanding of the sheer weight of a non-churchgoing population that, in reality, all of us faced.

Then it was, as if in answer to prayer, that the possibility of a Northern Initiative in mission began to take shape in the mind of the group. Thus the report of the meeting, in commending the papers, somewhat hopefully concluded, "If it were thought to be valuable, the Bishopthorpe Conference would need to discuss specific methods by which such a project might be evaluated and prepared."

CHAPTER 8

Whether or Not to Go Forward: A Second Gathering at Bishopthorpe

With May 1970 now in sight, preparation for the second meeting of church leaders at Bishopthorpe meant prayer and reflection among those surrounding Stuart Blanch. This time members, having consulted their constituencies, were presumably in a position to make the decision whether or not to commit their local church to a united mission in the North of England.

Among the Liverpool leadership there had been serious reflection on the likely chance of a negative reaction when the leaders met. Manchester certainly had support in thinking that evangelism had been tried in the past and had not proved effective. The York Evangelistic Committee had also said as much, and the North East had equivocated. Moreover, the press had now begun to talk of Britain as a post-Christian society, and recent sets of statistics on church attendance supported these views. Yet, given the commission of Jesus, evangelism still remained the prime task of the Church for the Bishop of Liverpool.

The second consultation

Early on the morning of 20 May 1970 there was just a hint of mist in the Yorkshire sunshine as I drove through the village of Bishopthorpe and entered the grounds of the palace that lay still quiet and deserted. I met David Blunt, occupying his ground-floor study looking out over the gardens in the older part of the house, and together we went up to the state rooms to prepare for the second consultation. It was not long before the great reception room, its refectory table clothed with coffee cups, came alive as the church leaders, gaitered or trousered according to the custom of the day,[81] prepared for their second consultation; the numbers gathering were impressive.

However, if the morning of the first Bishopthorpe Consultation had been trying, this of Bishopthorpe II was little better. A Free Church leader was later to write, "The problems we faced were almost insuperable, we met in conditions of almost chaos . . . the wide differences in views that emerged then had nothing whatsoever to do with denominational differences, but had everything to do with varied theological emphases." He was referring to the surprise felt by many of those present that each church had its radicals or Evangelicals, many of whom felt emotionally or spiritually closer to the radicals or Evangelicals of another church from whom they differed. In view of what others were to write or say, however, this view was perhaps too sanguine, as denominational differences and loyalties were still alive. We were vividly reminded of them by a letter from a Blackburn Methodist, who had written to reject the 1969 Bishopthorpe Statement "lock, stock and surplice". Suspicions of underlying questions of power were also evident.

Donald Coggan opened the consultation with a welcome to all the church leaders. After a time of prayer he sketched in the background of the meeting and spoke to the Bishopthorpe Statement. Once again, all parts of the North and all the major churches were in attendance. Then, in an effort to win a united response, the Archbishop affirmed that the Statement was the combined work of Aubrey Vine (for the Free Churches), the Archbishop of Liverpool, the Chair of the Newcastle Methodist District Kenneth Weights, and himself. The Statement, he believed, was the outcome of our vision to work together to speak a word from God. Now, he said, we would hear from those assembled today what response that vision had provoked. Their many local deliberations had already been forwarded, as agreed last year, to their secretary in Liverpool where they had been collated. He then asked for my report.

The report attempted to summarize the raft of replies. It set out both the anxieties and the uncertainties that the Statement had aroused. At the same time, the report also presented the enthusiasms and encouragements that the Statement had engendered. On balance it suggested that the

Bishopthorpe Statement had received a guarded welcome for some sort of united action. This was then undergirded by Leslie Fisher's emphasis on the importance of the media. Those who evaluate audience figures, and therefore influence publicity in the newspapers and on radio or television, would find a project embracing the whole North far more attractive to report than anything merely local.

Mission or maintenance?

The Bishop of Liverpool then summed up the objectives of the Consultation as the need to associate church leadership with mission rather than maintenance. Thus the local church might be stimulated to seize opportunities for effective witness. This would correct the impression that Christians were too divided and preoccupied with their own survival to be taken seriously.

The Consultation proceeded to debate the report. This session revealed not only the wide diversity of opinion, but perhaps more importantly, honesty in the expressions of fear and anxiety. "The clergy have lost their nerve," we were told. Another suggested, "We are all happy to approach our fellow Christians, but we're terrified of outsiders." A third speaker told the Consultation, "The exercise is seeking to open a shop which has nothing to sell." The North East protested that it was not prepared to be dragooned. Manchester confirmed that its great conurbation was quite unsuitable for evangelistic campaigns. Some protested that the gospel was not suited for a technological society, or that the North was too big, or that God could not be manipulated, that our churches were too different, that our boundary variations ruled out effective joint action, that nobody wanted to hear what we were saying anyway.

It soon became apparent, however, that there were few who were prepared to be overtly hostile, although many feared failure. A Newcastle correspondent had written that "the visible results will be disappointing except to the pessimistic who expect nothing". Another pessimist from Rochdale opined, "A campaign in two years' time would be so contrived and artificial that it is doubtful if the Church has any right to say anything." All, however, were agreed that our objective must be to awaken interest in the Christian faith as a live option for our contemporaries, and that this would involve motivating the laity of our churches who were in touch with the non-churchgoing community. This would mean first inspiring our clergy, and so through them gaining the laity's active confidence and support.

As the morning wore away, however, little or no progress was made. The leadership and their allies had hoped that the consultation would provide an opportunity for advanced thinking on ecumenical mission, and again that it might explore an understanding of the gospel using biblical insights to speak to modern society. This was not happening.

It was a situation that revealed the chair, Donald Coggan, at his most tenacious. By skilled leadership and perceptiveness, he piloted the ship of mission through the storm of opposition and overcame the leaden weight of doubt that fouled its hull. At one point when the debate had become totally negative, he sat steely-eyed at the end of the great table, until one by one all fell silent, except for two of the leaders talking away in a window seat oblivious of the silence about them. After that, things began to improve. Coggan later wrote:

> I had a deep longing that the untouched masses of the people of the North of England should be reached by the message of the Christian gospel. My conviction was that that message was muted so long as we remained divided. I believed that we should not wait for the day when full organic union was achieved between the churches. As I saw it the need was immediate, and I believed and still believe that the main branches of Christ's Church have enough in common to go to the man in the street and declare the gospel.

It was the strength with which Donald Coggan held to his vision of the whole Church being engaged in mission that made this exercise possible. Time and again when doubt and uncertainty appeared to embroil us in failure, the Archbishop's tenacity and serene confidence won the day. Such was the case when divisions opened up threatening the unity of the North, or when internal opposition appeared to threaten the validity of the Church of England in the eyes of its partners.[82]

The context and the gospel

The Consultation now had before it the two papers presented by the North West group, "Method" and "Message", of which every member had already received copies in preparation for the meeting. The first, entitled "Method", considered the ways in which we might proclaim our common gospel. This paper had first analysed what was preventing people from identifying with us today. George Andrew Beck had told us plainly that it must be "to those who have separated themselves from us" that we must speak.

This might involve us in discovering and changing things in ourselves that contributed to this situation. Only then might people's spiritual potential be fulfilled. Did we need to speak to the working class's natural desire for revenge for past injustices? Did we need to confess to the Church's silence? The facts suggested that perhaps those who had lapsed from the practice of faith were being kept from our doors, therefore, not only by personal decisions of belief, but by a series of complex sociological or even psychological factors. The divisions of Christianity, with different churches claiming to possess the whole truth, were often quoted by our critics. Others found claims for biblical inerrancy a hindrance. To many people the churches appeared to have little answer to the problems of evil and the facts of war and suffering.

A further factor considered was the possibility of an ebb and flow in religious practice being an explanation for today's flight from faith. Any survey of the history of religious practice in Britain over the last millennium appears to show that fluctuations have taken place in a regular chronological fashion. The highs and lows or booms and slumps of religious practice appear to have had a fairly regular incidence on a one-hundred-and-fifty-year cycle. If this phenomenon were to be shown to be statistically accurate, then our present distress might be part of this ongoing sociological process. The present decline in churchgoing experienced by almost all Christian churches would be related to this cultural process. The latter part of the twentieth century was perhaps facing the nadir of such a cycle. This would then have its roots in the nature of humankind acting over time in the large group. To seek for its cause, therefore, in the current aspect of scientific, industrial, or urban life might be to chase a chimera.[83] Perhaps we needed to seek to understand the causes of the cycle.[84] These forces, it was suggested, had to do with the character of our humanity.

The second paper presented was rather different. "Message" was an attempt to formulate an apologia which might form the basis of our proclamation. It sought to show that despite our differences we could proclaim a lively and contemporary message. Both documents came in for a fair amount of criticism. The methods might be acceptable but the message was felt to be too dated; there was no mention of war, or of abortion, or of student unrest. This led Stuart Blanch to intervene and to present the thinking of the group that had produced the papers.[85] First he pointed out that "the gospel is always the same, but the emphasis will change with the kind of society and the particular circumstances to which it is addressed."

He then expanded his point:

> One of the felt needs of twentieth-century England is the sense of meaninglessness or loss of personal identity. This has been caused by the progressive enlargement of political and economic structures and by the palpable absence of any generally accepted direction in which to steer national or individual life. The need is everywhere reflected in modern literature and the arts.
>
> Our message, therefore, must take seriously the needs both of the individual and of the society which conditions him, as indeed they are taken seriously in Our Lord's "preaching of the kingdom."

By the "preaching of the kingdom", Stuart Blanch explained, we understand in our own day:

1. The presentation of a way of life which makes sense of the individual in his relationship with God and with other people, and gives some indication of the means by which this life may be discovered and enjoyed.
2. It also provides a critical appraisal of the social forces which play upon the individual (i.e. the subjection of all human enterprise

to the profit motive) and then it makes an attempt to apply the teaching of the Bible to our national, social, and economic structures.

The Bishop emphasized that:

> the inalienable basis of our message is belief in Jesus of Nazareth as himself the presence of God in the world and the *logos* or inner logic of all creation, whose life, death, and resurrection are reliably described in the New Testament documents.
>
> Such a belief involved not only personal submission to our Lord but identification with his Church, seen as the agent of man's identity towards his true destiny and the agent for God's purpose for the whole created universe.

This was clearly no mere rewriting of a creed. Indeed, as the Bishop said, "we must look beyond the Nicaean and Chalcedonian foundations to see the *Logos*—the undoubted humanity of Christ and the undoubted fact that he was the vehicle of God's revelation."

Stuart Blanch then went on to spell out the gospel of the kingdom in the light of today's culture:

> Christ came into Galilee proclaiming the Gospel of God (Mark 1:14) and this gospel was "The kingdom of God is at hand" (verse 15), and the key passages to his interpretation of this Gospel are found in Luke 4:18 where he read the scroll in the synagogue and in Matthew 6 where he preached on the mount.
>
> In the synagogue, he speaks of "Good News" as the fulfilment of Isaiah 61—the coming time of blessedness when the present sick society will be healed through its transformation (verses 2 to 4).
>
> On the mount he develops the theme, and the kingdom of righteousness is shown to depend on right relationships between men, with things, and with God. Again it conceded that there will be a transformation of values. From this follows a summary of

the law (Matthew 22:37) and the parables which all start, "The kingdom of God" (or "of heaven").

The Bishop believed that:

> this teaching is curiously relevant today in a society whose economic dynamism is based on "money seeking" (Matthew 6:19 and 24); his words on the quest for security (Matthew 6:25ff) are entirely relevant to those whose insecurity lies behind many of our great strikes, the facelessness of organizational man.
>
> Jesus' words in Matthew 7:12 or to Peter in John 21:22 are a clear challenge to contemporary society's acceptance of competition as a virtue. His comments in Matthew 6:33, as well as his example in John 13:4, speak to those who believe in the incentive of ambition.

As the Bishop sat down, there was silence. It was a dramatic moment and it was clear that for the first time everyone felt that here was the message from God. Differences became hazed as a new sun of truth shone on the minds of the audience. Then Tom Morrow declared that if we could ground this vision at the local level it would enable us to give the North a "Christian consciousness". However, it was the intervention of the Methodist Chair of Newcastle that was decisive. Kenneth Weights had a forceful, never-inhibited personality. He was outwardly humorous, self-deprecating, iconoclastic, but had a pastoral and evangelistic passion. The son of one of the great Methodist ministers of the past generation, he now called the Consultation to listen to the Holy Spirit of God.[86] "What are the conditions governing the Spirit's actions?" he enquired. "Will He be working through our responsible laymen?" "The North," he challenged, "needs some sort of Pentecost. We face the North with a choice as Christ did: the way of materialism in which God is remote, the way of the kingdom in which God is nigh."

As he finished speaking, again there was silence throughout the room. It seemed to be a turning point in the mood of the Consultation. "This speaks to us," said Ivan Neill, Provost of Sheffield and representing his bishop, "of a movement of the Spirit of God." And in a rare intervention

Gordon Wheeler, Roman Catholic Bishop of Leeds, then quoted Cardinal Cardijn (Belgian founder of the Young Christian Workers) who called for "like to evangelize like, and group to speak to group".

The relics of yesterday or the beginning of tomorrow?

The ensuing debate was of high quality, and a very important contribution came from Manchester in the person of Bishop Ted Wickham, representing the Bishop of Manchester. "Is this," he asked, "the relics of yesterday, or the beginning of tomorrow?" He went on to call for the setting up of four research groups. These would look at our basic thinking on mission. The first would be the theological task of how we communicate Christian truth to the secular world; the second to think out what our missionary task might be; the third to study how the Church relates to secular institutions which mould society; and the fourth to discover ways in which the Church might play a real part in community developments. Wickham's proposed research groups put flesh on the Bishop of Liverpool's inspiration.

So the time moved towards four o'clock, and Donald Coggan asked if we wished to meet again. Once again there was silence throughout the room, and in the quiet the Archbishop of Liverpool returned a firm "yes". The Bishop of Newcastle, Hugh Ashdown, added, in words that seemed to sum up the sudden sense of euphoria which appeared to have overtaken the Consultation, "Yes, the occasion is historic; we must go on, it is important." There was a murmur of assent from every corner of the room.

CHAPTER 9

After Bishopthorpe II

Following the second meeting at Bishopthorpe it appeared, to the surprise of many, that the major and historic divisions of our English churches had not apparently posed any substantial problems to the Consultation. Moreover, it was clear that the Archbishop of Liverpool and his allies in the Roman Catholic hierarchy were warm in their support of the vision of ecumenical mission. The more powerful Methodist Chairs of District had also been wholly supportive. Again, although not everyone was enamoured by the vision of ecumenical mission, what opposition there was did not appear to be divided along denominational lines.

This trans-denominational accord was the more encouraging considering the history of the churches of the North, with its memory still well-entrenched. It seemed remarkable to those involved in the leadership that all three major Christian traditions, after centuries of conflict, were now committed to working co-operatively. Each of these traditions, however, had within them an opposition which was destined never to go away.

The Memorandum

After Bishopthorpe II, in May 1970, David Blunt and I, acting as secretaries for the new initiative, set about our task. In the first place, we constructed a memorandum which tried to set out fairly the arguments aired at the church leaders' consultation. This suggested that the leaders might return to Bishopthorpe in twelve months' time able to give a firm "yes" or "no" to the proposed Northern Initiative. We also hoped that the leaders' meeting might give some guidance to the two archbishops and Aubrey Vine as to how the project should then proceed. The memorandum was completed by June 1970 and sent to all members of the Bishopthorpe conference. Leaders were asked to report back on what they might say in 1972 if the project went ahead, and also what they might do.

The very fact that year had followed year of discussion in this way highlighted the endeavours of the three leaders to allow for a consensus to emerge. Archbishop Beck, in particular, consistently warned against any attempt to rush towards any decision. "Just as we have taken many months of discussion to come to our present position," he said, "so we must allow the minds of others to grow together." It was hoped that by refusing either to produce or announce any plans, this might reassure those cautious of any suggestion of archiepiscopal direction. At the same time, it might allow the movement to grow and develop its own direction out of discussion at the grass roots. The Bishop of Liverpool also consistently maintained that our patient waiting for general agreement to become manifest was deliberate. He insisted that "this is an exercise in leadership".

Nevertheless, such hopes were hard to sustain, as years of cultural tradition—not to mention suspicion—had to be overcome. The experience of the consultations had helped a sense of unity and trust to grow among those who attended. However, for that experience then to be shared among the hundreds of other leaders with lesser responsibilities for guiding their laity across the North took time. These were leaders who had not had the advantage of face-to-face discussion with those of other traditions, as had happened in Liverpool or at Bishopthorpe.

The Protestants and Rome

There had already been a reasonable working relationship between the Free Churches and the Church of England. But so far as Rome was concerned, the situation was different. The Roman Catholic hierarchy were sensitive to the attraction that the Church of England might have for their faithful. Rome therefore had to protect Catholic laity from heresy; they had been taught for decades that Anglican orders were "absolutely null and void".[87] Protestants were encouraged to convert if they wished to marry a Roman Catholic, or on occasion even to have a loved one buried by a Roman Catholic priest.[88] Priests firmly insisted that the Roman Catholic Church was the only true faith and instilled this into their laity.[89] For this reason Catholic discipline forbade Catholics to enter Protestant churches or to pray with Protestants.[90]

These strict rules apparently provided a winning ticket. Catholicism in Britain had recently enjoyed both swift numerical growth and generous bequests. Its churches were well attended; a plentiful supply of priests poured forth from its great seminaries at Upholland and Ushaw. The Church was able to maintain a steady expansionist programme of building new churches and schools, while reminding Protestant society not only of the injustice of its penal past but of its present success in attracting high-profile converts.[91]

At the same time many Protestant churches were not only experiencing declining congregations, but had adopted an inward-looking programme of maintenance and even of demolition of their now underused buildings. The Church of England alone demolished over a thousand churches in the 1970s. This had led them to feel under pressure from Rome. Moreover, the disciplined ranks of Catholics in the streets of our cities hurrying to mass Sunday by Sunday were a witness to the success of English Catholicism. It was a time when the division between the churches appeared permanent and complete.[92]

Anti-Catholic prejudice, however, still existed, and historic memories of St Bartholomew's Eve were not forgotten.[93] But no one at that time could then foresee or even imagine that the monolithic Roman Catholic Church would be transformed into a group of fellow Christians. Now, as a result of Vatican II, this very thing had happened. "*Semper eadem*" may have been the hallmark of Rome,[94] but Vatican II marked a watershed. As one Jesuit academic at St Francis Xavier in Liverpool commented to me, "It was for Europe and Ireland preventative medicine; without it we should not only have faced a massive slide from faith as we experienced in South America, but possibly a fresh schism in Europe." This had made Bishopthorpe possible.

I was fortunate in being able to talk about our church relationships with Bishop Joseph Gray, who lived in Wigan. He was always happy to accept a lift in my car, as we sped homewards across the Pennines after meetings in York. For England, perhaps more than for many Roman Catholics on the Continent, the shock of Vatican II had been more difficult to bear because of these differences in Catholic history. Just as some members of the churches informed by the Reformation found it hard to accept the new Roman Catholicism, so Vatican II's transformation of Protestants from heretics to "separated brethren" was difficult for many of the Catholic faithful, whether bishops, priests, or laity, to accept. Vatican II had challenged the whole culture of English Catholicism by its adoption of changes which many English Catholics, given their particular history and culture, found too abrupt and radical. In particular these involved the abolition of Latin in the mass, the bringing of the altar to the chancel steps with the priest now facing the congregation, and the sweeping away of treasured images and ornaments in parish churches.

The Roman obedience had taught a form of conformity, so it was believed, to eternally accepted standards and ideas. This was especially true for the older laity who clung to the past. "You have no idea, Canon," the gentle and godly Catholic Bishop of Lancaster told me, "of the flood of mail that arrives on my desk every day from our hardliners". Bishop Gray also complained that Catholic laity had warned him that these new ideas of Vatican II were "proving Cranmer to be right". This should have been music to my ears, naturally, but in fact I felt for Bishop Joe, a generous, good, and godly man, and I could not but share the trauma Bishop Joe's church was now enduring. However, I could not also fail to thank God for Cranmer and his courageous foresight and liturgy, although saddened by his terrible end.

In fact, the sense of spiritual unity, integrity, and accord felt between Bishop Joe and myself was no doubt repeated many times elsewhere, and it transformed the relationships between Rome and her Protestant allies across the North.[95] Many Roman Catholic priests, however, had been deeply shocked by this sudden reversal of the growth figures for the English Catholic Church, which had caught everyone by surprise; this led to priests leaving the priesthood, and then Catholic laity began to appear in Protestant pews.

The causes were not easy to analyse. Among them might be the movement of population within our large cities away from the centre, where Catholic strength lay, to the suburbs. This had stripped once powerful and populous parishes of their membership. Accustomed to numbering mass attendance by the thousand, parish priests now found themselves reduced to a handful in church. This had left them bemused and defeated.[96] However, not only had laity moved away, but now even those who remained no longer felt the old obligation to attend mass regularly. The political independence of Ireland in 1916 and its growing prosperity in the European Union meant that the children of the émigré Irish no longer felt their loyalty to the Catholic faith was necessary to resist Protestant England. With the removal of these constraints, Catholic laity found themselves subject to the same secularization pressures as their Protestant neighbours. Some, of course, undoubtedly blamed the flight from the Church on Vatican II.

However, Vatican II had, in fact, opened a window onto a new goal. Not that of converting the English one by one, which, as Cardinal John C. Heenan pointed out, would take centuries,[97] but rather of uniting our divided Christendom. It suggested that the logic of the Catholic claim to universality would inevitably draw their "separated brethren" into harmony with the Catholic Church. Hans Küng predicted, in *The Council and Reunion*, that if Rome itself were reformed, the churches of the Reformation would be facing a reformed Catholic Church from which they then had no need to remain separate.[98] Many in the Protestant churches welcomed the new relationship opened up by John XXIII, but had reservations about the obstacle of a conservative Vatican establishment and a series of unreformed doctrines, including Papal Infallibility and Transubstantiation, which still needed to be addressed. Others looked forward to reunion with Rome.

The fact that the wars of religion were now a thing of the past meant that no longer did the English fear conquest and subjection by a Catholic Europe. The defensive anti-Catholic prejudice which rejected Roman Catholicism as a foreign religion and had been the hallmark of English Protestantism had therefore now faded, allowing a warm response by the non-RC church leadership to the Archbishop of Liverpool's comment that we were now "beckoning to our partners in the other boat" (Luke 5:7). (The sad thing was that prejudice remained unmoved in the conservative minority of Protestants, as did the corresponding anti-Protestant prejudice in conservative Roman Catholics.)

A wider partnership

It was not only that partnerships were being discovered between Protestant and Catholic, but also within the Protestant churches; there was a new spirit of united purpose between the traditional Protestant denominations. Many Methodist leaders had set great store by the Anglican–Methodist Scheme.[99] Now the Northern Initiative appeared to open up a further path towards unity. As Rex Kissack recalled, "We worked on through the years, unresting, unhasting, even if not silent." What was true for the Methodists appeared to have even greater weight with the Presbyterians and Congregationalists as they moved towards the formation of the United Reformed Church. "They had to insert the word 'United,'" observed a Catholic bishop with a smile, "or they would have become RCs." It was no surprise that the first initiative of that new star in the ecclesiastical sky was to call for multilateral talks on unity. This bore fruit in the birth of the "Churches' Unity Commission".[100] However, and unfortunately, this did not include the Pentecostals—Elim and the Assemblies of God—nor the Independent Evangelical churches.[101]

The Church of England was not unaware of its lack of church growth, but preferred to focus on its role as the ancient and national Church of the country with a church presence in every community. The logic of this situation meant that none of the three great English traditions, Anglican, Free Church, or Roman Catholic, had any option but to go forward together in faith and work as one in obedience to the Great Commission of our Risen Lord (Matthew 28:19–20). Mission was proving to be the path to unity. So despite the tensions and difficulties of our meetings, we appeared to be on the edge of something both significant and unparalleled in the long history of the English Church and nation.

The Roman Catholic Church had finally agreed in June 1970 to a full report of Bishopthorpe II going to all church leaders in the region. The Memorandum had then followed. This was designed to be helpful in providing some form of possible timetable for those who were prepared to co-operate with the church leaders. As so many had complained of vagueness, the Memorandum set out possible ways forward as a basis for discussion in the localities. In addition, all Councils of Churches throughout the North had also been informed of the Bishopthorpe consultation and its subsequent memorandum.[102] The results were both varied and disturbing.

. . . and also confusion

An illustration of the latter might be seen in the bishop who wrote of his own advisor in mission that, "he believes this to be a piece of archiepiscopal shoving inspired by his Lordship of Liverpool." An archdeacon wrote that he had been told by his youth officer that a meeting of diocesan youth officers held in the South of England had been given a warning "to go cautiously in respect of anything to do with the Northern Initiative". As a result, he added, "Many of our Northern youth officers now are not prepared to do anything on a co-operative basis."

In one instance, the Anglican diocesan bishop expressed support for the Northern Initiative, and the Catholic bishop also wrote, "I want you to know that I am deeply interested in the project." Moreover, the Free Church leaders also expressed enthusiasm. Yet soon the Anglican diocesan staff were writing to say, "We don't seem to have much co-operation from the Roman Catholic and Free Church people, and the Methodists don't seem to want to co-operate." Then in November 1971 a cold blast came from the north as the priests of the Hexham and Newcastle Diocese voted five to one in favour of withdrawing from any contact with Call to the North.[103] A Baptist superintendent wrote, "We don't seem to have much moving . . . the initiative must come from the larger bodies." A Congregationalist moderator commented, "No one seems to be aware of any initiative being taken." Finally, the Council of Churches of that city wrote that, "We understand that the Anglican Diocese is not prepared to participate in the Northern Initiative, but the other denominations will want the fullest opportunity to take part." This added to the confusion.

It was this that led David Blunt, in exasperation, to pray for frankness, that people might really say what they mean. But it was difficult. At Bishopthorpe, no one whose experience of mission in the past had been unhappy wanted to be the one to say "no" to something that was apparently so right spiritually. This was particularly so when it was aligned to a belief that "the Church had nothing to say" to which the contemporary world would listen. Thus we had dignitaries making speeches at Diocesan Synods supporting the Northern Initiative, but in their Cathedral Chapters expressing doubt as to the value of the exercise. In my reporting to Stuart Blanch, we looked at the paralysing anxiety that was evident among many clergy, lest the Church had nothing to say to the world. Again, there was among others a fear that the Archbishops would force an initiative onto the churches. It also became patently clear that in some way we had to win the support of the frontline clergy if we were ever to mobilize the laity. This was important, as in the end our point of contact with the world at large was through our Christian laity.

Project or movement?

A group of Ecumenical Officers from across Yorkshire met at the Ripon Diocesan Retreat House at Woodhall in October 1970 with Monsignor Michael Buckley (then reputed to be something of a storm petrel in the Catholic establishment) in the chair. This group expressed fears that the project was "in danger of being talked out of existence" and maintained that "we must think of the whole Church re-examining its commitment to Christ. The Church is enfeebled by its lack of commitment."

The group further noted that "the leaders appear to commit themselves to a course of action at the Bishopthorpe meeting, then afterwards . . . begin to withdraw from that commitment". They also insisted that "the object of the exercise is the churches speaking to the world rather than a recruiting campaign. They must be prepared to sow the seed and not expect to see tangible fruit in increased membership or bank balances." "We recommend," the group concluded, "that in Holy Week 1972 there should be a pastoral letter from the leaders to all the churches calling them to renewed commitment and preparation for a special effort in the North starting in Holy Week 1973."

The final phrase of the statement was particularly noteworthy: "starting in Holy Week 1973". This underlined a concept of mission that the Archbishops not only accepted but made a keystone of their policy. "Starting in Holy Week 1973" meant that mission was to be seen not only to rest on a single initiative between the churches, but also as the continuing work of the churches acting together into the future. It meant that the Bishopthorpe Consultations were not intended to finish with the 1973 meeting, nor was the work of united mission to come to an end with the Easter of that year. One almost immediate result of the policy was that references to a "project" were dropped and replaced by the term "movement".

It was certainly becoming very clear through the debate, diffuse as it was, that any real hope of doing something effective in 1972 was receding. Moreover, the studious avoidance by the leadership of identifying any particular style the Northern Initiative might adopt had not prevented names like "crusade", "mission", "campaign", or "evangelism" being used by others. These names all aroused as much hostility among radicals as they generated support in the hearts of conservatives.

In the end it was Stuart Blanch who picked up the words of Kenneth Weights from our first Bishopthorpe Consultation. He had asked for a "Call", and so Stuart Blanch suggested "Call to the North". This was a brilliant title. It neatly sidestepped the anxieties associated with the well-worn titles associated with mission; yet at the same time gave a ringing affirmation of the eternal call of God to his people: in this case to the people of the North. It was to serve us well and was soon copied, as "calls" sprang up in other parts of the country, and indeed requests for information began to come even from overseas.

CHAPTER 10

Where Now?

Out of respect for the Archbishop of Liverpool and Roman Catholic sensitivities, the vision of the early Bishopthorpe meetings—together with subsequent traumas and confusions—was neither reported nor publicized. But now, after Bishopthorpe II and with Catholic agreement, the news of a possible ecumenical enterprise entered the public domain. Thus the challenges and tensions experienced by the Bishopthorpe leaders were soon replicated in the churches and meeting places across the Northern Province. Both radicals and conservatives in all the churches were deeply cautious, if not suspicious, about the proposals coming from Bishopthorpe.

The more conservative

Both within and beside the major denominations lay more conservative elements. These members clearly had grave doubts as to the compromises they would be called upon to make. The proposed exercise could clash with deeply-held beliefs concerning gospel truth. This was particularly true of Conservative Evangelicals. The Independent Evangelicals would have no truck with Rome. Similarly, the Pentecostals had so far shown no interest as their rank and file were unable to accept Roman Catholic participation. On the other hand, radical Liberals, while happy to work with Rome, were determined not to be compromised by being tarred with any Evangelical brush.

A further complication lay with local conservative groups such as Independent Evangelicals, the Brethren, and the Pentecostals who had proved cautious but not unfriendly. However, we now became aware that the northern ecumenical initiative had alarmed their southern counterparts. Letters had been received urging their congregations not to compromise their gospel witness by allowing members to be lured into working with Roman Catholics.

In contrast, this was not true of the conservative John Pollock, one of those whose vision had led to the Northern Initiative. He still hoped that Billy Graham, whose authorized biographer he was, might have a part to play. However, given the fierce opposition of radical Anglican opinion to the crusade style of evangelism, it was clear that Graham could not be invited to take a major part in the exercise. Despite this, some Conservative Evangelicals in the North longed to be able to invite Billy Graham back. Given the leadership's commitment to local initiatives, it was important that they be supported and encouraged. John Pollock had suggested that Dr Graham, who was on a private visit to Britain, might meet someone connected with the movement. The leadership approved the idea, and I was deputed to meet the evangelist and brief him.[104]

Soon, therefore, I found myself being taken by the side door of a London hotel up to the evangelist's suite. As we entered, Dr Graham, sitting in an armchair, rose to meet us. His pale blue, penetrating eyes surveyed us as he bid us welcome in a soft southern voice. He spoke of his endeavours and his hopes, if required to be of service to the work of the gospel in England. Having come to London following a visit to Northern Ireland, he appeared to have been well briefed and so fully understood the situation in the English North.

John Pollock introduced me, and I was then able not only to recall my role as the Liverpool Secretary to Graham's 1961 Manchester Crusade, but to outline what the Northern Initiative was hoping to do. All the famous names of his entourage were present and the atmosphere was warm, with a quality of sincerity and friendship that was disarming. However, Graham had clearly also been made aware that many of his closest supporters had grave misgivings about the ecumenical nature of the proposed initiative.

Although sympathetic,[105] Billy Graham appeared to be constrained by his understanding of the nature of the evangelistic movement he had engineered. This Northern Initiative clearly was not something that his organization could easily accommodate. The meeting with Graham gave us a further insight into the difficulties facing Conservative Evangelicals in joining any Northern Initiative in mission which had a universal ecumenical dimension. Dr Graham, meanwhile, took the opportunity to give me a personal invitation to an International Congress on Evangelism in Amsterdam.

The Christian Brethren were another conservative group, again deeply concerned with evangelism, but not always noted for their ecumenical spirit. It was therefore with real appreciation that we received a letter from the editor of their newspaper, *The Witness*, commending a member of the Brethren—Charles Oxley. Oxley was headmaster of a flourishing Christian private school, Scarisbrick Hall, a magnificent Pugin building modelled on the Palace of Westminster and set in woodland near Southport. The traditions of congregational independency among the Brethren and Pentecostal churches made their co-operation more difficult than with churches having a more centralized structure. Thus individuals in general spoke for themselves, and no one was in a position to commit anyone else. Charles Oxley responded warmly to our approach, but then surprised us, not only by suggesting that we might pray together for the health of our nation, but by suggesting that we invited Roman Catholic clergy also to meet for prayer.

This led me to invite one of my neighbours, Fr Bullen of Formby, to join us and Oxley welcomed us in a pleasant room overlooking a lake. He then introduced us to those present. Many were from churches of which I had not heard, but all appeared convinced of the importance of prayer if our co-operation in evangelism was to be blessed by God. Oxley, a tall, spare, and charming man, spoke briefly of the needs of the country, the need for prayer, and the need for us all to be united in our intercessions at the throne of grace. After a short Bible reading we fell to our knees in open prayer in the best evangelical manner. Then after half an hour or so, we rose for a cup of tea and planned a further meeting before departing. Charles Oxley gladly associated himself with Call to the North, believing evangelism essential for the health of the nation. He promised to make it known to Brethren groups throughout the North and, for himself, accepted our invitation to join the church leaders at their consultation at Bishopthorpe in May.

A further group, the Pentecostal churches, had so far shown little interest in the project. Although many Pentecostal churches were independent, most were linked to one of two groups: either the Assemblies of God or the Elim Church. The Assemblies had their headquarters in Nottingham but were unable to contemplate the sort of exercise we were engaged in. Their members had grave doubts as to the possibility of working with Roman Catholics in mission. In any event, each assembly was independent and so would have to make up its own mind in the context of the local area where it was set.

Elim, on the other hand, was more positive. Founded as a result of the remarkable evangelistic and charismatic work of the Jeffreys brothers in the 1930s, the church welcomed our approach. As a church it had its headquarters in Gloucester and was more structured than the Assemblies. The Secretary General suggested that we invite Cecil Jarvis of Barnsley, the District Superintendent of their North West Area, to represent the Elim Church at the next meeting of church leaders at Bishopthorpe. Meanwhile they warned us that much would depend on the views of their membership generally in so far as the future was concerned.

The Roman Catholics also had their conservatives. The diocesan bishops of Middlesbrough, Hexham and Newcastle, Salford, and perhaps even Leeds were all clearly very uneasy with any vision of ecumenical mission. For them, the whole concept was a break with centuries of Roman Catholic history and was not traditional Roman Catholicism. The Bishop of Middlesbrough never attended Bishopthorpe and never consented even to meet other Catholics officially connected with the movement. He possibly had his ear close to the Vatican.

Then George Andrew Beck, perhaps in an effort to reduce the anxieties of these conservatives, invited me to meet Cardinal Johannes Willebrands of the Vatican's Secretariat for Christian Unity. To have the Vatican's blessing on the enterprise might reassure the more conservative Catholic. The occasion was an informal tea party at the Archbishop's house. The Cardinal, a jovial Dutchman, was in good spirits, dispensing cigars. The half-dozen guests, all Catholic priests except for me, were entertained to a splendid succession of stories—many of them humorous—from the Cardinal's wide experience of ecumenism the world over. Then the group moved to discussing the somewhat radical developments in the Catholic

Church of the Low Countries. My ears pricked up, but the Archbishop as host steered the conversation into areas of ecumenical co-operation in this country, and so allowed the Cardinal to draw from me a picture of what we were endeavouring to do in the Northern Province. Willebrands' bluff and hearty exterior concealed a keen mind, capable of asking penetrating questions between the stories. It seemed to me that he viewed the initiative with real interest and showed confidence in the Archbishop's vision. I was to meet him again later, in Rome, in the somewhat different context of my visit to Pope Paul VI.

Although things appeared slow, progress was being made in some of the most difficult areas and thus Bishopthorpe III could yet prove exciting, and indeed positive.

The laity and study groups

One of the general criticisms the Christian churches faced in the twentieth century was that its divisions contradicted its message. Our divisions, and the divide between Catholics and Protestants in particular, denied our Lord's teaching on love and a God whose central aspect was unity in Trinity. A major step, therefore, towards common witness to the truth of the gospel locally required some high-profile united action that could be seen by the general public. This might be demonstrated, perhaps, through "common marches of witness" such as the Whit Walks of Lancashire. An alternative, less high-profile, but more effective method might be "ecumenical study groups". The latter, although discussed widely across the North, were a matter of some sensitivity.

Frank Amery, the Methodist Chair of the Sheffield District, clearly felt that such lay groups could help. He wrote:

> Many people most need to be convinced that such outreach is possible for them in their situation . . . the most urgent task is to stimulate in local churches the belief that outreach is possible.

It seemed that the project was moving towards a period of preparation that would involve ecumenical lay groups. Meanwhile Michael Parker, then Bishop of Bradford, had recently completed an exercise to celebrate the Golden Jubilee of his diocese. This was called "The Consideration" and again involved groups of laity. The Bishop had called on all the parishes of the diocese to "share in a sustained effort to discover how the church in their parish might become more realistic in its worship, fellowship, and witness".

With the aid of a specially prepared booklet, lay groups in the parishes conducted this self-examination within the context of their local community. The exercise concluded with a report, presented to the local congregation. This involved recommendations for implementation by their church council (PCC). The final great Jubilee meeting in the centre of Bradford received these reports and welcomed the Archbishop of Canterbury, Michael Ramsey, who took the opportunity to stress the importance of worship, mission, fellowship, and service in the life of the Church.

This experience led the church leaders of the West Riding to suggest that the way forward for any Provincial initiative might well lie in enabling similar but ecumenical local lay groups to meet across the North, so demonstrating the local unity of Christians. In meeting together, they could consider ways in which the theme of reconciliation might be worked out.[106] This would allow Christian people to think of ways of reconciliation across denominational boundaries, itself an experience and demonstration of unity. In addition, people might consider how to reconcile people to God, which was the fundamental purpose of mission. The Bishop was supportive of the idea of a Call to the North and asked his staff to advise us regarding lay study preparation, based on the hard experience of his "Consideration".[107]

It was recognized by the leadership that if we were serious in seeking to reach non-churchgoers in mission, this could best be done through the thousands of faithful laity in the communities of the North. These were men and women in day-to-day contact with those who were outside the life of the churches but within the love of God. The laity of all our churches, however, needed to be both inspired and prepared. Indeed, if many of our church leaders had evinced uncertainty about what to say, was it surprising that the laity—in the frontline, as it were—felt uncertain?

Such an instance was exposed at the Sheffield Council of Churches which had met to study "The work and witness of the laity". John Collie, the Vicar of Eccleshall, summed up the situation in a paper entitled *Mission in the '70s*, which he had prepared for the Council, and his words revealed the lay problem then lying at the heart of Call to the North.

> Christians must take the message of the Gospel to the world, the message which they know and can illustrate both from scripture and from their personal experiences of Christ.

However, Collie then went on to ask if this was realistic. A frighteningly high percentage of weekly worshippers in our church are "terribly ignorant and paralytically silent about their faith", he maintained. "These are quite unable to give a coherent, let alone a convincing answer to any who enquire the reason for the hope that is in them." "Was the Church," he asked, "expecting its laity to convey a gospel which, from personal experience, *they* had discovered impossible to communicate in the climate of today's conventional wisdom?"

These experiences led the church leaders to suggest that it became essential for the local communities of the North to meet in ecumenical study groups, so as to enable the laity to be inspired and informed. Only then might they find themselves effective in evangelistic witness to those outside the churches. The groups could be set up through Councils of Churches where they were strong, or through denominations where they were not. Mission was now being seen as the local manifestation of the Church in action. Bishopthorpe III would have to take this aspect seriously.

The aspect was underlined in a memorandum from an ecumenical group led by Geoffrey Lawn, Ecumenical Advisor to the Archbishop of York, in March 1971. "A massive highly-organized campaign would gain little support," the group wrote. "The message needs to be clear that it is a local initiative. The part played by the leaders and their staffs should be to help, support and encourage local work."

CHAPTER 11

Preparing for Bishopthorpe III

As minds began to focus on Bishopthorpe III, various groups across the North were active in their regions. In Liverpool Bishop Stuart Blanch began to consider the production of study material, the Manchester group met to prepare their paper on the "intellectual challenge implicit in the development of technological society and explicit in rival philosophies of life", and in Chester Archdeacon Leslie Fisher undertook to find out what part the mass media might play, and to decide what we had to say.

Gerald Ellison, the Bishop of Chester, had put a challenge to the North West leaders when they had met at Foxhill:

> If Bob Dylan, at the Isle of White Pop Festival last week, had given you the microphone with an invitation to preach the gospel to that vast crowd of youngsters, what would you have said?

He was greeted by silence, but the point had been made. Ellison was concerned with lay witness. If the leaders themselves felt challenged and silenced, what could we expect of the laity? Yet it was our lay men and women who faced this challenge day by day in their working environment. How could we prepare them, inform them, and inspire them?

This experience led Stuart Blanch to convene a lay conference to act as a "think tank"—a term much in vogue at the time. Its task would be to discover the Church's message for the world of the 1970s. It would be a meeting of those in touch with the common people, laity who might point the way for us. It was a radical decision, forced upon him by the experience of church leaders who had discovered themselves reduced to silence, or theologians who similarly appeared dumbstruck. It was clear that even the leadership had lost confidence in the Church's current apologia in speaking to contemporary men and women. However, if we were to explore the commitment of our laity who were in touch daily with contemporary secular society, the group, it was agreed, would have to cover the full range of denominational interests. Yet it would be charged with working out a common approach. George Andrew Beck was most concerned that anything that emphasized our divisions should be avoided.

The Bishop of Liverpool promised to edit the resulting document and to present it to the next meeting of the North West church leaders at Whalley Abbey. If approved, it could be submitted to the following Bishopthorpe Consultation in York. Assuming Bishopthorpe accepted the document, it could then be offered to the churches of the North as a study guide and used over the next two years by ecumenical study groups to prepare our laity for their common witness to non-church people. The two Archbishops and whoever was chosen to succeed Aubrey Vine, who was on the point of retiring from his role of leader of the Free Churches, could commend it to all the churches, so giving it authority. Bishopthorpe might then call the church people of the North to prepare for mission at Easter 1972.

In preparation for this lay initiative, considerable trouble was taken in the selection of its members. These had to be drawn from the widest possible spectrum of churchgoers, from shop floor to management. It would need to include professional people and housewives, so providing the best possible mix both of occupations and denominations. The invitation read:

> The conference is planned to cover as wide a range of age, church allegiance and occupation as possible. I am writing to you therefore because we believe that you have a distinct and individual contribution to offer.[108]

Members of the group were selected by the leaders of the church traditions involved. The results included three teachers (university, grammar, and junior), a lorry driver, two social workers, two from management, two from the professions, two students, two lay church workers, a customs officer, two shop floor workers, two engineers, and a housewife, together with four clergy.

When it met at Foxhill, the conference was first divided into four groups, with one of the clergy allocated to each group. This was designed to help members come to a common mind in their thinking on the gospel. The objective was to stand aside from the work of those engaged in professional apologetics, of whatever camp. Further, it was an attempt to uncover the answers that lay Christians might have discovered themselves in their day-to-day struggle to live by and witness to—in their non-Christian secular working life—their own personal vision of the Christian truth they themselves embraced.

So the invitation explained:

> You will be asked to come armed with a script of about 250 words prepared as if for a talk on local radio. Imagine this is the only chance you are ever going to have of saying in public what you understand by the gospel. Be yourself, don't strain after orthodoxy.

The conference met at Foxhill on Friday 5 February 1971, and at the first session the Bishop of Liverpool bravely set the scene. He pointed to our concern for society as a whole, of our lack of communication with our fellow men and women, and to the failure of the professionals, leaders or theologians, to find an adequate answer. "Too often we rely on just turning up the volume," he said; "now instead we look to the laity."

Of the twenty-four original manuscripts produced, most bore the mark of orthodox teaching. There were some that called for a restatement of the gospel in new thought forms, leading to the development of a new Christian "style of life". These spoke of justice "as the hope of the deprived", of truth, love, and peace, and the need to build the kingdom, of making the gospel relevant to wage claims and the new technology, of bringing Christ's concerns into working lives. Others, however, confessed to uncertainty and spoke of a lifetime's work with no shortcuts, and yet others spoke of a "simple faith". All the manuscripts dealt with the problem of death, the new life in Christ, and personal commitment.[109]

When the Bishop came to sum up, having read the scripts, he commented on our real unity:

> I have a script before me, which from internal evidence I was sure must have been written by a Baptist. When I looked up the name, it turned out to have been written by a member of the Roman Catholic Church. Another script which had all the hallmarks of orthodox Catholicism turned out to have been written by a Presbyterian.[110]

The conference was then divided into four groups, each with the task of producing a composite script. These scripts were then discussed in open session. Following the conference Stuart Blanch used the scripts to produce a Study Guide and entitled it *The Six Gospels*.[111] The Bishop added an introduction, Bible readings, and a commentary. The subsequent meeting of the North West group at Whalley Abbey received it warily, but commended it to Bishopthorpe III.

Chester takes the lead

In the North West, Chester Diocese had been ahead of the rest in its thinking on mission. The Bishop of Chester, Gerald Ellison, had appointed as his new archdeacon Leslie Fisher with a remit for mission for the diocese. Fisher was an able administrator with a rare vision for mission. He established a "College of Mission", clerical and lay, and in 1969 announced a year of training for the diocese. This followed a successful exhibition devoted to mission and evangelism, held in Chester Cathedral, which had attracted some 10,000 people. Bishop Ellison therefore welcomed news of a Province-wide ecumenical initiative. He proposed to use the structures of the diocese to make it part of diocesan life, and wrote inviting me to address Chester's Diocesan Synod in October 1970.

Bishop Ellison had designed this session of Synod as an instrument to involve the whole diocese in mission and then set it within the ecumenical programme for the Northern Province. The nave of the ancient sandstone cathedral, once a Benedictine abbey, was filled for the occasion with

Synod members. The Bishop, a splendid figure with a shock of white hair, spoke powerfully, directing the attention of the diocese to mission in the 1970s. He then invited me to set the scene for the North of England. I sought to give the members present a picture of the Northern Province and of their role as the Diocese of Chester. Here was an opportunity for them to unite with their partners in the Roman Catholic and Free Churches to speak to those who were without active membership of any church. It concluded with a reiteration of the Bishop's own advocacy of mission related to the society and culture of the 1970s. The response of Synod was positive, and the debate concluded with the unanimous adoption of the resolution:

> That this Synod commends that Deanery Synods and Parochial Church Councils be invited to take part in a planned study of the Mission of the Church at home and overseas beginning in Lent 1971, with the object of co-operating with other Christian Communions in the Northern Province in a project to present the relevance of the Christian Faith in Holy Week 1972, and instructs the Bishop's Council to set up a committee to make all necessary arrangements.

At the informal buffet that followed in the Bishop's House, a gracious eighteenth-century townhouse, the spirit of unanimity in the diocese was striking. All gradations of churchmanship appeared to hold the Bishop in equal affection and respect and to support fully his vision of mission for Chester. The positive response of Chester was followed by similar resolutions of support from Anglican Synods in Liverpool, Ripon, Wakefield, and York.

Meanwhile, the Roman Catholic Church

In September 1971 a significant conference of secular priests took place in Liverpool. This, the second National Conference, took seriously the question of Christian unity that had been addressed by the Second Vatican Council. The bishops of the Catholic Church on that occasion had spelt out a new vision for Catholicism: "Concern for the establishment of unity is a matter for the whole Church, faithful and pastors alike. Each individual is affected according to his ability."[112]

After debate the Liverpool conference passed a resolution which reflected the emphasis of Call to the North in recognizing mission as the incentive for unity. The resolution read:

> This conference recognizes that the search for unity is at the heart of Christian mission, that we share this mission with other Christian communities, and that we will work with our brethren of other Churches for the evangelization of England and Wales.

This provided a remarkable impetus within Catholicism for serious co-operation at ground level for Christians working together in mission. Indeed, the resolution could not have better expressed the vision that George Andrew Beck shared with Stuart Blanch.

Unbeknown to those outside the Catholic Church, however, it exposed a rift with the thinking of the conservative north-eastern dioceses of Middlesbrough and Hexham and Newcastle. This problem was not ignored by Catholic authorities. A pamphlet issued by the Catholic Information Office stated:

> We must also say with the same honesty that in many parts of the country Catholic involvement in the ecumenical movement is not significant. Where this is the case there is without any doubt a widespread feeling that the cause is lack of leadership by the clergy.[113]

No one was more conscious of this situation than George Andrew Beck, and following the success of my meeting with Cardinal Willebrands, his concern with Middlesbrough and Hexham and Newcastle led him to sound me out concerning a possible visit to Rome. This, he hoped, might involve an audience with Pope Paul VI. He felt that such an occasion could provide papal endorsement and so help the more conservative Catholics of the North of England to have confidence in the ecumenical mission that he was proposing to undertake with the Protestant Archbishop of

York. I readily assented to George Andrew's suggestion, hence in October 1971 I found myself on a plane to Rome.[114] Here I was met at the airport by Monsignor Frank Frayne, a friend of the Archbishop, with whom I was to stay for the fortnight. The Monsignor was kindness itself and arranged for me to meet Canon Purdy of the Secretariat for Promoting Christian Unity. In turn, Canon Purdy arranged for me to spend time at the Secretariat, meeting staff members, and to talk again with Cardinal Willebrands.

The discussion with the staff proved agreeable. Cardinal Willebrands, however, was no longer the jovial Dutchman I'd met in Liverpool, but a cool, almost hard administrator, setting York, or perhaps I should say the Liverpool Province, within the context of world Catholicism.[115] The Secretariat curiously, so it seemed to me, treated the Church of England and the Methodist churches as one entity, and in discussions at the Secretariat I gathered that the C of E would carry more weight in Rome once it had achieved reunion with the Methodists. Further, I noted that then current issues of the *Church of England Newspaper*, the *Methodist Recorder*, and the *Church Times* were neatly stacked together on the Cardinal's desk. My efforts to outline the advantages of all the English churches of the North being united in mission left the Cardinal unmoved. I left the Vatican wondering why Willebrands was so utterly different from the man I'd met in Liverpool and why the Vatican appeared so cold towards the vision of Call to the North.

Undeterred, Monsignor Frayne had meanwhile also arranged for me to spend time at the Venerable English College, meeting staff and students then led by Cormac Murphy O'Connor, later to become the Cardinal Archbishop of Westminster. Cormac was enthused by the vision of a movement towards Christian reunion based on mission, commending it to the students as he introduced me prior to my addressing the student body. I spoke with vigour of our common purpose in winning England for Christ and his kingdom. Similarly, judging by the questions I then fielded from these Catholic seminarians, the cream of English Roman Catholicism, the students appeared also to grasp the vision that had inspired George Andrew Beck. There was a real concern among the students to understand and work with their "separated brethren", and a refreshing absence of Roman Catholic triumphalism. Here, indeed, lay the future for the Christian faith in Britain if God were to bless our unity in diversity and see his Church recover and grow again.

My visit, however, also included a rather splendid reception hosted by the Archbishop of Westminster, Cardinal John Carmel Heenan. This, I knew, was significant, as I had come to Rome on the initiative of his successor as Archbishop of Liverpool, George Andrew Beck. Further, the reception turned out to be one of the most magnificent I'd ever experienced. I knew that Cardinal Heenan's reception was viewed by Monsignor Frank Frayne as most important, and coming on the initiative of George Andrew, I felt a sense of warmth and appreciation as my taxi swept me through the incredibly crowded streets of Rome. Finally we arrived at the splendid residence of the English Cardinal. As I entered the room, the usher on the door, somewhat to my surprise, proclaimed in stentorian tones, "The Revd Canon John Gaunt Hunter, special representative of the Archbishop of York".

I crossed the room to greet the Cardinal warmly and looked forward to sharing with my fellow English people in Rome the ideals of Christian unity and mission that Call to the North promised. But it was not to be; the Cardinal shook hands, smiled, and then swiftly passed on.[116] Clearly the Cardinal had other things on his mind.[117] The reception was an agreeable occasion, and I made many useful contacts, but the whole episode left me with a sense of unease and deep disappointment as no one seemed interested in a Call to the English North. It appeared to me that Rome now took a different view of ecumenical mission from that of George Andrew. My sense of regret was, I believe, shared by Monsignor Frayne.

My presence in Rome also allowed me to attend a mass in St Peter's, where the Holy Father was celebrating, and between these significant events some sightseeing was encouraged, including a visit to Assisi. Finally there came a public audience with Paul VI.

My first experience of the Vatican took my breath away, as our limousine sped right into the papal building and then up internal roadways to the floor where my meeting was to be. The splendour of the occasion and the enormous bureaucratic organization was most impressive. Guided by George Andrew I sought to share the ideals of Call to the North with the Vatican. However, although my welcome was courteous and generous, I found the Roman Curia to be icily inflexible. I thought it injudicious to mention this to Monsignor Frayne, but did comment that I thought Pope Paul VI had a problem following John XXIII, to which Frank replied, "Yes, I agree, but then John XXIII would have had a problem following John XXIII!"

The visit gave me an insight into what lay behind the attitudes of the priests of Hexham and Newcastle, but particularly the Bishops of Middlesbrough and, indeed, Salford. As I flew back from Rome, I could not help but wonder if George Andrew's initiative had paid off.[118] Both Cardinal Heenan and Paul VI had been cool towards this concept of ecumenical mission.[119] Indeed, I felt that George Andrew Beck had taken the vision of *Gaudium et spes*, Vatican II's "Constitution on the Church in the Modern World", far more seriously than did Cardinal Heenan or even Paul VI, John XXIII's successor. If the Cardinal Archbishop of Westminster's usher had refused to accept that I was in Rome on behalf of Liverpool, and so had substituted York, then it suggested that the godly George Andrew did not represent the official Roman Catholic Church of England and Wales.

I reported my visit to both George Andrew and Donald Coggan. Stuart Blanch, meanwhile, asked me, "Did you travel as Archbishop's Advisor in Evangelism or as a special emissary of the Archbishop of Liverpool?" Curiously, this suggested that Stuart Blanch had not been involved in this approach to Rome. In reality, I knew my sponsor to be George Andrew Beck, but Cardinal Heenan had clearly preferred to distance me from Liverpool Catholicism.

The Call is postponed

The Archbishops now began to feel an urgent need to consult, particularly as developments were moving at an encouraging pace in some parts of the North, whereas in other parts little movement appeared discernible. As the Archbishop of York was to be in Blackburn on 11 October, he arranged to come on to Liverpool to meet George Andrew Beck. Stuart Blanch was happy to offer hospitality. Donald Coggan and George

Andrew therefore met over supper at Bishop's Lodge. David Blunt had accompanied the Archbishop, and I was also invited.

Donald Coggan had decided that the next Bishopthorpe must be "D-Day", although I personally realized that George Andrew needed more time. York suggested that we had to make up our minds in the light of the evidence available, before the Province tore itself apart. We had to think out a clear programme and arrive at a title. We also needed to come to a common mind on some form of structure which we could present to Bishopthorpe in May, or else the whole exercise would founder. Coggan was certain that we could not afford another inconclusive gathering of church leaders. Despite the Chester resolution it was decided to put the exercise forward a year. This allowed a further twelve months to win the hearts and minds of the clergy and people. Under God, this incredible project of mission was founded on the sense of unity, respect, and Christian love that three outstanding church leaders had for one another.

The Archbishops then turned to me to prepare a draft programme. This, I was advised, should provide the maximum possible detail to allow those who wished to go ahead to do so within some guidelines. At the same time it also had to provide the maximum flexibility to meet the constraints imposed by those who viewed the exercise with anxiety. Again, the programme had to meet the caution of those who feared rushing our fences.[120] It was clear that anything like a tight programme, even if initially agreed by the Bishopthorpe Consultation, would in the event fail to attract enough support among the general run of churchgoers to make it effective. Stuart Blanch took the realistic view, expressed in a letter: "However long we wait and however careful we are, we are not going to achieve a 100 per cent response to anything that we do."[121]

Easter 1972, therefore, instead of being the date for the launch of the exercise became the date for an encyclical from the church leaders, to be read publicly to their people, calling them to engage in mission. The following year would then be spent in developing this strategy by the formation of local ecumenical groups which would use the ideas provided by the Bishop of Bradford's "Consideration".

Firstly, clergy groups would meet. These were designed to help clergy come to a common mind, to think out how to work together in mission given the local context. Only then would lay groups be formed to help laity learn to work together in mission. This use of study groups was to assist Christians, clergy and laity across the North accept what was new for many—the idea of lay involvement in mission and ecumenical mission. Once the ecumenical lay groups had concluded their programme, the strategy then was for the laity to focus on engagement with their non-churchgoing neighbours.

Spring 1973, therefore, covering the period of Lent, would be when these lay groups would be encouraged to engage in a five-week exercise along the lines of the highly effective "The People Next Door" campaign. This, the leadership hoped, would take church people into the homes of their neighbours, so breaking down inhibitions concerning talking about faith.[122] All preparation was designed to lead up to Holy Week, which was then planned to be marked by ecumenical projects of mission undertaken by local church leadership in the population centres of the North, the projects being locally designed and clearly directed towards those outside the churches. If we were to profit from media exposure, it would be wise for us to time our "Call" when the media was likely to report what the churches were doing. This programme would now be put to Bishopthorpe III.

CHAPTER 12

Final Decision Time: Bishopthorpe III

So 19 May 1971 became our "D-Day". A day indeed—perhaps one to provide the final opportunity for the church leaders to gather and decide on whether some united action in mission was possible. Prior to the meeting the Archbishop of York had asked David Blunt and me to meet him and brief him on the state of play. He was generous with his time and listened carefully to what we had to say. It was clear that Donald Coggan hoped for a positive response, but was determined not to go ahead unless there was a clear resolution shown by the leadership in general for some form of united action.

The day for decision

The Archbishop proposed to put a question to the Consultation: "Do you want to go ahead and endorse the plan for a Call?" This he would do, if possible, before lunch which would have the advantage, if the answer was positive, of allowing members then to spend time in prayer for the undertaking. After lunch, the afternoon could be used for planning. If, however, the response was inconclusive or negative, Donald Coggan, having discussed the possibility with Archbishop Beck and John Marsh, was prepared for the Consultation to disperse.[123] It was clear that the possibility of a negative decision and consequent dispersal was taken very seriously. Both Archbishops were aware of powerful negative groups in every church. Nevertheless, it seemed from the Archbishop's demeanour that he would try very hard to ensure a positive outcome to the work of the past three years.

It was agreed that if there was a positive decision, we would need to pray for guidance, so some sort of structure might then be set in place to enable the enterprise to function effectively. This might take the form of a committee that could oversee the movement and make suggestions for the use of Stuart Blanch's study guide, *The Six Gospels*. It was also clear that the second-tier leadership, those to whom church leaders would look to take executive action, would need some inspiration and guidance. In addition, Leslie Fisher would need to be asked to look after our publicity, including a press statement which could set out what was proposed. This, it was hoped, would bring public clarity to the present somewhat confusing scene. David Blunt then drew our attention to the financial implications of the exercise. These, too, would need to be addressed.

So the morning of Bishopthorpe III dawned. Once again church leaders from right across the North converged on York. Our numbers, for the first time, included members of both the Pentecostal and Brethren churches. The two Archbishops chaired the Consultation together with Dr John Marsh, who now represented the Free Church interest. John Marsh was a distinguished Congregationalist who had been asked by the Free Church Federal Council in London to speak for the Free Churches as "the third Archbishop".[124]

After prayer, Donald Coggan reviewed the three years of discussion which had brought us all that morning to Bishopthorpe. He spoke of the decision to postpone any united action, but proposed a "call to mission" for all church people to be issued at Easter 1972 by the two Archbishops and John Marsh. He then bluntly asked the Consultation to decide on whether we might, after two further years of preparation, launch this movement of mission in Holy Week 1973. He made it clear that what was needed was a movement of mission rather than a short-term project lasting a week.

Archbishop Coggan then asked me to comment on the present situation, and I introduced the paper on "The Programme". Members had been supplied with this so had it in their files. They were now given some understanding of how the proposed programme had emerged from many different sources across the North. The leaders listened intently, and then four further speakers illustrated the situation.

First, Father Dennis Corbishley, the Archbishop of Liverpool's representative, spoke of the situation in Cumbria, and in particular, how the proposed movement was viewed from the point of view of the Roman Catholic Church.[125] Secondly, Archdeacon Leslie Fisher reviewed the situation in Lancashire and Cheshire and spoke to the need for good relationships with the media. Then Tom Morrow, Chair of the Methodist West Yorkshire District, spoke of the situation in Yorkshire and presented the Free Church point of view. As a Methodist, Tom Morrow would have been aware of the recent Westminster meeting of the Methodist Commission on Evangelism which had heard Dr Leslie Davidson emphasize the determination of the Home Mission department to "intensify Mission in every possible way".[126] Finally, Stanley Linsley, Archdeacon of Cleveland, outlined to the Consultation the situation generally from the standpoint of the Church of England.

At this point Stuart Blanch introduced the study material *The Six Gospels,* with a word on how it came to be written. He gave a gentle reminder of the need to win hearts and minds through enabling people to see for themselves the value of, if not the imperative for, mission. But this must be done, he insisted, in company with those belonging to other churches. This led to the morning's general debate, a session which turned out to be as confusing and disappointing as any of those in previous years. At times, as the hours passed away, it seemed that despite all the work that had been put in, there would be no alternative but to conclude our Consultation and disperse after lunch.

No one appeared antagonistic to the idea of mission or ecumenism. But there was nevertheless a general antipathy to anything that might trap members into some ongoing evangelistic programme. Some leaders appeared primarily to be concerned to preserve their own freedom of action. The Methodist Chair of West Yorkshire warned against any programme that imposed restrictions on local churches. The new Bishop of Bradford spoke plainly about the anxieties that the movement had aroused, and which the programme as now outlined would not dissipate.[127] The Chair of the Sheffield Methodist District called for the leaders to commit themselves to one another in local action rather than in a northern project such as was being proposed. Such a universal programme, he argued, could only be of a temporary nature. The felt need was to have freedom to be able to meet future local problems in the way which might then appear to be best for the local church. The

Bishop of Durham was gloomy. "There was," he said, "no enthusiasm for anything like this in the North East."

The most encouraging feature of the whole debate, however, was that the Christian leaders of the North were taking these proposals so seriously. There were few absentees. Twelve out of the fourteen Anglican bishops were present, and the absentees had sent their archdeacons. Eight of the fourteen Methodist Chairs were in attendance. Four of the six Roman Catholic diocesan bishops attended and, again, those not present had sent their auxiliary bishops. All three Baptist Superintendents arrived, as did the four Congregationalist and Presbyterian Moderators, together with representatives of the Salvation Army,[128] the Christian Brethren, and the Elim Pentecostal Church. It was a formidable gathering, a gathering of those whose personal qualities had led to their appointments to leadership, and who now, having consulted their constituencies, were prepared to speak openly, frankly, and at times even trenchantly.

So it was that, after a morning of confused and somewhat negative debate, the Bishop of Chester, Gerald Ellison, took the situation in hand. Standing by the vast open fireplace he castigated the assembly for its obtuseness and called in no uncertain terms for the churches to commit themselves to their vocation and "say something to this sick world". "If in this, our third Consultation," he added, "we are not prepared to pull together, then some of us are determined to go it alone."

With this intervention, the Consultation warily agreed to take the plunge. There was no sense of euphoria; even to speak of enthusiasm would be out of place. The Consultation, however, suddenly faced reality and made up its mind after a sober three-year assessment of the situation. It well knew that there would be large areas of uncertainty, as clearly expressed in the North East. There were many who had heavy reservations, but then came the quiet intervention by the Archbishop of Liverpool: "Be aware when the finger of God is in a movement of his people," which apparently gave waverers the courage to go forward together.

A way forward

This led the Bishop of Middleton, Ted Wickham, in what appeared to be a remarkable change of heart, to introduce his paper which both justified mission and suggested a structure. "The instinct for mission at this time is sound," he affirmed, commenting on the "malaise in our society that can be evidenced . . . by the widespread disillusion about the 'democratic process', affluence that has bought off social protest, and mass sports and television which have become narcotics on a national scale".[129] He then called on Bishopthorpe to establish "ongoing" mission, which is inseparable from renewal and reform, and contrasted it with sporadic or spasmodic "mission events".[130] Such ongoing mission, however, Wickham insisted, must be backed up by "good analysis and theological thinking". He therefore called on the conference now to appoint a small executive committee which would set up working parties on different aspects of mission. In addition, he suggested that each "diocesan mission area" should have its own ecumenical group which would relate to the executive.

As the morning concluded, prayers were led by the Archbishop of York in the chapel of the house. This was a simple fourteenth-century building, pewed in the collegiate style, and had a complete absence of fussiness. Essentially dignified, it was in the Reformed tradition, tranquil and peaceful. The prayers that day led many to feel a new sense of purpose and unity that had until then evaded the Consultation.

After lunch the Consultation agreed to the setting up of a Co-ordinating Committee (the word executive was purposely eschewed), consisting of nine members, three nominated by each of the Archbishops and three by John Marsh. Its task would be to oversee the development of the movement under the authority and guidance of the annual Bishopthorpe meetings. The study guide *The Six Gospels*, later renamed *Say Your Piece*, was welcomed and commended to the churches. The four research groups proposed by Wickham's Manchester paper were accepted with real enthusiasm. The new Co-ordinating Committee was given the task of setting up the groups.

The committee was also asked to keep in touch with the local situation through a series of local co-ordinating committees, one for each region.

They, like the central committee, would consist of three members, one from each of the three Christian traditions nominated by the local church leaders.[131] These would be the effective arm of the movement in the localities and would be responsible for carrying through the agreed programme. Thus the movement was earthed in the localities and had a structure. The local co-ordinating committees would also oversee the initiatives in Holy Week 1973. The North East then decided to use the North East Ecumenical Group as its co-ordinating committee.

The need for prayer

Finally we came to discuss our next meeting. George Andrew Beck reminded everyone of our common experience in chapel. He suggested that he had felt the need in our meetings for more time to be spent in reflection and prayer. With this in mind might we, he asked, next year in 1972 have a two-day residential conference? The first day we could spend in prayer and meditation, and on the second day we could attend to our business. There was much fumbling with diaries before the fifty or so church leaders could find two clear days for their programme. Eventually it was agreed we should meet again on 28 February and 1 March 1972.

In order to finance the new committee, Roman Catholic and Church of England dioceses agreed to send £50 apiece to David Blunt, who became Treasurer to the movement, while Free Church districts agreed to contribute £25 apiece.

The Call to the North

Leslie Fisher was asked to act as the movement's Press Officer and to communicate the news of the Bishopthorpe decision to the media. The following statement was subsequently issued to all the churches and the public media:

CALL TO THE NORTH

At a meeting held at Bishopthorpe, York, on 19 May 1971, fifty-two leaders of the mainstream churches of the North of England, believing that there is a word from God to be spoken to the world of the 1970s, met to examine the Church's Mission.

Under the Chairmanship of the Archbishop of York with the Roman Catholic Archbishop of Liverpool, the leaders of the Anglican, Baptist, Congregational, Methodist, Presbyterian, and Roman Catholic Church, with representatives from the Salvation Army and observers from the Christian Brethren and the Pentecostal churches:

1. **decided** to commend to the consultative Councils of the Churches a period of ecumenical study and preparation of the task of making known, in word and action, the relevance of the Christian gospel in the lives of people under the peculiar pressures of life in the '70s;
2. **hoped** that this study and preparation would issue in evangelistic action of various kinds throughout the North of England, in many cases during Lent and Holy Week, 1973;
3. **acknowledged** that various areas and differing Churches would, understandably, follow different patterns of study and preparation, and that this would result in a variety of expressions of mission where action, demonstration, and proclamation are concerned;
4. **undertook** to set up an ecumenically based network through which information about this great undertaking and its development, and the kinds of action contemplated, would be made available to the public at large.

20. 5. 71.

With this announcement, the enormous and significant undertaking in mission across the whole of the North of England was launched into the public domain.

PART 2
Thinking It Through

CHAPTER 13

Taking Things Forward

The leadership acts

Once the members of Bishopthorpe III had dispersed in May 1971, the three senior church leaders began to plan for the future, in particular the ecumenical network outlined in Paragraph 4 of the press statement.

The two Archbishops, together with John Marsh, first nominated the membership of the Central Co-ordinating Committee which would oversee the future general administration of the movement and the development of the ecumenical network.[132] To chair the committee Donald Coggan asked Archdeacon Stanley Linsley. He also appointed David Blunt, his lay chaplain, to act as Treasurer to the movement. I was invited, as Secretary, to be the third member. Together we formed the Church of England's contribution.

The Free Churches were led by John Marsh, a Congregationalist, who joined the committee himself and in addition asked Bill Walker Lee, Chair of Leeds Methodist District, along with the Baptist Sydney Clark, Superintendent of the North East, to join him.

Archbishop Beck nominated his auxiliary bishop, Joseph Gray, together with Hugh Lindsay, the Bishop of Chester-le-Street and Coadjutor Bishop of Hexham and Newcastle, for the committee.[133] He also invited Dennis Corbishley, parish priest of Ambleside, the Cathedral Church, to be my opposite number for the Roman Catholic Church and so join the committee.

The Local Executives

The leadership then turned to the critics who had complained that "those who are going to have to bear the burden at diocesan level" need to be involved.[134] The leadership was aware that if the whole North was to be mobilized, then those local executives already active in mission would play a vital part in driving the movement forward. This local leadership therefore needed to be affirmed and mobilized, so a letter from the Bishopthorpe leadership was sent to all church leaders, inviting them to nominate someone with executive responsibility for ecumenism or mission to meet with the Archbishop in York. The meeting would be designed to inform and enthuse local executives with the Bishopthorpe thinking, so they could convey that thinking to their local clergy and people.

The first meeting took place on 23 June 1971 at King's Manor in York, a delightful Tudor building close to the Minster used by the Church of England for meetings of its Northern Convocation. This first meeting, chaired by the Archbishop of York, was attended by fifteen Anglicans, three Baptists, eight Methodists, a Presbyterian, and six Roman Catholics. In addition the Archbishop had invited his Lay Chaplain David Blunt, Archdeacon Linsley, and me.

Donald Coggan opened the meeting by outlining the vision of the Bishopthorpe Conference, and a very full discussion followed. This was a very positive occasion, with Roman Catholic members stressing the need for prayer; many Methodists emphasized the importance of social witness, while Anglicans were conscious of existing avenues of ecumenical work and the importance of the Councils of Churches. David Blunt set out the proposed structure of a Central Co-ordinating Committee with working parties, the local co-ordinating committees, and the financial basis of the enterprise. The local executives then left York, having been commissioned to set up local Call to the North structures or networks in their areas, and a further meeting was arranged for the following January.

The Central Co-ordinating Committee

Stanley Linsley, as Chair, called together the members of the Central Co-ordinating Committee in July, and it assumed practical day-to-day oversight of the Call to the North project. At David Blunt's suggestion, members chose to meet in the village of Bishopthorpe itself, as this might identify it with the Bishopthorpe Consultation and so lend authority to its work. Although no one commented on the amazing fact that the churches were now working together on a common project for the first time in four centuries, the members were very conscious of the uncommon and perhaps alarming path we were treading together. Again, although it was never discussed, the occasional comments made in the ongoing debates revealed identity anxieties still lying beneath our willing co-operation.

Anglicans saw themselves acting as hosts, anxious for the future of the faith in the North, now seeking help as it was clear that no longer could the Church of England pretend to be the only traditional Church of the Nation. That faded image might, however, still hang in their background. Methodists, having forged an independence from the established Church, saw themselves to be in the vanguard of those meeting the spiritual needs of the common person, uncluttered by bureaucracy and the pretentions of establishment. They could bring reality to the scene. Baptists thought of themselves as true to the original vision of New Testament church life and were anxious that it was not betrayed. Catholics, on the other hand, believed that in reality they were the one true Church, yet were driven forward by *Unitatis redintegratio*, Vatican II's Decree on Ecumenism (1964). They just hoped that the movement might become a step towards England being restored for the Catholic faith. Meanwhile traditions were muffled, suspicions stilled, and hopes enlarged.

The Co-ordinating Committee found itself facing two issues. The first was organizational: an ecumenical structure needed to be established across the North. Such a network had to allow each local (diocesan) area freedom to develop its own structure which could then network with the thirteen other local areas, assisted, but not dominated by the Central Co-ordinating Committee. The second was to understand the local cultural context in which the churches would be speaking, and so to advise on the message or apologia that CTN would present.

The first issue was dealt with primarily by members of the committee helping their own denominations develop local structures and so enabling them to work with their fellow Christians. However, it soon became clear that in this task, local leaders would find support from the Central Co-ordinating Committee to be helpful, if not essential. A further letter, therefore, was sent to all church leaders of the North and their executives, this time from the Central Co-ordinating Committee, outlining the objectives of Call to the North. The letter also made suggestions for the setting up of local organizations and stressed the importance of the CTN as "a co-ordinated attempt by local communities to speak to their local societies throughout the North".

The letter was accompanied by material designed to assist the establishing of a Local Co-ordinating Committee in each (diocesan) area, outlining its composition, tasks, and function. Attention was drawn to the importance of these Co-ordinating Committees relating to local Councils of Churches.[135] Once formed, many of these Local Co-ordinating Committees were chaired by a bishop or a Free Church leader. Members of the secretariat encouraged these committees, once established, to be pro-active in arranging for groups of churches in their areas to meet together. These were then asked to form clergy study groups in their locality in preparation for Holy Week 1973. Here the committee looked to the local Rural or Area Dean to take the initiative. Study guides for these clergy groups were made available by the Central Co-ordinating Committee.

From the outset the leadership had held that the role of the laity was vital in reaching those outside the churches. This made it all the more important that the clergy be inspired by the movement and so be able to affirm and train the laity.[136] Thus the clergy were asked to complete their study group's course and then to set up ecumenical lay study groups in preparation for Lent 1973. The letter stressed the importance of adequate preparation in each locality for the launch at Easter 1973. This was essential if the new movement was to stand any chance of being heard by the non-practising general public of the North.

It then fell to Dennis Corbishley and to me to travel across the North to meet church leaders in person, explaining the CTN vision and encouraging the setting up of the Local Co-ordinating Committees.

These endeavours met with varying results, generally positive although sometimes lukewarm—but never palpable—rejection.

The Central Co-ordinating Committee also believed it important to inform and mobilize local Councils of Churches across the North, and therefore consulted the British Council of Churches in London. The Council asked Bob Jeffery, Secretary of their Department of Mission and Unity, to assist the Committee. In response, he wrote to all Northern Councils giving them guidance on what Call to the North was attempting to do. The letter emphasized that this was a co-ordinated attempt by local Christian churches to speak to their local communities, rather than a grand campaign with charismatic speakers. As a back-up, the Department's leaflets on mission were sent to all Councils to help them see mission as an imperative.[137]

The second issue, concerning the relevance of the gospel, was then addressed by the Committee. Members had to ask themselves how to restate "the relevance of the Christian Gospel in the lives of people under the particular pressures of life in the '70s". This was a fundamental task, the importance of which was illustrated by the defeatism expressed by the weight of complaints from those discussing Bishopthorpe that "the Church has nothing to say". This was the reality of church life in the 1960s, felt by many, suspected by all. As a result, the laity of the participating churches felt equally unable to speak openly about their faith. How could the Committee now assist the clergy to unlock their lips, and so help them commend their faith in today's sceptical climate while being true to the gospel and to biblical evidence?

Bill Walker Lee, Methodist Chair of the Leeds District, was a prophetic voice, believing firmly that the primary task of the Central Co-ordinating Committee must be the duty of thinking through these issues. He saw its role to be a think tank and this work, he believed, took precedence over its tasks of seeking to sponsor organizational structures or producing study material and making programme suggestions. Might the Committee, he asked, be able to provide an acceptable presentation of the gospel which would be relevant and so heard by the general populace to which it was addressed?

CHAPTER 14

The Context

What people were saying

Walker Lee, in taking the lead, suggested that the Central Co-ordinating Committee should address the current cultural and religious climate of the early 1970s. It was a context, he suggested, where the churches felt they had nothing to say that the world would listen to, but was also illustrated by the saying, "Jesus I can understand, but don't give me the Church!" This was true particularly for the younger age groups. In itself the saying was unremarkable, but it had significance in the context of the various religious surveys that had been completed since the Second World War.[138] These had all indicated a persistent decline in Protestant religious practice across England. The late 1950s accentuated the situation, when the Roman Catholic Church of England and Wales also faltered and moved into decline.[139]

The statement issued by the Bishopthorpe leaders, therefore, acknowledged the situation. Article 1 insisted on "the relevance of the Christian gospel in the lives of people under the peculiar pressures of life in the '70s". This was a focus that sought to address the residue of faith in modern society. This residue showed itself in a number of ways. One of them appeared to be the unwillingness, revealed by all the surveys, for people to deny the existence of God. Again, there was a general readiness by the majority of the general public to accept the designation of "Church of England" when asked for a religious allegiance for hospital, military, or similar registrations. Further, the desire for a religious funeral remained strong. The succession of surveys, however, suggested that this veneer of religion was becoming thinner year by year and was indeed, perhaps in the more distant future, threatening to disappear altogether.

The credibility gap

The saying "Jesus I can understand" therefore represented something rather new. It suggested a discernment that had not been visible before. It was as if the youth of the land were becoming newly aware of the person of Jesus. This discernment, however, also revealed a credibility gap between the Jesus that interested them and the churches which professed to serve him. It suggested that the abandonment of churchgoing did not necessarily mean the abandonment of religious faith. In some strange way it seemed that the churches themselves were beginning to be judged by the words and standards taught by Christ Jesus. It was as if people sensed that there was a discontinuity between Jesus and his Church. There appeared also to be a few who went further, and while still prepared to accept the words of Jesus as authoritative, were curiously at the same time prepared to question the existence of a God. "I am afraid, Canon," Bishop Foley of Lancaster told me at this time, "that we can no longer hold our youth." This was something the Church of England and the Free Churches had learned to live with, but it was clearly a new experience for the Roman Catholic Church in England and Wales.

Yet even as the drift from the churches continued, the interest in Jesus as a person appeared to increase. It was as if a fresh Jesus was emerging from the tomb of the churches into the light of a new day, sometimes with the assistance of non-Christians like the director of the 1964 film *The Gospel According to Matthew* Pier Paolo Pasolini, a Marxist. This was no post-Christian world we were experiencing; young people were interested in Jesus. He was now a serious talking point, but it was post-Christendom. The churches would never be the same. The person of Jesus seemed to become more real as the churches witnessing to him receded, like shadows moving uncertainly behind the reality of his teaching and life.

The saying appeared to reveal a cultural development not limited to young people. The same thinking could also be discerned among both working people and intellectuals, perhaps a strange parallel to the contemporary student-workers alliance of the Cohn-Bendit revolutionary struggle of the period.[140] Keith Jackson, economist and Head of the Social Studies Division of Liverpool University, himself an atheist, told a group of Liverpool clergy, "If I were ever to consider becoming a Christian, it would be the words of Jesus that convinced me. 'Blessed are the pure in heart' seems to me to be the most real statement ever made."

The same problem of a tension between faith in Jesus and membership of a church was evident at this time within the churches themselves. Individual Christians such as Jim Punton of the Frontier Youth Trust, a Christian network dedicated to helping young people experience life in all its fullness, found themselves deeply committed both to Jesus as a person and to their fellow Christians, yet at the same time very critical of the historic churches as they knew them. Some, such as Jim Hart of the Evangelical Urban Training Project, an organization for training laity of Urban Priority Area parishes in Christian witness, were prepared to call themselves Christians but felt unable to participate regularly in the life of the local church community, the church on the High Street. Thus they became solitary Christians, finding fellowship in groups of the like-minded from time to time. These were men and women who were searching for new and more realistic groupings which reflected Jesus as they knew him rather than as he had been presented by the church in the past.[141] They found themselves estranged from the regular worship of the Church, be it in the vernacular, the charismatic, or the Church of England Series 1 or 2 or 3.[142]

Moreover, despite often coming from different backgrounds, they came to discover that all their traditional churches had similar problems. By the same token, sensitive Christian academics were expressing their own misgivings. Harry Williams, a Cambridge don, wrote, "I wondered how much I had thereby contributed to the emptying of the Churches by making the Christian gospel appear unreal and irrelevant to people's lives."[143]

Those in church leadership with a concern for integrity, however, had an interest in the Church as representing the essential corporate nature of Christianity. They felt exercised by the style of Christian life these dissidents represented. Some argued that those who had discovered a reality in Jesus would be forced to come to terms with the Church, social anchorites or hermits though they might be. Yet their existence was a challenge to the churches. In time past such a challenge might have been met with instruments of repression. Today, when the churches had become irrelevant not only to outsiders but now to some insiders as well, the issue was forced onto the agenda of groups such as Call to the North. These were groups which were struggling to understand society within the context of the New Testament. They were found not only in the Church of England, but also in the Free Churches and the Roman Catholic Church.

The Committee accepted Walker Lee's assessment and believed that the four working parties proposed by Bishop Wickham's Manchester paper, and endorsed by Bishopthorpe, might help us address this situation. The Co-ordinating Committee, in setting them up, sought to ensure that each working party had members representing each of the main traditions together with a fair geographical representation across the Northern Province.

The first Working Party

To chair the first Working Party the Committee looked to St Joseph's College, Upholland. This was perhaps the largest of the seminaries of the Roman Catholic Church in England and Wales. Prior to Call to the North I could never have imagined I would ever set foot within its portals, let alone be invited to preach to the seminarians. Father William Dalton was a member of the seminary staff and accepted the invitation to chair the Working Party. In the words of its brief, the Working Party was asked "To understand and explicate the essentials of the Christian faith in terms that are intelligible and capable of commanding the consideration of secular man." Some fourteen theologians, including Michael Taylor of the Northern Baptist College, Manchester, and John Montague, an Anglo-Catholic Residentiary Canon of Wakefield, formed the panel.

The resulting paper produced by the group started with the person of Christ: "We believe in Jesus Christ;" and continued to declare his purpose: "his whole life was devoted to establishing the rule of God his Father among men." The paper consisted of four studies which sought to enable people to understand:

1. the uniqueness of Jesus,

2. the meaningfulness of the world created by God,
3. the place of the Church, and
4. the way forward, as the power of man grows within a frightening future.

The paper took careful account of the anxieties and developments of the contemporary world, yet was wholly orthodox. Some traditional readers, however, were alarmed by its apparent abandonment of a primary focus on the cross.

The second Working Party

The second of the working parties was chaired by Ted Wickham, Bishop of Middleton, and his brief had been "The intellectual and theological task of discerning God's will for man in contemporary history". Its report was entitled "The Task of Prophecy and the Uses of Technology" and declared:

> Biblical Christianity does not allow us to reduce the faith to an unchanging "religion". It requires us to hear God's word and to discern what his will might be for man in the contemporary and tumultuous history of our time.

Whereas the first of the papers had provided four studies with questions attached to each, this report dealt in a firm and authoritative way with prophecy and technology in the light of the word of God, reserving its final page for questions for groups to discuss. The paper maintained that:

> Prophets were concerned to say forthright and . . . hard words, and to point men to the moral demands of the living God in their own day. God still speaks to the world, addressing men through the events of contemporary history, through crises in human affairs. This is in order to win an obedient response, the response of love, in our handling of the world's affairs and in our service to one another. Prophecy quite simply is about the

discernment of the will of God in our day, in all the secular affairs of men. Clearly it earths the Christian religion.

Referring to the prophets of Israel, it then suggested:

> Blessed is the Church that is prophetic, and condemned is the Church that fails to prophesy in a wayward nation, and then presumes to judge.

The paper then turned to consider technology:

> Technology happens to be the single greatest fact of our time that underlies all the most acute problems of our contemporary world. That is why CTN has singled it out for special study. There is today a widespread disenchantment with technology. This finds sharp focus in the radical sociologicalist's [*sic!*] attack on economic growth as the mainspring of a rapacious society. We take for granted . . . the fruits of social wealth created by technology. The failure to produce them adequately then breeds social cynicism. The attempt to provide them without an increase in real wealth not only fails but adds to inflation and inflation rots a nation.

And the paper concluded:

> The true logic of technology is clear. It cries out that man should grow in wisdom and moral stature, to mature manhood, measured by nothing less than "the full stature of Christ". (Ephesians 4:13)

The third Working Party

Dr David Charley, a Baptist and a surgeon from Leeds, chaired the third Working Party, consisting of a Roman Catholic priest and three lay members in addition to the Chair. The group had been set the task of looking at "the range of moral and social questions that faced people as individuals in all advanced technological societies".

This particular group encountered considerable difficulty in coming together and proved unable to produce evidence of a corporate statement on the issues allocated. The Central Co-ordinating Committee decided, however, that the ecumenical importance of a Baptist contribution outweighed the advantages of trying to find a new Chair.[144] In a letter on behalf of the Working Party, Dr Charley showed an understanding of the need to help Christians adapt to local problems:

> This is an age of discontinuity in employment, domicile and education. We must help people adapt to these changes and to the idea of creative retirement. Drugs, delinquency, violence and permissiveness should be regarded as symptoms of underlying disease. The good society is one which allows growth to full stature.

The group then asked for guidance from the leadership as to whether it should concentrate on new problems such as drugs, discontinuity, human power over life, death, and personality, or focus on the old problems of poverty, violence, and housing. It drew the attention of the leadership to the importance of the assimilation of immigrants, finally urging that action be taken on these issues, as the positive value of debate and decision-making is lost without action.

The fourth Working Party

Hartley Victoria Methodist College in Manchester provided the Chair for the fourth Working Party in the person of R. C. Jones. Its report was entitled "Enabling the Church for Mission". The group had been given a brief which called for "searching questions to be asked and studied about the church's own life and work and organization".

Hartley Victoria College was an amalgamation of two Methodist colleges and so was a significant venue for this particular group. The Methodist Church had had to struggle more than most churches with the realities of structures over the recent fifty years. This struggle had involved the uniting in 1932 of the three different strands in the Methodist tradition (Wesleyan, Primitive, and United Methodist Churches). It was a development which had led to the consequent rationalization of many chapels and institutions inherited by the newly united church.

The college itself, Victorian in feel, had a sense of vigour and life. The benches of its dining hall were boisterous with young men training for the ministry. The report opened with the words:

> We want to stress the significance of church organization and the physical shape of church plant and buildings—all of which we can term rather loosely as structure—for determining the way in which Christians themselves view the mission of the church.

It continued by examining the example of the effects of different styles of church structure on the thinking and life of church members. It looked at the possible ends of Christian mission, and its nature, and confirmed that "the Christian faith, as such, is not under wholesale rejection, as there remains considerable latent respect for it; however, the organized church, as an expression of Christianity, most certainly is." The report went on:

> It is critically important for the churches jointly to develop regional ecumenical bodies which have some effective power and are not merely consultative. There is value in calls like this one "to the North"; they force us to face up to awkward nagging

questions, while offering common objectives which local groupings of churches can latch on to.

The report then called for ecumenical mission teams and the encouragement of other forms of Christian presence than that of the local church congregation, but warned that "study programmes can exist without anyone actually doing anything".

The printing of these four reports was arranged by the Co-ordinating Committee and they were made available across the churches of the North at ten pence per copy. They were designed for the ecumenical groups to study in preparation for the launch of Call to the North at Easter 1973.

The Local Executives

The Local Executives met again in January 1972 at King's Manor in York. The meeting was once more well attended: four Baptists, two Congregationalists, fourteen Anglicans, six Methodists, and six Roman Catholics, together with some new members—representatives from the Brethren, the Elim Pentecostals, and the Salvation Army completed the contingent. In addition there were observers from the Bible Society and the Liverpool Ecumenical Council, together with staff and the Chairs of the Working Parties which had been set up by the Central Co-ordinating Committee.

The picture of progress that emerged showed immense variation, often reflecting the commitment of the leadership. Some areas, such as Liverpool, Chester, or Manchester, were forging ahead, having set up the local ecumenical infrastructure, but in other areas, such as Bradford (under its new leadership) or Southwell,[145] little or nothing appeared to have happened. Visits by Dennis Corbishley or me to church leaders had varied results. Bishop Ellis of Nottingham, although in the Birmingham Roman Catholic Province, was very encouraging. However, despite our united efforts, neither Bishop Cunningham of Hexham and Newcastle nor Bishop Brunner of Middlesbrough could find time to meet us. On the other hand, outside the "official North", Cyril Bowles (Bishop of

Derby) and his opposite number, the Methodist Chair of District, made it clear that, despite being in the Canterbury Province, they would like the northern part of their diocese to take part in Call to the North.[146]

Even in places fully backed by the bishop and his staff, wide variations in response across the local area were recorded. Archdeacon Leslie Fisher wrote:

> As you will realize response to Call to the North is very patchy. In some places the laity are keener than the clergy. On the whole I would think the clergy are more keen than their laity, and in some places finding it hard work in getting it across to them.[147]

The Diocese of York itself appeared to have some areas of enthusiasm but others of complacency. The Diocese of Durham presented itself as representing the whole of the North East, although Newcastle was to offer an independent picture. Yet, given this wide variety, undoubtedly the whole of the North was in some way involved, and that itself was a remarkable achievement.

Dennis Corbishley, in August 1971, produced a paper for the Roman Catholic Ecumenical Commission, excellently summarizing the work done by Bishopthorpe I, II, and III. Given the caution of the Roman Catholic Dioceses of Middlesbrough, Hexham with Newcastle, and Salford, it was a most sensitive and valuable attempt to get the English Church alongside CTN. My own visit to Rome, however, suggested— from the coolness of Paul VI and the Curia—that this would not be an easy task.

The response of the North East

In the North East Bishop Ian Ramsey had been as good as his word, and once the leaders at Bishopthorpe had agreed to launch Call to the North, he invited me to a meeting of the churches of the North East in the Council Chamber of County Hall, Durham. Speaking himself, he clearly addressed the current divorce between the churches and the contemporary world. As he saw it, this was the result of the gap between religious attitudes and the scientific outlook.

> Call to the North is a mnemonic for the concern that the Church has for the outside world. Our task is to relate society into a whole as it once was.

Ramsey went on to say that division in society came with the Cartesian separation between theology and science . . . a wonderful and imaginative idea with disastrous consequences. Cartesian separation, which appeared for so long to be a methodological success and, indeed, a political triumph, was now turning into a disaster. On the other hand *Lux Mundi* turned theology into transcendent paths,[148] while science became increasingly concerned with secular problems, so that people were now questioning whether science could have any transcendence at all.

The Bishop challenged:

> We stand today at the dividing of the ways—the way of life, or the way of death. Science now seems to have lost its way and to be looking for a moral basis for its actions, while the common people have imbibed a view of life and society from the Tyneside shipyard that is very far indeed from the Christian Faith.

The Bishop was heard in silence, his auditors not altogether sure whether they knew where he was going while being deeply impressed by his words. His address came at the opening of the meeting. Representatives from all the churches of the North East were present (with the exception of the Catholic Diocese of Hexham and Newcastle).

The meeting had been called in response to Call to the North, and a new body—"Action North East"—then came into being. It had been clear from the inception of our talks that the North East would wish to operate in parallel; to provide something designed to meet the needs and opportunities of the region, but not necessarily being beholden to Bishopthorpe.

Next the Bishop asked me to set the scene. This led me to give an overview of the North, setting out clearly Christ's preaching of the kingdom, as he strove to create a new Israel, a community of love. His clear commission to his followers was to make disciples and so to embed his teaching in society. Thus the vocation of us all as Christians was mission. With this I was able to point to the needs of contemporary society and the value of all our churches speaking together with one voice. As the conference moved into discussion, members struggled with the idea of mission: clearly it was not palatable.

Indeed, the discussion revealed that the main concern of "Action North East" was to improve the quality of the present life for the people of the North East. A project might be undertaken, designed through local church initiatives to lead up to a "Church and Community Festival". This would culminate in a great "United Service of Thanksgiving and Dedication" in parallel with Call to the North. It was a brave start, although not having the focus on mission that Bishopthorpe had planned.[149]

CHAPTER 15

The Think Tank

Bridging the gap

After setting up the working parties, the Central Co-ordinating Committee then turned to Bill Walker Lee's primary objective that it should act as a "think tank". This led it to set itself the task of trying to understand the reason for the gap in the public consciousness between the person of the historic Jesus and his contemporary body (the Church).

Members considered what people meant when they said, "Jesus I can understand, but don't give me the Church!" and asked themselves what this had to teach the churches. In some ways it seemed that today we were facing a version of Bonhoeffer's "religionless Christianity", something now not only felt by a godly German theologian but curiously by the youth of our land. Their restless, newly liberated spirits saw in the rigmarole of elaborate ceremonial and dress a contrast to the simplicity of the man of Galilee and the teaching of the Sermon on the Mount. Moreover, the wealth of the Church Commissioners, although originally given to support poor clergy and parishes, was viewed by the working class of the nation as an offence, contrasting as it did with the man "who had nowhere to lay his head".[150]

Education and economic prosperity with (comparatively) full employment had produced an independent generation with enough knowledge of the Christian faith from their schooldays to be able to ask questions from an alternative foundation, the authority of reason or science, and so to question the religious assumptions of their fathers. Walker Lee, therefore, asked if the committee could produce a specific answer to this question, in a form that the Bishopthorpe leadership meeting in 1972 might endorse. Stuart Blanch's masterly addresses to

Bishopthorpe II needed to be unpacked. Such an answer might then provide a basis for a common message from all the churches to the people of the North.

This led the committee to look at the public perception of Jesus as contrasted with the image that the Church itself presented. The image of Jesus in the minds of those unconnected with the Church was drawn from the evidence of surveys and comments by the general public. This image appeared to be the man who loved the poor, who had "nowhere to lay his head", who had remarkable wisdom and common sense in his teaching. Thus Jesus himself was generally admired as the compassionate teacher whose wisdom was accepted, but it was commonly said that you didn't have to go to church to be a Christian.

The Central Co-ordinating Committee discussed this image and contrasted it with the common perception of the churches as places for baptism, marriage, and burial, and whose great buildings were significant landmarks across the cities, and the common criticism of a church leadership that enjoyed rich perks and lived in comfort in contrast to the lifestyle of Jesus. The gospel the Church proclaimed primarily focused on an afterlife in heaven, in contrast to the gospel of God that Jesus himself proclaimed with its emphasis on kingdom values for this life.[151]

Members of the Committee, particularly those with experience of the world outside the Church, whether in industry or elsewhere, were now convinced that Christianity, if it was to mean anything in the future to the people of the North, other than a tiny religious remnant, had got to change its style radically. Its present message and presentation meant little or nothing to most non-churchgoers. The Student Christian Movement (SCM) founded in 1889 had struggled with this question and had failed to attract enough members to continue its life in the student field. The author of the 1963 bestseller *Honest to God*, John A. T. Robinson, having faced the chasm between Church and people in London's East End, had sounded a trumpet blast, but hadn't been able to move the establishment. The Oxford don Maurice Wiles had gone beyond what was theologically acceptable to Christendom. Yet, we knew that within the Church were legions of the faithful, including clergy, who held to existing tradition but at the cost of ignoring the challenge of modern secular life. They would need persuading, if Bishopthorpe was ever to endorse our somewhat radical thinking, as it could appear to threaten their faith.

From seeing that gap the committee turned to ask how the gap had arisen. A variety of answers presented themselves. In the first place, it was suggested that in every era Christians were moulded by their contemporary culture. That process then became part of the witness and life of the Church, inherited by subsequent generations. The style of most Anglican ecclesiastical buildings, until recently, had been dominated, not by contemporary congregational needs, but by romantic concepts of medieval architecture. These pseudo-Gothic buildings now imposed huge financial burdens on contemporary congregations struggling to maintain structures unfit for purpose. Advanced clerical dress had been inherited from pagan classical Rome and impregnated with medieval doctrines which were now difficult to justify and baffled the non-churchgoer.

The fourth-century Constantinian recognition of Christianity had led to the leadership of a pagan society converting to Christianity. This had enabled that leadership to maintain its social status and wealth, although its members brought with them into the Church the cultural and religious mores of their pagan past, including monarchical structures. The Church then sought to "baptize" the non-Christian cultural mores of its contemporary society, its social and financial distinctions, its religious nomenclature, doctrines, dress, and structure. This allowed the leadership to be absorbed by the Church, so becoming the leadership of the faith. In the process, it failed to resolve the conflict of pagan culture with the gospel of God as proclaimed by Jesus and practised by the early Church (Mark 1:38, Acts 2:43ff.). Feudal class distinctions were still maintained in modern church life, as were capitalist distinctions in the payment of clergy.

Further, in our own day, some on the committee noted that the political power centres were no longer controlled by the traditionally rich and powerful, but now alternated between middle class and working class.[152] However, the churches—apart from the Salvation Army—appeared to be supported by and led by the middle-class social elite and so had lost touch with the working class, where Labour, the party of the working class and the poor, now provided leadership. This enhanced the gap between church and populace.

The more theologically-minded members of the Central Co-ordinating Committee, such as John Marsh, drew attention to the Church's apologetics, which had got out of step with the changing needs of society. They believed there was evidence that this had happened in our own century. The writings of the New Testament have been a store from which Christian apologists have drawn throughout the centuries to heal the world. The gospel thus preached by the contemporary Church had been designed to meet the primary needs of a pre-modern society. It concentrated on the good news of an answer to the problems of sin and death.[153] But this was a need that was no longer felt by our present-day culture.[154] The culture of the world steadily changes, and it needs to change. Was the Church's apologetic appropriate for today? Asking this question revealed that assumptions had been made that the message of the Church was unchanging.

Tradition and change

Members of the committee saw evidence of this religious ossification in the creeds used in public worship. Although not all churches used the creeds in this way, all appeared to use them as a standard of orthodoxy. For centuries they had encapsulated the message of the Church to the world. The Nicene Creed, produced in the fourth century, makes no reference to the central work of Jesus in preaching the kingdom, its mores, values, and commandments. It reflected the struggles of the Church at that time and the needs of its contemporary culture. Since then, however, this statement has been imposed on believers in churches that use the Creed in worship, and assumed by many others as a faithful summary of revealed truth.

Jesus had declared that the reason for his incarnation was, unlike Nicaea, the preaching of the kingdom. "I have to proclaim my message ... that is why I have come." (Mark 1:37). His messianic manifesto in the synagogue at Nazareth (Luke 4:18ff.) emphasized proclamation, in particular to the poor, and Jesus underlined this importance to Pilate: "My task is to bear witness to the truth, for this I was born, for this I came into the world." (John 18:37). The Committee came to the conclusion that this teaching was probably "the gospel" that today's world might find relevant,[155] but at the same time realized that many conservative Christians, Protestant and Catholic, would see it as a betrayal of the gospel they had been taught and to which they were committed.

By bitter irony Jesus was crucified as a Jewish pretender on the grounds that he had spent his life, like John the Baptist before him, preaching the kingdom. By friend and foe alike his proclamation was heard as a call to revolution, promising the overthrow of the existing political order (John 11:48–50). "We had thought it was he who would liberate Israel." (Luke 24:21). But for those who had ears to hear it was the preaching of a kingdom that "was not of this world" but of the reign of God in human hearts, demanding a new and costly way of life in a new relationship between human beings and God. Yet the traditional creeds, stating the essence of what Christians believed, totally ignored the teaching of Jesus and over the years the Church had come to regard that teaching as something different from "the gospel" it had to proclaim.

The preaching of the gospel Jesus proclaimed was indeed a call to revolution, but a revolution in human hearts which would lead them to perfection. It was a call to repentance that sinful human beings would find hard to live with, had Christ not died. His resurrection made it possible by providing grace by which they might become children of God. This had to be applied to the modern Western capitalist society in which we were living and speaking to the North. Human beings were sinful because they knew the teaching of Jesus, even if sketchily, but refused to live by it (John 13:2). While pointing a finger at the Church, human beings preferred to give themselves to ambition, self-interest, acquisitiveness, and competition. By this they hoped to acquire for themselves treasure in this life, in the comfortable assurance (with Nikita Khrushchev) that there was unlikely to be any life to come.[156]

But members of the Central Co-ordinating Committee now felt convicted as they, in our own day, were members of churches which accepted the contemporary culture as part of our Christian heritage. Few leaders saw any conflict between Western society and the teaching of Jesus, although it was accepted that the conflict between God and Communism appeared clear. "How can you compromise with Communism?" an American theologian was said to have asked a Czech political leader.

"How can you compromise with Capitalism?" is said to have been the reply. Perhaps the latter compromise was possible because the teaching of Jesus had dropped out of the Church's basic apologetic. The message "Christ died for our sins" allowed that compromise.

It is more surprising that his teaching receives no mention either in the so-called Apostles' Creed, which again passes directly from the birth to the death of the Saviour, or—more significantly—in the Eucharistic Prayers of our churches, which rehearse his memory as their central act of worship. The great Prayer of Consecration thus also passes directly from the birth to the death of Jesus. It was here that the committee generally began to feel that the credibility gap between the Church and its Lord lay in the minds of thinking people. What had happened to the central work of Jesus preaching the kingdom, the new society of love?

Both our Roman Catholic and Baptist members, however, now began to express anxieties lest our thinking became too radical. However, they could not deny that many outside the life of the Church placed considerable stress on the teaching and example of Jesus, yet the Church itself placed its greatest emphasis on the great acts of God in Christ, his birth, death, resurrection, and ascension. This made it difficult for the Church to preach the gospel it was commissioned by Jesus to proclaim (Matthew 28:20). Was it this that led some to say, "Jesus I can understand, but don't give me the Church"?

This meant that the way of the kingdom had ceased to challenge the Church itself in its own structure and life, so opening it to the charge of hypocrisy, blunting its witness, and making it irrelevant in the eyes of contemporary society. The Saviour who died to save the world replaced the Lord who had lived to teach the way of life, that the world might be saved by his death.

The gospel of the kingdom

The question of how the gospel of the kingdom had faded from the churches' message was under discussion in the committee on one occasion when Donald Coggan was present. It appeared certain that the very experience of the resurrection was so breath-taking and astonishing to the disciples that they burst upon Jerusalem and the world with this news. At first, it might be that the gospel of the kingdom was carried along with their new message, but over the centuries it became submerged by the glorious news of the resurrection and that of forgiveness and eternal life through the atonement on the cross.

Donald Coggan observed that the idea of the kingdom was unacceptable politically in the context in which Paul was preaching to the diaspora. To the Greek world the idea of a Jewish kingdom was meaningless, thus it was the message of the atonement that had traditionally dominated the Church's apologia. The German doctor and New Testament scholar Albert Schweitzer, however, had summed up the situation half a century earlier:

> This enthusiasm went hand in hand with a misunderstanding of the Lordship of Christ which increasingly ignored the obedience of the community and came more and more to look upon Jesus merely as Lord over all powers who guarantees eternal life to all who believe in Him.[157]

In a society dominated for centuries by the problem of death this may have been inevitable. Thus the Church's message became fixed in this mould until the present day. Dr Ken Rice of the Tavistock Institute, speaking from outside the Church, had declared that "the primary purpose of the church is to prepare men for death",[158] a view from the world that is salutary. Yet this is the message that the Church has conveyed to the world through its apologia in mission, a mission that was tailored to meet the dominating needs of people prior to the eighteenth century.[159]

The Catholic members of the committee were not offended by such open discussion, nor were Free Church members when we discussed the Reformation's doctrinal struggle over "Justification by faith", then seen also in terms of answering the human plight concerning death. Since that time Christian apologists have explored the answer to humanity's greatest and most intractable problem and have found it in the atonement of Christ. Indeed, in their zeal some Christians have been tempted to exploit human anxieties about death. This was true both of the sixteenth-century sale of indulgences in order to build St Peter's, Rome, and of Victorian times through hellfire preaching in order to save souls.

However, since the late eighteenth century Western civilization has not had the afterlife as a priority in its thinking.[160] With the coming of modern medicine, the dark clouds that had oppressed human beings down the centuries rolled away, and death's horizon receded with longevity and the steep decline in levels of mortality. At the same time, during the eighteenth century serious questions were asked about the existence of hell as a place of everlasting torment.[161] It was during that period that many among the elite of society rejected the concept of hellfire both as unproven and also, given a God of love, rationally unacceptable.

The perspicacity of nineteenth-century science led to the general mind also rejecting the concept of hellfire, and subsequently the idea of a heaven of everlasting bliss lost the immediacy that it once had. The concept was now seen by many as having value in assisting mourners come to terms with the death of loved ones. With these developments the Church's gospel, designed to reassure human beings faced with the terrors of hell but with an assurance of heaven, took on the appearance of irrelevance. Indeed, to attend church in order to achieve such objectives appeared to be an expensive option; or as Mr Justice Avery put it, a doubtful "fire insurance".[162]

However, when death actually comes it may well be in the guise of a friend whose pale hand closes the eyes of those who live in our geriatric homes and for whom the pleasure and purpose of living has long since departed. Euthanasia is advocated on the one hand and abortion practised on the other, both concepts challenging the right to life. Both can lead some to conclude that the Church's irrelevance today lies in the fact that its apologia was designed for an age where the terror of death was an ever-present reality.[163] That age has now passed silently away, and, as with philosopher David Hume, many moderns face their personal death with equanimity.

The discussions of the Co-ordinating Committee around the vestry table at Bishopthorpe were interleaved by members visiting church leaders in the field. Here some of our thinking was tested against the reality of church life. The Dean of Manchester, Alfred Jowett, encouraged us. "One of our principal problems today," he commented, "is that the words we use no longer mean very much, even to well-disposed non-Christians."[164]

CHAPTER 16

Motivating and Informing the Clergy: Bishopthorpe IV

In 1972 Scargill House in Wharfedale provided the church leaders with a new venue for their fourth annual meeting. George Andrew's intervention at the last church leaders' gathering at Bishopthorpe, calling for a residential meeting to allow more time for prayer and reflection, was now met by Scargill. In preparation for the occasion, the Central Co-ordinating Committee had looked at a wide range of suitable Free Church, Roman Catholic, and Anglican retreat houses. Finally, however, members—Free Church, Roman Catholic, and Church of England—came to believe that the ecumenical holiday, conference, and retreat centre of Scargill House provided both a neutral and appropriate venue for the Call to the North movement.

The church leaders met together from 31 January to 1 February 1972. The weather was fine and the situation remote enough to avoid distractions. The house was comfortable, with an impressive chapel designed by the architect George Pace (1915–75). Everyone was invited to spend the whole time together, although it became clear as the acceptances were returned that some would be coming only on the second day for the business meeting. As the leaders arrived, they gathered in the chapel of the house, a dramatic and inspiring place. Here John Tabor, Warden of Scargill, welcomed them, and the afternoon was spent in meditation and worship. The worship was non-eucharistic, in deference to the discipline of the Roman Catholic Church and in order to avoid any sense of division. Three devotional addresses followed, interspersed with periods of quiet. George Andrew Beck led the thinking for the first session, followed by

Donald Coggan, and finally, after supper, John Marsh. Afterwards hot drinks were provided in the lounge as the leaders relaxed together.

The following morning the Scargill Community gathered for Communion, celebrated by Donald Coggan, in which members of the Consultation were invited to join if they wished. After breakfast our business meeting, chaired by the Archbishop of York, was held in the Marsh Lounge, a fine timbered room named after the second Warden of the House who was killed in a climbing accident in 1962. Gordon Wakefield, Methodist Chair of Manchester and Stockport, spoke first of the purpose of our united endeavours, then Dennis Corbishley, the Roman Catholic Secretary, reported on the work of the Central Co-ordinating Committee. Stanley Linsley, as Chair of the Committee, followed and spoke about the progress of the Call to the North across the Province. Finally the Consultation considered reports from the four Working Parties.

After coffee the floor was open to a general discussion of the principles behind Call to the North and the planned programme. It fell to me to draw attention to the need for prayer, if hearts and minds were to be won for the evangelization of the North.[165] Pastoral experience had convinced me of the wisdom of William Temple's aphorism on prayer and I introduced the prayer card which had been designed for Call to the North.[166] David Blunt then spoke to the financial situation and Leslie Fisher the importance of publicity.

Following the decision of Bishopthorpe III, the three leaders (the two Archbishops and Dr John Marsh) had set about composing a letter to be read from all pulpits on Easter Sunday 1972. This proposed Easter letter was introduced by George Andrew Beck and discussed. Once a final version was agreed the Consultation commended it to be read across the North on Easter Day. Considerable attention was paid to the Working Parties, and they were asked to produce study material to equip local ecumenical groups throughout their localities. It was hoped this would allow their use by the Local Co-ordinating Committees.

The Bishopthorpe Consultation was concerned to motivate and inform the clergy. Thus ecumenical clergy study groups were planned throughout the North in preparation for the launch. These would use the study guide *Say Your Piece* and were designed to help clergy come to terms with the idea of personal witness. This experience was also designed to inspire them to encourage their laity to meet ecumenically too.

The atmosphere of this, our fourth Consultation, was quite different from its predecessors. There was a purposefulness about the debates, and while the anxieties and doubts may not have vanished, they were no longer clogging the discussions. Indeed the enthusiasm engendered by this Consultation led to clear demands for the Call to the North to be a continuing process.[167] There were many who felt that the Working Parties should remain in being.[168] One of the church leaders confided as we were leaving, "I thought the conference was by far the best we have had, and the atmosphere was both relaxed and positive."

The wider scene

Following the second Bishopthorpe meeting of church leaders in 1970, the Roman Catholic Church had felt able publicly to acknowledge its engagement in negotiations with the Protestant churches. The possibility of a united exercise in evangelism was therefore now public knowledge. This was to lead to wider implications, from those unacquainted with the warmth of the Scargill and Bishopthorpe meetings.

In November 1970, as CTN Secretary I received a guarded but anxious letter from Bill Persson of the Church of England Evangelical Alliance (CEEC), whose chair was John Stott whom I knew well. The Alliance was a moderate but quite definitely Evangelical organization, alert—as they saw it—to Anglo-Catholic pressures seeking to unpick the Reformation. Thus for many, a joint exercise with the Roman Catholic Church in evangelism was a paradox, and one that would weaken and confuse their Evangelical witness. Clearly the CEEC wished for Evangelicals to be positive and to engage in evangelism, but felt that Donald Coggan ought to be aware of possible negative reactions. I shared the letter with the Archbishop and wrote a positive reply.

The following April a further anxious enquiry arrived on my desk, this time from the Church Society, one of the most conservative and Protestant of Anglican bodies, but a significant group due to its influence across the Church of England with the network of Diocesan Evangelical

Unions. Again, the Society expressed concern at the involvement of the Northern dioceses in this proposed ecumenical exercise. In response I travelled to London to address representatives of the Unions. A relieved Michael Benson, Secretary to the Church Society, wrote to thank me for the "excellent talk which helped to silence the fears of many and win the sympathy of all".

Towards the end of the year, however, Canon Harry Sutton of the South American Missionary Society, perhaps the most evangelically Protestant of the Anglican missionary societies (understandably so, given its work in that predominantly Roman Catholic continent), was in Liverpool. He spoke on behalf of all the Anglican mission societies, many of whose supporters lived in the North, expressing deep anxiety over this attempt to work with Roman Catholics in mission. Again I travelled to London, this time to address the secretaries of the missionary societies. They provided what proved to be an understanding if somewhat puzzled audience. There was sympathy for my presentation, but incredulity that such a paradox of Evangelicals working with Roman Catholics in preaching the gospel should be attempted.

Then, in June 1972, Gordon Landreth of the Evangelical Alliance, a very responsible body representing Evangelicals across the whole spectrum of the Protestant churches, wrote to enquire about Call to the North. "We have had," he wrote, "conflicting reports down here." This led him to enquire what proportion of Evangelicals actually supported Call to the North. Although his question was impossible for me to answer, he seemed grateful for the long and careful reply he received. These reiterated expressions of concern from London concerning the Northern Province's approach to mission did not disturb the leadership overmuch, as they might have been anticipated. However, they were an indication of the anxieties also affecting some of our own northern Evangelicals. Fortunately both Donald Coggan and Stuart Blanch were trusted and held in great respect.

Of course, the Pentecostal churches played no part, and no doubt there were individual congregations in all denominations who would not feel able to compromise their traditions. This was also true of the Catholic Church, despite the warm leadership of the Archbishop of Liverpool. The western dioceses of Liverpool, Shrewsbury, and Lancaster were all positive, but not so the eastern dioceses of Hexham and Newcastle, Middlesbrough, and Nottingham. Nottingham was friendly but, protected by its position in the Birmingham Province, took no part officially. Leeds appeared to keep quiet and do little, while Salford loudly protested the old orthodoxy, although engaging warmly in discussions.[169]

The new press officer

The discussion at Scargill on publicity now led to the appointment of a "Free Church executive" as Publicity Officer to match the work of the Roman Catholic Dennis Corbishley and myself.[170] In the event, as the disparate Free Churches discovered difficulty in financing the new officer, the Church Information Office (CIO) in London was consulted. As a result a post was advertised, a short list of five candidates drawn up, and these were then interviewed by General Adam Block (head of the CIO), John Miles (the Archbishop's Press Officer), and me. As a result Kevin Logan was offered the post, which he accepted. A professional journalist from Blackburn, Logan took up his role in June 1972 and had his office and base in the Methodist Central Hall in Liverpool. As with Dennis Corbishley's and my own appointments, his was part-time, three days a week, so allowing him to continue his professional work as sub-editor of a Lancashire evening paper.

Vision versus tradition

Despite the warm atmosphere of the Consultation, loyalties, customs, and attitudes died hard. In the warmth of the generous atmosphere of Scargill, many found themselves dropping their guard. Once away from Scargill, however, traditional attitudes appeared to reassert themselves. George Andrew Beck's constant warnings that we should be patient in waiting for the old climate of suspicion, local loyalties, and separation genuinely to dissolve were well founded. "The further north, the more intransigent," he once commented to me.

The Archbishop knew from experience that the twelve months of discussions held in Liverpool in the privacy of Bishop's Lodge had enabled the three major traditions to come together in a trust and a common purpose for evangelism hitherto unknown. This slow process, he believed, needed to be repeated at every level: executive, the clergy, and above all with the laity. If the enterprise were to be successful and, in particular, if it were to lead to a permanent change in the spiritual outlook of the churches across the Province, much work still needed to be done. George Andrew's prescience was well founded. Nevertheless, the three leaders backed by significant Free Church leadership carried the day in Holy Week and Easter of 1973.

CHAPTER 17

Articulating the Vision

The problem

Bill Walker Lee, the Methodist Chair of Leeds, had made it clear that the key role of the Central Co-ordinating Committee must be to produce a message which could be heard by the common people of the North, those who no longer came to or belonged to a church. Such a Christian message, he believed, clearly needed not only thinking out, but above all communicating to the North in a succinct and acceptable way, perhaps by some form of agreed declaration.

The Central Co-ordinating Committee had already spent some time on this issue. Bishopthorpe IV now gave members an opportunity to discuss the matter informally with their leaders. It seemed clear that the lack of a convincing Christian message apposite to people today meant that a number of leaders remained wary of Call to the North, feeling that "The Church has nothing to say that will be believed," despite agreeing to go forward together in faith. It had become patently clear that our traditional apologetic was no longer speaking to the general population. Curiously, the universality of this experience appeared to come as a surprise to some, yet time and again we experienced defeatism: the complaint "The Church has nothing to say" or else "Whatever we say, people will take no notice" was widespread. Yet the faith and optimism of our top leadership remained unswerving.

John Marsh pointed out during our discussions in the Central Co-ordinating Committee that the German-American theologian Paul Tillich (1886–1965) had commented, "A theological system has two poles—tradition and the present situation. It serves the two different functions of stating the truth of the Christian message and of interpreting the truth for every generation."¹⁷¹ The latter was the issue that confronted us all, and so far had defeated us.

The American evangelist Billy Graham had won many thousands of converts, both in the USA and in the United Kingdom, but it was clear that in some significant quarters his message and method remained profoundly unpopular.¹⁷² This was disappointing to those, both Catholic and Protestant, who were aware that Call to the North had its origins in response to the inspiration of Graham's UK crusades. However, his critics directed their attacks against what they saw as a lack of ethical application in Graham's message. We were reminded of Tillich's further observation, "An existential theology necessarily implies ethics, and so no separate moral theology can be admitted: in every theological statement the ethical is not only necessary but often the fundamental element."¹⁷³

Fortunately Stuart Blanch had produced a message which had taken the ethical dimension seriously and had been accepted by Bishopthorpe III in 1971.¹⁷⁴ In addition, the four Working Party reports inspired by the Manchester Group all made their contribution to the Committee's task of applying the cultural implications of the gospel to the needs of today's world.¹⁷⁵ George Andrew Beck had written:

> I think we must consider such things as a recall to the sanctity of Christian marriage, condemnation of racial discrimination, concern with human problems concerned with unemployment and if possible, some joint defence of the sanctity of human life particularly with regard to terrorism and violence, euthanasia and abortion.¹⁷⁶

But the message had to be rooted in human need and inspired by biblical evidence which "interpreted the truth for every generation". Stuart Blanch's message pointed a different way in reminding members of Jesus's words in the synagogue at Nazareth. Our prime point of address, Blanch had insisted, must therefore be, as Christ's was, "this world and the lives of men in it". The Committee, particularly its Protestant members, felt, however, that this vision needed to be spelt out. Following Bishopthorpe III the members of this Committee asked themselves, not what the Church had tried to say in the past, but what the Church should be saying today. To answer the question the Committee looked again at what Jesus himself was trying to do.

The New Testament evidence appeared to suggest that Jesus concentrated his ministry on proclaiming by word and action his gospel of the kingdom. His mission appeared to be to transform contemporary society through teaching—he accepted the title of Rabbi—into a community of love. Could this, the Committee asked, be applied to the North of England today? Might we sum up our thinking and reflection, as Walker Lee had suggested, in some agreed statement—perhaps we might call it our manifesto? Such a statement would be designed not only to declare the truth of the gospel, but to set it in the context of the reality of modern society, a reality which might indeed convict the world, leading the non-churchgoer to identify with the Church's search for truth. If this could be done, it would give those engaged in Call to the North a unity and their gospel a relevance to British society.

Problems of modern society

Any proclamation, however radical, had to start with the experience as well as the words of Jesus. Christians experience Jesus in their lives. Indeed, the contemporary Charismatic Movement focuses on this aspect of Christian life. Moreover, the teaching of Jesus in his own day spoke to and met the needs of his contemporary society; here John Marsh was the Committee's theological guide.

What problems, the Committee asked, might have been exposed by the Working Parties and so be relevant to modern society? These were problems of society such as unemployment, poor productivity, and also inflation. Might these problems, the Committee asked, yield to examination using the criteria of the kingdom? These were indeed problems of the marketplace, of the boardroom, of politics, or of the trade unions, but not until now of the Church. Despite their relevance to society all the churches had been silent, indeed fearful of speaking. Our secular society did not expect the Church to speak to these fields.[177] The Church was thought of as a privatized sphere meeting the needs of religious individuals, not a challenge to the values and ways of modern life. Indeed, within the Church itself it was widely supposed we had not the expertise to speak.

Yet if God were king of all the earth, if he were to be shown to be relevant to the modern world around us, if the Church were to help modern men and women discover in Christianity a faith to live by, we had to demonstrate that the person of Jesus had something pertinent to say today. His teaching on righteousness needed to be shown as not only addressing holiness of living, but the corporate issues of the family, of poor housing, and of crime. His words might address the life of spirituality in prayer, but they were also pertinent to those fundamental economic issues from which sprang the contemporary ills of society. Debate on these issues, therefore, led to a paper designed to bring hope, excitement, and reality to our mission.

The Committee termed it our manifesto

If Bill Walker Lee was right in suggesting we needed a short paper which the "person in the street" might read and discover that issues in society he or she knew needed addressing were being faced, we might term it "our manifesto". Jesus, in his gospel of the kingdom, taught human beings to seek first the righteousness of God and in pursuit of this to be single-minded (Matthew 6:33). Not being compromised over anxieties concerning money or security, still less revenge for injustice, Jesus called human beings to perfection in serving others in love.

Following Stuart Blanch's paper at Bishopthorpe 1971, it seemed to us that, in direct contradiction to the teaching of Jesus, competition, acquisitiveness, ambition, and self-interest were accepted as essential dynamics of modern Western society. Society generally assumed that on them depended our prosperity. Exposure to these dynamics, however, meant that many people could not honestly then call themselves Christians. Working men and women hate hypocrisy and so avoid churchgoing, as it suggests they live by these standards. Businessmen faced with the choice between kingdom values and making money, leave churchgoing to "the wife".

The Committee suspected that the ills of low productivity, now clearly destroying our British industrial base together with inflation and unemployment, sprang from these very dynamics of corporate society. Because there had been so little said—from a Christian point of view—in this field, the Committee felt it right to stress how the word of God might be relevant, even if unwelcome in the context of Western secular society today. We were aware that that society—as with Baldwin and the bishops in general, but William Temple in particular—would probably be more than anxious that the Church should have nothing to say.[178]

In seeking to apply the teaching of Jesus to our modern culture, Committee members were not suggesting that the Church or the gospel provided any alternative system to the problems of modern society, but that kingdom values should permeate modern society. Thus Jesus, in illustrating his teaching with an attack on the custom of Korban (Mark 7:11ff.), was not seeking to provide an alternative system to the ills of his own time, but rather to infuse the accepted scriptural truth with divine insight as to its application. The Committee, in analysing these modern problems, was illustrating what could be done by Christian people in their contemporary world, using their own expertise in their own field. In so doing, it was hoped the Christian laity of the North would be stirred to a more effective witness, using the teaching of Jesus to open the ears of their contemporaries in their daily work at desk or bench.

Paul, in introducing "his gospel" to the Greek world of his day (1 Corinthians 15), did not ignore the gospel of the kingdom which we see him teaching in Rome (Acts 28:31). We had now to discover ways of presenting the very gospel of the kingdom as preached by Christ himself, but in a modern context. This was a gospel which answered the problems of insecurity (Matthew 6:34), which gave freedom from anxieties over money (Matthew 6:19), which allowed people the liberty of seeking each other's good, and enabled them to enjoy the wonder of becoming sons and daughters of God. It was the good news that some today were seeking through the alluring byways of the drug culture, the guru, or the mystical experience.

The gospel that Jesus commissioned his disciples to proclaim in the towns and villages of Galilee was this gospel of the kingdom. The Seventy returned with joy from preaching this gospel, declaring that even the devils were subject (Luke 10:17–19). This is the gospel that Jesus finally commissioned the disciples to preach "beginning at Jerusalem and away to the ends of the world" (Acts 1:8). This gospel spoke to the community about their way of life and their relationship with one another. Although it was a gospel which called people to repentance and to make peace with God, the outcome was that God's righteous judgment must be mirrored not only in the life of the individual but corporately in the life of the community, the nation.

Although any statement produced by the Committee might not be agreed by all church leaders, we hoped that if endorsed generally by the leaders it might give laity a challenge to think seriously about their message to their neighbours. To listen to what God wanted them to say to the people of the North in the light of the gospel of Jesus. The manifesto itself was reduced to an A4 sheet, folded and containing a dozen propositions which set out the traditional message of the New Testament in the context of modern Western society. It was a serious attempt to be faithful to the traditional gospel, but also to gain the ear of non-churchgoers by enabling them to see the importance and relevance of the Church today.

The notes

The Committee was aware, however, that the twelve propositions of the manifesto itself were terse, and so set its hand to produce a booklet— with notes on the manifesto—so that groups might understand what the manifesto was setting out to do.

It seemed to be the case that individuals were influenced and moulded, as Stuart Blanch had suggested, by the economic structures of society. Mission, therefore, as an expression of God's saving grace in the world, must seek to influence these structures. The aim, the Committee felt, would be to create a righteous nation, pleasing to God and used by him in the life of the world. We might start with the North, but the Committee hoped that if people heard and responded, then this vision would soon be embraced also by the South. The "manifesto" therefore dealt with matters of society as well as with matters of faith. Describing itself as "a call to ordinary men and women of the North to hear greatness, perfection and glory through and in the steps of the perfect man Christ Jesus", the manifesto, in a prophetic manner, affirmed the good of society and the truth of the faith, but in addition it examined also the ills of society.

Inflation

Bishop Wickham's Working Party, to the surprise of many, had singled out the issue of inflation. Inflation thus became the first "ill" to be looked at by the manifesto. Its manifestations were the current regular price rises, which were inevitably reflected in regular demands for higher wages. The general explanation for these price rises was to blame the increasing costs of raw materials from overseas. The Working Party, however, in identifying the problem led the Central Co-ordinating Committee to believe that this explanation was false and that inflation was not the result of external costs, but rather stemmed from UK monetary policy. The expansion of the money supply, normally by printing extra money, met the desire of governments to provide rewards for people without the pain of taxation. In 1972 this was prophetic; inflation was hardly recognized as such, as it was in single figures. Inflation was generally believed to be beyond the control of government or the competence of national monetary authorities.

However, following Wickham, the Committee was not prepared to accept this defence and prophesied, accurately as it was to turn out, that inflation would become a major scandal that would threaten the fabric of our democratic society. Bishop Wickham, in a striking phrase, declared, "Inflation rots a nation," because fiscal dishonesty destroys people's trust in the currency which is part of the government's public face. A people who cannot trust their MPs finds that the loss of public trust is followed by the destruction of private trust. This had been witnessed in the 1930s in Germany. The process is corrosive, leading people to turn to political extremism.

At the time, however, many church people were puzzled by its inclusion in a Christian paper, particularly as one of the sins of society. They expected the Church to attack the sins of drink, crime, gambling, and sexual misdemeanours. However, the Committee believed that the cause of inflation lay in the money supply.[179] As the classical economist Ricardo observed 150 years ago:

> ... neither a State nor a Bank ever have had the unrestricted power of issuing paper money, without abusing that power.[180]

Legislation, prior to 1939, had controlled the issue of money, so there was no inflation for the inter-war years.[181] The term "inflation", the notes of the Working Party observe, "is a modern term for a practice for which past rulers, including Henry VIII, were criticized: the 'debasement of the coinage'.

At first, inflation appeared to benefit everyone, providing (as in the Soviet Union) that it was never allowed to rise above five per cent, so people would retain faith in the currency. The government had a free source of income, business benefitted by selling with prices rising, as did employees now able to demand rising wages. It appeared that the state, like the sorcerer's apprentice, had discovered a scheme which benefitted everyone. There were, however, losers: those on fixed incomes, those dependent on savings, and those without access to the new money created by the monetary authorities. A proportion of the real value of their capital in the bank or their income had, by stealth and so "painlessly", been transferred from the citizen owners to the state.

As Stuart Blanch had commented, the prophet Amos spoke out against those who dealt with "the balances of deceit", so this section of the notes concluded:

> We must challenge inflation because of its intrinsic offence to the righteousness of God, and because we are engaged in speaking the word of the Lord.

Unemployment

From inflation the Central Co-ordinating Committee turned its attention to unemployment. This was another area on which public attention was to be riveted in the years to come. However, in 1972 the subject was well down the list of priorities for the churches, even though unemployment in a sophisticated society such as our own denied the teaching of Jesus on service and love of neighbour. The manifesto therefore stated that "Unemployment is both wrong and unnecessary."

This sprang from the theological conviction that it was the will of God that people should enjoy the privilege of work. Human beings were made in the image of God the Creator. Work today involved a far wider spectrum of activity than paid employment. The housewife worked, often very hard, if not harder than her husband in the factory. The work she did was unpaid in economic terms, but in most cases it proved satisfying and rewarding, sometimes, indeed, more rewarding than her husband's work at the mill or counting house. However, the fact that in the UK there was now approaching a million unemployed, meant, from a family viewpoint, close on a million households suffering psychological and financial deprivation. This represented a waste of resources for any community. The notes commented:

> Labour is a valuable asset and a national resource. Germany has found it profitable to import nearly two million foreign workers to keep her economic miracle fuelled. Moreover, East Germany was forced to build the notorious "Berlin Wall" to retain labour which otherwise would have drained from its industry to the West.
>
> Theologically speaking labour is a reflection of the doctrine of creation. Genesis teaches that God works; Christ tells us that he works as his Father does. Man is made in the image of God and unites himself to the creative and sustaining activity of his heavenly Father. Work is not only the right for everyone; it is also a theological necessity for people to achieve their full stature.

In 1972, the unemployment problem of the UK was almost unique among the European powers. Britain appeared alone in being unable to compete with its industrial competitors; its productivity was the worst in Europe, but the solution to the problem was thought to lie in financial, fiscal, and economic measures.

The Committee believed this view to be materialistic as it regarded people as units of labour to be manipulated by measures taken by others. The fact that these measures were proving ineffective, the Committee felt, was due to the failure of management (and government) to understand the culture of industry. The repeated emphasis on the financial bottom line taught working people that they were being used for the benefit of others. Instead of giving the workforce a vision whereby it worked with management for the benefit of the consumer, that culture today meant that for many ordinary people, work was regarded as something to be avoided as it merely served the oppressing class. The churches needed to assist society to see work as a good serving the whole of society.

Work or a job?

This led the Committee to look at the question of work itself. With the exception of the Roman Catholic Church,[182] this was a topic scarcely ever heard addressed by the churches. Few sermons were preached on the subject, and it was rare for work to be the subject of one of the many conferences or studies that engaged contemporary church people. The Committee believed that it was important, in understanding the problem, not to confuse work with the desire to hold a job.

Most people did appear to want a job. The possession of a job in the 1960s provided status and financial reward, but the possession of a job did not mean work. A job might involve spending the working period playing cards behind a pile of packing cases.[183] In contrast to the "Samuel Smiles" image of work in Victorian times,[184] by the 1960s work had become a "Non-U" activity.[185] In fact, the days when the French philosopher Montesquieu (1689–1755) could write of Birmingham where Englishmen "worked as if they could get rich today and die tomorrow" had long passed. "Do not blame providence," Montesquieu told his fellow

Frenchmen, "for the prosperity of England in giving her good harbours and rich mines, for the wealth of Britain lies in the hard work of her people."[186]

The problem the UK faced was not limited, as was popularly supposed, to the working classes and the frequently blamed trade unions. The Committee was aware that the White Paper on Industry and Trade published by the then Government in 1928 directed its criticism at management and ownership. That paper had made it clear that the work ethic was no longer effective in British management. This factor, more than any other, accounted for the poor levels of productivity and the sluggishness of growth in British industry.

As Stuart Blanch had shrewdly observed, in place of the work ethic of old there had come a money ethic, which dominated the thinking of both sides of industry. In industry it resulted in the practice of asset stripping and the gradual growth of corruption, and in the mushrooming of the gambling industry which targeted too often those already poor. The manifesto took a prophetic line, calling instead for a service ethic in line with the teaching of the kingdom, although it fully recognized the value of capitalism providing service and integrity were its motors, rather than wealth acquisition. Perhaps it was here, above all, that the Christian faith was tested for validity. It was in failing to enter the marketplace in terms of service and motivation in the past that had led to charges of pietism and hypocrisy by some, or resulted in a Marxist alternative being offered by others.

The flight, in the United Kingdom, from the idea of the goodness of work had many bases, but it was common to both management and labour. On the management side, the early start Britain had in the Industrial Revolution had given UK industry an overwhelming position in world markets. Local overseas (Third World) industries had collapsed under the fierce weight of British competition, and by the twentieth century Britain had established a reputation for excellence of design and a cheapness of product born of efficient production unmatched elsewhere. The United States was fully occupied in supplying her own swiftly expanding home markets, the Continent had yet to catch up, and Japan had not even started.

Perhaps as a result, by 1928 the Board of Trade's White Paper on Industry and Trade showed an astonishing complacency in the United Kingdom. Firms, it declared, did not feel any need to win markets as the world beat a path to Britain's door. More ominously, firms did not feel the need to invest in new products to protect their existing markets. This complacency, the White Paper warned, would lead to the loss not only of our South American markets, which were already under pressure from the United States and from Germany, but ultimately to the loss of all our markets except those which were colonies of the British Empire.

The subsequent collapse of the motorcycle, motor, shipbuilding, and other British industries became examples of how this warning went unheeded. These were not the cases of traditional heavy industries going to the wall, but of modern industries which failed to keep pace with contemporary design and investment, and which failed completely to motivate their workforce. Management, in effect, sat back enjoying the fruits of the drive and efficiency of their Victorian forebears rather than pursuing the example of their great Creator. On the labour side, the story—although different—produced the same results. Those made in the image of God were destined to share his concern for righteousness. Commercially motivated injustice therefore bred resentment which might not be godly but which could have been anticipated. R. H. Tawney had drawn attention to this very fact in 1926:

> Both the existing economic order and too many of the projects advanced for reconstructing it break down through their neglect of the truism that, since even quite common men have souls, no increase in material wealth will compensate them for arrangements which insult their self-respect and impair their freedom.[187]

An alarming and bitter resentment was latent within the labour force of British industry. This was deep-rooted and was born out of a sense of injustice experienced under ruthless employers in the past.[188] The resentment manifested itself in a desire for revenge on the employing class and coloured the unconscious philosophy of the worker. So much so that in place of the Industrial Revolution, now in Britain we had an unrecognized Industrial Civil War between management and labour. As early as 1931 Pope Pius XI drew attention to this phenomenon:

> With the leaders of business abandoning the true path, it was easy for the working class also to fall at times into the same abyss; all the more so because very many employers treated their workmen as mere tools, without the slightest thought of spiritual things ... for from the factory dead matter goes out improved, whereas men there are corrupted and degraded.[189]

The demise of the UK as a leading industrial power that we were now experiencing was a direct result of this "civil war".[190] This was something to which the Church had to speak. Unfortunately Labour in 1945, whilst promising Socialism, had instead delivered State Capitalism, under which the civil war continued.

The work ethic described so admiringly by Montesquieu in the eighteenth century had been replaced, by the twentieth century, with poor productivity, restrictive practices, wildcat strikes, high labour turnover, and the other ills of the "English disease". This development can only be understood against the background of what people believe about themselves. Their corporate philosophy coloured their attitude to each other, to society, and to the churches. It was generally accepted by the workers that the employer's objective was to make as much profit as possible by extracting from the labour force as much work for as little pay as could be decently done. Workers therefore took the opposite view, which sought to extract the highest pay for as little work as could safely be done within the boundaries of keeping their jobs. This led to the anomaly of a labour force that wanted jobs but not work, and to the sense of dissatisfaction with work as a means of earning money.

The consistently low level of British productivity and dissatisfaction contrasted with the much higher levels of productivity enjoyed by Germany and the United States. These nations enjoyed historic factors which encouraged a high work ethic. Despite this, there had been almost a conspiracy of silence in the UK to cover the glaring basic factor of an increasing fall in prosperity suffered by Britain. Economists, employers, and unions alike chose to ignore the problem or even refused to acknowledge its existence. The Church needed to speak in this silence.

A sense of social injustice is communicated by word of mouth; it is transmitted by the group and imposed by corporate loyalty or workers' solidarity. It was this "view of life and society" that the Bishop of Durham, Ian Ramsey, spoke of as being imbibed by the workforce and their families from the Tyneside shipyards. This was a view to which, despite Durham's clear analysis and influence, no church appeared able to relate, let alone counter.

These were but few of the reasons for the breakdown of trust within British industry; savage and self-inflicted wounds had led to economic weakness and to the collapse of great firms. "If the Church is to fulfil its role as the voice of God in the community," the notes to the manifesto suggest, "it must seek to restore the concept of work to its rightful place in the life of the nation . . . it means that the Church must repudiate the comfortable assertion that religion and business do not mix and insist on the restoration of love as the true relationship between employer and the employed." This aspect of "love" might have a striking spinoff in the fields of marriage and divorce. "The Church must demand that individual self-interest linked to the profit motive is subordinate to the needs of the community as a whole and that we are all made for one another." The development of the best technology must therefore be encouraged to create the wealth to provide, through taxation, the income to pay those no longer engaged in industry. However, such a service ethic would not be viable unless people themselves saw work to be good.

Industrial democracy

Such a view would demand that churches actively support the movement towards economic and industrial democracy. Lack of participation in decision-making, and the resistance of those in power to share that power, heighten the sense of division. Further, they heighten the sense of division between the two sides of what should be a corporate enterprise designed to serve the consumer. William Temple, in his remarkable work *Christianity and Social Order* (1942), called on the government—among other objectives—to provide "opportunities for workers to have a voice in the running of their firms".[191] Temple had called for five reforms, and four of them were enacted as a result of the Beveridge Report in 1942. The only one not to be enacted was the fourth—industrial democracy. Yet in seeking to help Germany recover from the disaster of the Second World War, Britain advocated just such a scheme which Germany absorbed to its great industrial benefit.[192] In not embracing this fourth point ourselves, we ensured the continuation of the industrial civil war not only in private enterprise but also in the nationalized industries, leading to the collapse of that brave experiment.

Without any stake in the running of its firms, labour sees itself as being primarily concerned with the wage packet. Democracy is the expression of trust and ultimately of love. These are the virtues that Jesus commended to the world through his disciples. In showing them to their Heavenly Father in the first instance, they might show them also towards their neighbours. It was essential that the gap between management and the worker be closed, that the worker be listened to, and his or her contribution to the industry or business acknowledged. Love also means that the Church must be prepared not to tolerate "boring, degrading, unpleasant work as the inevitable lot of the most poorly paid". There was a case for this type of work, rather than that bearing responsibility, attracting the greatest rewards. But perhaps that ideal will have to await the coming of real understanding of the kingdom in the industrial life of Britain.

In its analysis of inflation, unemployment, and work, the manifesto was seeking to apply the teaching of Jesus in the Sermon on the Mount to the contemporary world. It was an attempt to help create a society where people might *serve* one another as the prime dynamic for society. A society whose people are a holy people, with factories which turn out the most excellent products for the benefit of the consumer, both at home and overseas.

Crime

In a similar way the manifesto went on to deal with the problem of crime. This was the speciality of Stanley Linsley, the Chair of the group. His concern lay with the record crime levels that our society had suffered, annually and incredibly, since the Second World War. This led the Committee to analyse the situation we faced, beginning to question the policy of spending ever-increasing amounts of money on prison building, police equipment, and the forces of containment. The true answer lay rather in reducing the psychological pressures to commit crime which were latent in our society. These might be thought of as the glorification of wealth rather than work in our media, the emphasis on the "taxman" as an oppressor rather than an enabler, so that our community might contribute to the good of all. Our society needed to give our people objectives other than money, in a positive desire to live and serve the community. There was much evidence that the potential was there in the wealth of good works and benevolent activities that existed within the community already. It needed release, both by destroying the evils of social injustice and also by positive teaching. This included reducing the element of punishment in the legal and prison system, and focusing more on the element of rehabilitation—a matter of love rather than hate.

The family

Then the manifesto dealt with the family. This was an issue close to the hearts of Bishop Gray and Bishop Lindsay. The institution of the family was under increasing pressure in society as a whole, as individual satisfaction replaced corporate love. Individualism placed family life under enormous pressure, with the emphasis on rights rather than responsibility, on sex rather than love. Media interest in the exposure of infidelity and marriage breakdown gave an impression of public acceptability quite contrary to traditional teaching. The churches found themselves called upon to endorse a way of life accepted by the state but contrary to accepted traditional morality. Questions of birth control, abortion, divorce and remarriage, and euthanasia all reflected the intense period of moral re-examination the nation was undergoing. Nationally, there was a struggle to find new mores to replace the traditional culture. Neo-liberalism's promise of freedom had permeated down to the poor where marriage breakdown contributed to homelessness, one-parent families, drug dependency, debt, and crime. These were questions the Committee struggled with in attempting to find some message for partners in distress or children in trauma.

...and the Church

It had been clear in the mind of the original Liverpool group which had met at Bishop's Lodge in 1969 that the structures of the churches themselves were also involved. They needed to be patterned on the gospel of the kingdom, if they were ever to be able to fulfil their true role. At this point CTN was venturing into an area that was foreign to traditional thinking. Committee members were aware that many within the Church would be anxious over this attempt to ground the gospel in modern society. It was therefore decided to submit this thinking to significant figures in the economic and business sphere. Members were encouraged by the reaction of specialists.

The industrialist George Goyder, a significant Anglican layman and member of the Standing Committee of General Synod, wrote to the Central Co-ordinating Committee:

> Thank you for sending me the notes on the proposed manifesto. I find this an exciting document and wanted to cheer at many points. I think I can honestly say that I agree with every word of it... if people think what you say is too political I think that the right answer is that it is biblical and expresses the righteousness of God.

And Keith Jackson, an economist and Head of the Social Studies Division of Liverpool University, wrote:

> I think you are courageous and very right to work out a manifesto such as this, although as you know I do not find it possible to see the solution to our problems being discovered or achieved with the help of any divine agency.

Jackson himself was an atheist. Support also came from the Archbishops' Council on Evangelism. John Poulton, the Council's Executive Secretary, wrote:

> What you are proposing is, of course, a charter for revolution, as the gospel must always be.

Baden Hickman, the highly respected religious affairs correspondent of *The Guardian*, also wrote enthusiastically in support of the manifesto.

However, as the Committee had feared, many clergy were alarmed at this venture into a critical appraisal of contemporary secular culture, however relevant it might be to society at large. Indeed, Bishop Lindsay felt that we were going beyond our brief, as it was up to the church leaders to define policy, and that the church people of the North were not ready for this sort of appraisal. Bishop Gray also expressed doubt as to whether such a declaration ought to come from the grassroots rather than the leadership.[193] Despite these doubts the Chair of the Committee, Archdeacon Linsley, insisted, "The manifesto is a most useful tool for today's Church."[194]

A more socially oriented theology of mission

The second part of the manifesto dealt with the positive aspects of our society and faith, believing that what the evangelist says must be all of a piece with what the evangelist is. It must also reflect the institution the evangelist represents. The structures of a church, or indeed a nation endorsed by the Church, can disqualify the evangelist in the eyes and ears of their hearers. However, if our people were to have the insight and courage to speak, they themselves had first to find God as Saviour, as Jesus himself had taught: "Seek and ye shall find" (Matthew 7:7), based on the Deuteronomic text "If ye seek me ye shall find me" (Deuteronomy 4:29).

Thus the manifesto had to speak to the nation on behalf of the Church in the name of God. Only in this way could the Church be heard and laity be given the confidence to speak about the kingdom to their fellows in the industrial and commercial life of the nation.

It was hoped that Bishopthorpe V in 1973 might endorse the manifesto and so give a clear message to the North. Indeed, the Archbishop of York, on occasion privy to our meetings as time permitted, encouraged this new direction and vision.[195] However, it soon became clear from the wide range of reactions we were receiving that conservative churchmen found this sociological interpretation of the teaching on the kingdom alarming. The Bishop of Blackburn wrote, "I must say I do not find the manifesto on my wavelength . . . it sounds as if we are presenting the gospel as a cure for the ills of society, whereas I believe the right reason for preaching the gospel is that it is true." Canon Ronald Preston of Manchester, the highly respected Professor of Social and Pastoral Theology, wrote a very helpful analysis of the arguments of the manifesto but concluded that it was too negative. Finally, it was clear from David Blunt that the Archbishop himself had become concerned lest it might be regarded as naive, perhaps over-simplifying and pietistic.

Bishop John Habgood, newly appointed to Durham, defended the document as "an attempt to work out a more socially-oriented theology of mission". However, it was agreed that the manifesto might be relegated to "study document" status rather than anything endorsed by the CTN leadership.[196] In the meantime, Archdeacon Linsley used it to great effect in his frequent speaking around the North.

CHAPTER 18

The Trumpet Sounds

The message

On Easter Sunday 1972 a message was read in all the churches of the traditional Christian denominations across the North of England. The message was from the leaders of the churches of the North, the Archbishop of York, the Archbishop of Liverpool, and John Marsh, to the people of the North. This was a call to action in preparation for a United Mission to the North. All clergy throughout the North (and where there were no resident clergy, lay preachers or senior laity) had received two copies of the letter, one for reading at the services on that day and the other for the notice board of the church or chapel. The text of the "Call" had been drawn up, hammered out, and finalized by the three church leaders. It was a call to all church people to make ready during the coming twelve months for the launch of Call to the North.

Whatever the letter did, it surprised the North. People and press alike had never heard of such a thing before. No doubt some clergy, priests, or ministers forgot to read it, some may not have liked the idea and quietly put it aside,[197] but undoubtedly from most pulpits, on that fine and clear Easter morning, the message of the churches, united in mission as never before, was heard. The message declared a concern that church people should become effective in the proclamation of the gospel. First, we must together speak a word from God to men and women . . . "God lives, God reigns, God cares . . .", read the Archbishop of York himself in a television broadcast from the Cathedral at Blackburn. "God is calling his people to action everywhere."

Even church leaders who had doubts as to the wisdom of the movement gave their support and encouraged their congregations to hear the letter.

From its reading, there then sprang into existence the many hundreds, if not thousands of lay groups throughout the North, ready to study together in preparation for Holy Week 1973. Meanwhile church leaders in all denominations had received a copy of the *Handbook for Church Leaders*, which set out the "aim and principles of CTN" together with its organization, so no one would feel that things had gone on without their knowledge.

The media

To give a public edge to their "Call" Kevin Logan had arranged for the three "archbishops" to meet the press at the home of Patrick Rodger, the new Bishop of Manchester, for a "photo call". The picture appeared in both national and local press, allowing the world at large to see the three leaders standing together with the letter heard throughout the North that Easter Sunday. After the photo call the leaders were entertained by the BBC at its headquarters in Manchester. John Miles, who had replaced General Block at the Church Information Office, and Stewart Cross, then the BBC's Northern Religious Adviser, had arranged lunch. This allowed the leaders to meet the media specialists and share with them their hopes for the work of the churches together in the coming twelve months.

Over lunch the senior TV departmental head drew our attention to what he felt to be the need for some "dramatic shape to be given to the movement". This would enable the media to "home in" on the work that was going on. Given such a key, he believed, the interest of radio, and more especially of television, together with the press, both local and national, would be stimulated. Their reportage, in turn, would undoubtedly stimulate discussion and concern in places where people congregate. This would give church people greater opportunities to talk about their Christian faith. The suggestion was exciting and was treated seriously by the northern leadership.

As a senior lay TV specialist had commended it, the churches would now have to act. Call to the North needed to make religion a talking point in the secular world and so release Christian people to talk about their faith in factory, office, home, and club. Church people had felt inhibited,[198] but with television reaching into every home this would open doors for Christians to share their faith. Manchester was the centre of the mass communication industry in the North and so would be the venue for action.

The plan was put to the Manchester Council of Churches. Ray Colley, the regional television manager for the BBC in the North West, joined me as the "secular technical expert" to meet the Council. The Council of Churches, led by Bishop Patrick Rodger, warmed to the idea. "Could we," asked Ray Colley, "pack the Albert Square with people, young people and men in particular? Could we then use our church leaders to deliver an inspiring message and surround it with the best build-up material the churches could provide?" Put in these terms, the Council thought it could. With all the churches co-operating, there would be little difficulty in producing the crowds. We had twelve months in which to prepare, and if this is what the BBC felt ought to be done, then the Manchester churches would see that it was done and done well.

This was a positive response to a secular initiative. However, once the idea reached the corridors of power in Broadcasting House, London, it was quickly vetoed as being just the sort of thing "the Church must learn to avoid for the sake of its own credibility and image". This reaction from the South was not an easy pill for Manchester or its northern colleagues to swallow.[199]

Lay groups

The church leaders' letter, however, had now been heard in the pews and through the media across the North. This led to an immediate and sustained demand for material from the secretariat by lay study groups. The clergy groups had already completed their study of *Say Your Piece*, and now the Central Co-ordinating Committee was encouraged that local ecumenical lay groups had already been formed. The Roman Catholic bishops believed that the key to getting any movement under way lay in an effective response by local lay leadership to clerical initiative. Shortcuts which avoided lay leadership on the grounds that it might be difficult would lead at best to half-hearted endeavours. The sympathetic Roman Catholic bishops were prepared to finance their groups.

This part of the programme, however, was not the overall success hoped for by the leadership. Although the lay group programme was widely taken up, there were clearly some areas where nothing at all happened. George Andrew had warned that it takes many years for a new idea or vision to become acceptable across the board; he well understood the conservative culture of the Catholic Dioceses of Middlesbrough and Hexham and Newcastle. Again, denominational differences left some congregations cautious. Moreover, clergy who were themselves in the process of coming to terms with the ideas of CTN were not anxious to expose their laity to a similar ecumenical challenge. For others, commitment to the study groups proved new and uncomfortable; moreover, it was demanding of time, which some felt unable to give.

By late summer, nevertheless, orders came flooding in from all over the North for *Say Your Piece*. In addition, some areas were developing their own material. The Bishop of Chester, under the leadership of Archdeacon Leslie Fisher and Captain Cecil Clarke (Church Army), was producing a massive weight of study material supplied by specialist groups from right across Cheshire. Sheffield, under the leadership of Provost Ivan Neill, had drawn up a useful set of studies, which were used in South Yorkshire, North Nottinghamshire, and North Derby. York itself had produced an attractive study guide, beautifully illustrated, entitled *Things People Say* (by Michael Wright). The North East Ecumenical Group had also produced study material. All these studies were designed to help laity meet their counterparts in the other churches and think through with them what mission meant today as they prepared for Call to the North.

This, however, was the preparation; action was to follow in Lent 1973 when the groups turned from study to meet and engage with their non-churchgoing neighbours.

Enabling lay witness and Working Party 5

The Central Co-ordinating Committee realized that encounter with Jesus requires more than the publication of his words; fundamentally, it required an encounter with witnesses who have themselves met Jesus. Essentially, Call to the North, although led by a leadership united in purpose, was fundamentally designed to be spearheaded by lay people united by conviction. They were then able to witness to the non-churchgoer—this was believed to be where mission would really take place. These meetings would be in the factory, the leisure centre, the home and neighbourhood where non-church people were to be found. The key to the success of CTN lay in releasing the laity of all our churches to be able to speak. In the words of Jesus, "to testify what they had seen".[200]

Planning this lay initiative across the North led the Co-ordinating Committee to suggest that a group of specialists be established under a competent chair. This led to a fifth Working Party being set up, and the Archbishop was asked to invite Miss Pamela Edis, Secretary to the Bishop of Liverpool, to lead the work. Membership of this Working Party was widely drawn from across the North and included the Vicar of Leeds (Graham Foley), Mr Martyn Hallsall (a journalist), the Jesuit Ralph Woodhall, Dick Williams (author and Rector of Woolton, Liverpool), together with Roy Lawrence of St George's Hyde, who was to prove a veritable mine of ideas and literature. Also contributing were John A. Coyne of Aughton Park, Ivor Jones of Hartley Victoria College, Manchester, Don Lewis (St Peter's Hale), and Don Roberts (Vicar of Parr).

In addition, assistance was provided by the British and Foreign Bible Society (B&FBS) General Secretary, Neville Cryer, who seconded an outstanding member of his staff, a Baptist minister newly home from East Africa, Tom Houston. He made the regular inter-city journey to Liverpool to assist the Working Party. It was probably one of the most hard-worked of all the groups, its members not only having the burden of regular meetings in Church House, Liverpool, but a good deal of homework as well. Without the assistance of the publishing expertise of the B&FBS, its task would have been impossible. The secretarial resources of Church House, Liverpool, were also generously made available to the work of the group by David Orman, Secretary to the Diocesan Board of Finance.

Pamela Edis, in setting up the Working Party, wrote to each member describing the work as "bridge-building and barrier-breaking"; the focus must be on enabling laity to become effective witnesses. She referred to the exercise "The People Next Door", created some years previously by the British Council of Churches (BCC). In the report on that exercise the authors of "The People Next Door" made two points which were particularly relevant to Working Party 5. These were:

1. Many Christians did not know any non-church people; and
2. if they did, they had no idea of how to talk to them about the Christian faith.

It was clear that this was an area of enormous importance. If our own Christian people were unable to make use of the opportunities provided by their contacts with non-churchgoers, there would be little purpose in encouraging the mass media to make religion a talking point during Lent and Easter 1973. Working Party 5 therefore had to seek ways to help Christian people articulate their faith.

The Working Party was asked to consider producing a "kit", "whereby ecumenical parish lay groups might use Lent 1973 in meeting their non-churchgoing neighbours on their own ground and talking about their faith". The concept of a kit, consisting of aids for lay witness, was drawn from the earlier "The People Next Door" exercise. Some 11,000 copies of *Say Your Piece* had already been printed and sold. This suggested that there would be a considerable demand for some solid material to help members of the lay groups to speak to their neighbours during the following Lent. So a kit, including the pamphlet *Communicating the Christian Faith*, was produced, together with a leader's booklet. This kit was described as "an instrument for action", and its six sessions were designed to help Christian laity understand how to communicate with non-churchgoers. To bring local group members into contact with people outside their normal range of interest, a survey of their local area was promoted.

Good news for the North

The Central Co-ordinating Committee believed that in addition to approaching the outsider, a helpful reinforcement might be for the laity to give local people something which could be valued for its own sake, and would continue to work after the visitor had left. With this in mind, Tom Houston of the British and Foreign Bible Society promised to produce a special edition of a Gospel in the modern "Today's English Version" translation. The Working Party liked the idea and suggested that it might have a special CTN cover and be supplemented by illustrations and quotes from well-known people. In other words it would put into the hands of non-churchgoers something that was new, but something which had the gospel as its core.

St Mark's Gospel was chosen because it set forth, perhaps more vividly than any other New Testament book, a picture of Jesus himself. It was the person of Jesus that CTN was seeking to commend, in the hope that in meeting him people might be led to reflect on his gospel of the kingdom and be led to follow his way of life. Mark was short, racy, readable, with sufficient material about Jesus to make people want to discover more about him and his teaching from Matthew, Luke, or John. Mark also shows Jesus challenging the culture of his own day; then the gospels of Matthew and Luke fill this out. CTN had to help people who saw Jesus in the lives of their contemporaries discover Jesus for themselves. The pages of the Gospel might well help them not only to read about him but to experience him in their own lives. Mark, then, it was. The Working Party sought to make Mark a talking point and the rest of the work revolved around the Gospel of that Evangelist.

So the B&FBS produced this edition of Mark's Gospel, illustrated by the cartoonist Bill Tidy and the drawings of David Charters, both of Southport. In addition, the text was supplemented by words of commendation from people whose names were well-known: men and women who could testify to their faith—Violet Carson of *Coronation Street*, Andrew Cruickshank of *Dr Finlay* fame, the cricketer David Sheppard, George Cansdale, well-known for his animal talks, and Cliff Richard, whose pop songs were heard by the youth of the land. They all gladly agreed to contribute. Roy Lawrence produced a theme song for the movement: "Stumpy fingers", owing its title to the belief that Mark had short fingers. Its catchy tune and words gave it wide, albeit brief popularity. The Gospel was bound in paperback with a cover in red on a blue ground depicting the North Country, and the whole made a very handsome package.

Meanwhile, Working Party 5 was busy on a study guide to St Mark. This again consisted of six sessions, and was designed to enable ecumenical lay groups to do some serious thinking on the Gospel they would be commending to the local population in the weeks that lay ahead. Neville Cryer, General Secretary of the B&FBS, was now redeeming his promise to the 1972 Bishopthorpe Consultation. He met with the Bible Reading Consultative Group (formed of the Bible Reading and Publishing Societies). In consequence, they published for Lent 1973 a special CTN lectionary on St Mark, together with a booklet and commentary on the Gospel for the forty-nine days of Lent. Like the Gospel text, the booklet had a bright and attractive cover illustrating the North and was published under the joint imprint of the Societies.

Always was there the consciousness that only the Holy Spirit himself could unlock the hearts and ears of the people of the North, that they might hear. Despite this generous backing of the resources of the churches of the North, there was an awareness of our own poverty, particularly in prayer. This led Pamela Edis to approach Dick Williams, Rector of Woolton and author of *The Gospel in Scouse* and *Prayers for Today's Church*. Williams readily agreed to write a book on prayer using St Mark as his central theme. So *Pray around St Mark* appeared, to stand alongside the other publications and to support those groups who wanted help with prayer in their studies of the Gospel.

Lent prior to the launch

A vast number of groups had come into existence largely as a result of the 1972 Easter Letter. The groups varied from tiny rural gatherings to large urban groups. The Vicar of the Dales village of Abbeystead in Bowland, with the support of a Methodist local preacher and the Catholic priest, had gathered the scattered Dales folk into his vicarage to work on the study material. In the cities of the North, clergy working together were able to set up strings of groups, particularly—although not only—in the well-to-do middle-class suburbs. In less sophisticated parishes we discovered requests being made by laity to set up their own meetings. Sometimes their clergy were asked not to attend, as lay people feared that the presence of a professional theologian would inhibit discussion by their non-churchgoing neighbours. Although widespread, however, the response to Call to the North was still patchy, and much depended on the enthusiasm (or lack of it) of the local leadership. Correspondence which flowed in at this period from all over the North nevertheless showed that even in areas where the movement received little official encouragement, inspired groups of clergy and laity wanted material in order to meet together.

Lent 1973 was the time it was planned that study would be replaced by action and that church laity would reach out to non-churchgoers. The Working Party therefore focused on seeking to equip these ecumenical study groups already in being. Working Party 5 produced a range of material to cater for different needs, in the form of a kit containing three alternative outreach programmes for Lent 1973.

The first programme, "Good News", was designed for a group engaging in a door-to-door visitation. The programme had six sessions and started with preparation and training. Then followed briefing, the distribution of the Gospel of Mark, now in its bright colours and entitled *Good News for the North by a Man called Mark*, and finally an assessment evening. The programme was designed for churches strong enough to have laity who could face up to knocking on doors in order to meet their non-churchgoing neighbours.

The second programme was entitled "Face to Face". This was a programme for house groups and was designed to enable an ecumenical Christian group to invite non-practising neighbours—perhaps met at work, through sport, or while shopping—to the group meeting. These six sessions included training in running group meetings, a study of the needs of the area, an evangelistic evening, and a final assessment.

Then there was a "Publicity Dinner". This made use of the "stewardship dinner" idea but used the event for evangelism, with after-dinner speakers talking about faith to the guests. The programme was designed to encourage church laity to invite non-church friends out to a free meal in a local restaurant, where they not only met with Christian fellowship but also heard interesting Christian witness.[201] The event was set within the context of the "Face to Face" programme of preparation. As with the house meetings in the second scheme, each of the guests was given a copy of *Good News for the North by a Man called Mark*. In all, some half a million copies of the Gospel were printed during this period. In addition, programmes for the study groups were provided in the form of a handy kit which could be bought as a unit.

Ten local radio stations across the North, from Radio Newcastle to Radio Sheffield, ran a series of programmes during the six weeks of Lent supporting Call to the North, including news of local events in their new programmes. Ivor Jones of Hartley Victoria College, Manchester, was largely responsible for co-ordinating this work.

The need for a logo to identify Call to the North was suggested by John Marsh, so the Co-ordinating Committee set up a North Country competition and invited a comprehensive range of people from across the country to submit designs. The attractive modern design which won first place used the "T" of CTN in the form of a figure embracing the "C" and the "N"; this became widely known and used throughout the North. The CTN symbol adorning the front of our publications was the product of the Chester group. Chester, interestingly enough, also provided the second most popular design—"The Cock of the North"—which the county itself preferred and continued to use for most of its own publicity. This provided some most attractive posters.

The Central Co-ordinating Committee was astonished by the sheer amount of material that CTN stimulated in this period across the North. Not only was the study guide *Say Your Piece* still selling well, but of Working Party 5's publications, handled by the British and Foreign Bible Society, some three-quarters of a million items were reported to have been ordered from all parts of the North, including the North East. It was a magnificent achievement for the Working Party and its Chair. In addition, the various areas had been producing their own materials which were now being used locally; moreover, there were the four major reports of the Working Parties, which sprang out of the Manchester Paper, together with the Manifesto and its Notes. This clearly demonstrated the potential rewards for clear leadership in the field of mission and unity; moreover, it put the Central Co-ordinating Committee in good heart as Bishopthorpe V approached.

The real heart of the action, however, lay in local areas, many of which were well able to develop a range of mission activity under the banner of CTN without reference to the publications inspired by the Committee. Even so, there were other areas that needed and called for assistance. At this period, with the support of our Bishops, three of us—Stanley Linsley, Dennis Corbishley, and I—were engaged in almost continuous travelling throughout the North, listening, advising, and publicizing.

More working parties

As different needs surfaced in local areas, the Central Co-ordinating Committee set up a further series of working groups to meet the needs and provide support. The proposal to set up the big "media" event in Manchester led to the suggestion that similar events might take place in other population centres. Working Party 6 was therefore created and headed up by Ray Colley, the Regional TV Manager for the BBC in the North West. However, when the concept was vetoed in London, that Working Party was wound up.

The need to relate the work of CTN to the youth of the North Country led to Working Party 7. Members met in the Catholic Chaplaincy of Liverpool University under the leadership of Alan Ripley, the Anglican Youth Chaplain. The Dean of the Anglican Cathedral in Liverpool, Edward Patey, immediately gave the work his full support. The cathedral was preparing to receive the BCC's Youth Conference in the autumn of 1973. The Working Party's efforts resulted in one of the liveliest incidents of CTN preparation in the youth field: the organizing of a pop song contest, "Sing around Mark". Cliff Richard judged the event and presented the first prize. There was a heavy response to the invitation to enter songs relevant to the work of Call to the North. Ultimately, the winner was a boy of 14. He was given a hero's welcome in Liverpool Cathedral, and the competition's widespread publicity provided encouragement for the study of Mark taking place in ecumenical groups across the North.

The importance of CTN relating to the Christian societies of the universities and to the denominational chaplains led to Working Party 8, headed up by Douglas Brown, the Methodist Secretary for student work in Manchester. Furthermore it was clear that Kevin Logan, our publicity officer, would be helped by a support group, which led to the creation of Working Party 9 to oversee our publicity. In an early report Logan pointed up the difficulty CTN publicity faced: "No tangible product to sell and an existing antipathy to the product we are selling!"[202] The group at first focused on local radio stations, encouraging the use of St Mark's themes to provide back-up programmes during Lent. Kevin Logan met regularly with the panel of local religious advisers for this purpose. From the Working Party sprang a large variety of posters, stickers, tee shirts, beer mats, cards, even a tie and suggestions for a special Post Office stamp. Floral displays in public parks were planned and executed with the co-operation of local authorities.

As with practically all the work of CTN, given its financial stringency, many of these initiatives had to be self-financing and people were encouraged to purchase the range of materials now available. Despite the agreement reached without dissent at Bishopthorpe, it seemed incredible that not all church leaders proved willing or able to contribute financially. David Blunt struggled to cope with the financial demands of this now enormous organization. As a result, a necessary caution trimmed back some of the more imaginative suggestions. Unfortunately it also contributed to the frustration that Kevin Logan began to experience in his work for CTN and which led to his sudden and dramatic departure within weeks of Easter 1973. He confessed later:

> I worked willingly within the tiny budget, though I wished for more. I had hundreds of pounds for a job that demanded hundreds of thousands of pounds. However, this in no way led to my eventual disenchantment with Call to the North. I accepted that funds were limited and we had to do the best we could.

Knowing a professional poster/display campaign was very limited, throughout the North I tried to set up DIY media/publicity teams in as many towns and cities as possible. Stewart Cross, Brandon Jackson

(Bradford), Michael Wright and many others were of great help, and they called together local media teams with great enthusiasm. It was a delight to work alongside the local teams and give advice and training where necessary.

The last Working Party to be established was number 10: "Ongoing Mission in the Seventies". This was again chaired by Pam Edis, with the remit to plan ahead for a programme of continuous ecumenical mission for the Northern Province after Holy Week and Easter. This was where the heart of Stuart Blanch lay. If this was successful, then CTN—created largely on his initiative—would have achieved his vision: to transform the culture of the church of the North—right across the denominations—from maintenance to a focus on its divine calling of mission. The North would never be the same.

The Working Party didn't fail him; its Yellow Paper ("Call to the North: Its Future") was a carefully thought-out response to the question "Where do we go from here?" and bears the hallmark of Stuart Blanch's thinking. It was a practical vision for the ongoing work of CTN, uniting all the churches of the North in mission into the future for the salvation of the whole North.

Anxieties and cold water

As the pace of the work increased and more and more column inches were appearing in the local press, so Call to the North became talked about throughout the churches and local communities. Even in factories and public houses, and across denominations and beliefs, CTN had become a talking point.

This widespread interest naturally led to local media exploiting the opportunity. Tyne Tees Television networked an ecumenical CTN (Action North-East) service from St Hilda's, South Shields. The programme was excellently produced and widely watched, and the leadership was pleased. CTN was now becoming accepted across the region. However, just as the North began to appear united in mission, the North's very effectiveness raised alarm bells in quarters which so far had stood quietly apart, perhaps hoping and assuming such a mission venture could never happen.

As a result, a number of anxious voices now began to protest to church leaders that the churches were being too hasty in seeking to launch so massive an ecumenical enterprise in 1973. Some leaders then turned to the secretariat to point out that we could not guarantee that everyone was ready for such an event. It would be wise now, they suggested, to call a halt in case the movement were to fail. One leader wrote:

> I am sure that the success of an ecumenical mission to the North depends more than anything else on the support of the clergy of all denominations. That support will only come from clergy who have had the experience of working together. This might take as much as two or three years . . . and to my mind Lent 1973 is premature.

For members of the Central Co-ordinating Committee who had travelled the North meeting local clergy, this was no surprise. The concept of working together in mission was very new and for some it was also alarming. There were those who believed that the church identity for which they had lived and had given their lives was now being betrayed. For others, CTN was dangerous as it might fail and so damage all the churches. George Andrew Beck himself had cautioned that more time was indeed needed for minds to adjust themselves to this new ecumenical concept. He knew his fellow diocesans, and indeed the Vatican. Yet the movement had already been postponed once, so to attempt a second postponement might prove to be a death knell for the whole enterprise. The letter, however, reflected starkly the anxieties of a senior church leader, perhaps keen to move in the direction he knew to be right yet aware that by moving too quickly he could isolate himself from those who looked to him for care and guidance. He was not the only one to express concern.

Anxiety was now also being expressed in Roman Catholic quarters as to the rightness of exposing Catholic laity to Protestant challenges in ecumenical study groups. For Catholics this was something that had historically been anathema. Questions of the sacrifice of the mass, abortion, contraception, or clerical celibacy and the like might disturb the faith of loyal Catholic laity. There was uncertainty also as to whether a programme which included scripture distribution might prove unwise, as the concept of reading the Bible was very new for Catholic laity. George Andrew discussed these problems with me.[203]

At the opposite end of the scale the Elim Pentecostal Church was also having doubts, as its membership was questioning the rightness of being associated with Roman Catholicism through CTN. Although the other main Pentecostal Church, the Assemblies of God, was never prepared to be part of CTN, at least the presence of the Elim Church in 1971 and 1972 had completed the spectrum of Christian traditions making up the English Church of the North. A letter on 21 February from Cheltenham, where Elim had its headquarters, therefore carried disappointing news. The North-Eastern presbytery, the Chair explained, had requested that the church should take no further part in CTN, and "this attitude . . . seems to be fully supported by our whole movement. Sadly therefore they had to request that the name of the Elim Church be deleted from the membership of the conference." Cecil Jarvis had meanwhile, I noted, been translated to Guernsey.

Moreover, the Church of England was not without its own problems. There had been a number of episcopal retirements, and newly-appointed bishops coming into the Northern Province found they were inheriting an exercise in the formation of which they had had no part. One new diocesan bishop found the concept of CTN against his principles, so with a large and cheerful grin he confessed, "I'm declaring UDI,"[204] and promptly closed the door to any further CTN activity in his diocese. Another newcomer warned me that he was certainly not allowing any "take-over bids" for mission in his diocese. This was sad, as until then his people had been supportive.

The irritation felt by new church leaders on coming into their responsibilities and finding their independence threatened by this unexpected Provincial network was, for some, intolerable. Nothing in their previous experience in the South had prepared them for this. Some, unfortunately, proved incapable of seeing that the good of the whole outweighed the good of their own independence. The glory of their particular tree prevented them seeing the glory of the northern woodland they were now called to inhabit. The bishops who had assisted in bringing Call to the North to birth had, in most cases, had long years in their sees; they knew the issues.[205] Indeed, they had discussed the original concept in Convocation, and so had been confident in their contribution. Newcomers, however, accepting new and heavy leadership responsibilities, inevitably required time to find their feet. Fortunately, some who expressed the greatest reservations at first later became firm supporters of the movement. Although all leaders appeared prepared, indeed keen to come to the annual Consultation, some also proved determined to maintain their own vision for their diocese or district, and in some cases this proved less than helpful for CTN.

The church leaders of the two main episcopal churches, Anglican and Catholic, again related very differently to this ecumenical venture. Catholic bishops felt their prime responsibility was to the Vatican, and there was a deep loyalty to the Pope of the day. It was commitment to the vision of Vatican II, the Decree on Ecumenism, and John XXIII that led George Andrew Beck to work with his opposite numbers in the Reformed traditions. But a similar loyalty to current Vatican tradition and to Paul VI allowed Middlesbrough and its allies to stand aloof.

Anglican bishops, on the other hand, felt a prime responsibility to their own see, so it depended on their personal vision of that responsibility as to what extent they were prepared to surrender their independence to this common enterprise, despite their Archbishop's views.

David Blunt, as Treasurer of the CTN, could not but feel that there were leaders who were deliberately withholding financial support. He wrote:

> If they are not going to provide the money, it is not going to be easy to continue Call to the North through to the 1980s, as had been agreed by Scargill 1973. If they give the impression of supporting Call to the North indefinitely, then they must back this by ongoing financial commitment; one without the other does not seem possible. Our total budget is absurdly modest for so large an operation.[206]

The Central Co-ordinating Committee was already concerned that our budgets were not being met by the church leaders, and thus the work was suffering, particularly that of Kevin Logan. However, Stuart Blanch was opposed to any fundraising to support CTN, believing that CTN was an exercise in leadership. The leaders themselves needed to back their public commitment by financing the operation.

Loyalty to their own ecclesiastical tradition inhibited members of the Committee from discussing this openly, yet it appeared that all three traditions had leaders who were fundamentally opposed to mission or united witness. However, they apparently felt unable to express their views publically at Bishopthorpe. So publically they agreed to the contribution, but in fact sent nothing.

Meanwhile a suggestion was made that CTN appeal to the pew to meet its financial needs. It was suggested that every congregation throughout the North be invited to contribute £1 to CTN. The Co-ordinating Committee, after consultation, responded positively and contacted church leaders with this suggestion. The Catholic dioceses generally agreed, as did most of the Anglicans and some of the Free Churches. But fierce opposition was also encountered from some Free Church leaders on the grounds that decisions on financing had been made by the leadership at Scargill. The Co-ordinating Committee, they believed, had exceeded its remit by suggesting such a request.[207] However, given the financial stringency faced by the movement it was decided, with the assistance of the B&FBS, nevertheless to press ahead with a letter to all participating congregations across the North.[208] If the leaders who had agreed to contribute at Scargill had fulfilled their solemn pledge, there would have been no need to appeal to the pew now. Fortunately, the pew was generous, so sustaining the network and secretariat. It was a measure of how CTN was valued by the laity.

Further anxiety was being expressed in the South, particularly London, about this ecumenical evangelistic movement in the North of England. That the North was taking this initiative was proving disturbing to southern church leadership, particularly the Evangelicals. The CTN secretariat began to receive more letters reporting these concerns. Senior Evangelicals in the South were writing to their northern counterparts expressing concern that Evangelicals were supporting Call to the North. They feared that its close liaison with Roman Catholicism would lead to confusion in the evangelical movement. These fears were fanned by a communiqué from the Catholic Information Office in London in August

1972, urging northern Catholics to work with their Protestant fellow-Christians in Call to the North for the Christianization of the North of England.[209] This display of Christian unity in mission encouraged the northern church leaders, but it equally alarmed some southerners. A letter from the Evangelical Council expressing deep concern over whether the Call to the North was "sound" was received by the secretariat, calling for their assurances.[210]

Even more disturbingly, however, in the autumn of 1972 a large-scale Conference on Evangelism was mounted by leading London Evangelicals. This, for the first time, had the declared intention of choosing a northern venue, ostensibly to "strengthen evangelism in the North of England". Without any consultation with northern Evangelicals,[211] a venue was chosen, and the event took place at Morecambe under the leadership of famous names in the London Evangelical world. A large number of evangelical clergy and laity from London and the South East arrived by car and train; Evangelicals from the North were also warmly invited to attend the conference, but none were invited to contribute from the platform.[212] Northern evangelical members then had the galling experience of being told about important and exciting projects of mission taking place in the South of England, on the Continent, and even in the United States, with not a word about evangelism in the Northern Province itself. All efforts by North-Country Evangelicals to secure any reference to evangelism in the North or Call to the North were most courteously brushed aside.[213] The conference, having done its work, then dispersed. The London Evangelicals, apparently well satisfied that the North had been given the inspiration and guidance it needed, were happy to return south.

These developments—anxieties over Rome, the withdrawal of Elim, new leaders suspicious of the movement, and calls for postponement—led the Central Co-ordinating Committee to express some anxiety in briefing the leadership. All efforts of the senior leadership were now geared towards Holy Week 1973, only some six months or so away. Despite these widespread anxieties, however, the Committee was convinced that a further postponement would now be a disaster. Fortunately, given the unity of the senior leadership, that likelihood was remote. Moreover, the Archbishops' Council on Evangelism (situated in the South) gave vital support, and the Council included impeccable Evangelical names such as Gordon Landreth, General Secretary of the Evangelical Alliance, and M. L. Rowlandson of the Billy Graham Evangelistic Association.

Perhaps the greatest shock of all, however, was the sudden and unexpected resignation of CTN's press officer. Kevin Logan had done an outstanding job on the smallest of resources. He had spent three days a week in Liverpool, commuting from his home in Blackburn, and a further three days working on the *Lancashire Evening Telegraph*, an important local paper with a large circulation. Since his appointment CTN had become news, not only in the local press and radio throughout the North, but in the national press too. Moreover, with a series of useful conferences at Foxhill House in Cheshire, Logan had been able to inform and assist the local press officers in the regions throughout the North. He felt, however, that poor quality office facilities and indifferent financial assistance were paralysing his efforts. The Church Information Office to which he was accountable did not seem able to help, and he shared his anxieties with me. I too was a part-timer with a parish to run, so I was unable to do much more than commiserate; Dennis Corbishley was in no better position. Indeed, it was one of the astonishing triumphs of CTN that its vision inspired Christians throughout the North to a level of dedication to mission unparalleled in the modern history of the Church. It was at the end of January, when we were at full stretch, in preparation for Bishopthorpe V to be followed by the Easter launch, that the news of Kevin Logan's departure became public and he went.

He had not arrived for a meeting of his support group, Working Party 9, but the members were not unduly anxious as they were aware of the pressures he was under. But then Kevin did arrive, late, to say that he had come to the conclusion that Call to the North was merely a cover for the Roman Catholic Church to take over the Protestant churches. He had therefore written to every editor in the North to expose the situation and filed a copy with the Press Association; this explained why he felt he had to resign. To say that members of the group were dumbfounded would certainly be to sum up their immediate reaction. However, they retired to communicate with the Church Information Office in London and to inform the Archbishops and John Marsh. A short statement expressing appreciation for Kevin Logan's work, understanding for his concern, and good wishes for his future was released.

Unbeknown to us, Kevin was a recent convert from Roman Catholicism to the Church of England. His doubts about contemporary Rome had finally brought him across to the English Church. Bishop Joe Gray commented to me privately afterwards that we should have been aware that converts were often unstable in this way.[214] An immediate search was undertaken for his successor, and within a week Eddie Neale, the religious advisor to Radio Merseyside—having first been interviewed somewhat carefully by the Archbishops of Liverpool and York—had been appointed by the Church Information Office.

CHAPTER 19

Clearing the Decks: Bishopthorpe V

The 1973 gathering of church leaders at Scargill turned out to be one of the more promising of the series. On the morning of 1 March, the "three archbishops" arrived at Scargill House early to meet over coffee in the library. This was an intimate room with a low roof and exposed beams, quiet lighting, and comfortable chairs, the whole embraced by bookshelves with volumes on everything from theology to climbing.

It was now five years since the first Bishopthorpe meeting in York and six since the idea was first mooted at Lambeth. Much would now depend on the inspiration of this consultation as to how things went during Holy Week and Easter, and hopefully for the following decades. So, led by George Andrew Beck, time was to be spent in prayer as well as in debate. The three senior church leaders had finished their meeting just as cars started to come up the long tree-lined drive of Scargill House, bringing church leaders from across the North. The Warden of the House, John Tabor, welcomed the guests, and Donald Coggan spoke a word on the purpose of this day of quiet and recollection together.

The first session met in the chapel and was led by George Andrew. Two hours had deliberately been given to each of the devotional sessions, and members of the consultation were invited to spend the time after each address either in quiet in the chapel itself, or else in walking about the grounds with other members. George Andrew was quite clear that it would only be in this way that a harmony of spirit between the leadership of the churches could grow, so allowing the Spirit of God to lead the churches forward in their role of mission. After tea John Marsh led the devotional session in the chapel, and the Archbishop of York followed him after dinner. By the time the leaders were enjoying their hot drinks in the lounge before retiring, it was already evident that there was a new spirit of fellowship and co-operation that could be felt and wondered over in the life of the consultation.

The morning of the second day was due to start with worship. However, many of the Anglican and Free Church leaders felt uncomfortable with the idea of a Communion service, as they knew that Catholic discipline would prevent the Roman Catholic participants from joining them. This could split the consultation at a very important time. Meanwhile, the Scargill Community made it clear that they would be very happy to welcome the church leaders to their regular devotions, and such an invitation would allow all to meet for non-eucharistic worship together.

However, the Archbishop of Liverpool, after consultation with the Conference of Northern Bishops, indicated that the Catholic bishops, although they could not take part in a Eucharist, would wish the conference to share in eucharistic worship at which they would be present. So it was, with George Andrew's encouragement, that the whole membership gathered early the next morning for Communion, celebrated in the chapel with what he described as a *logion*[215] from the Archbishop of York himself. There was a spirit of unity at the service such as we had not experienced before.[216]

Down to business

After breakfast the rest of the conference began to arrive for the business sessions. The 1973 consultation was richly enhanced by the presence of Harry Morton, then President of the Methodist Conference. Morton, a scintillating figure in any company, came as the guest of Lincoln Minshull, Chair of Darlington District. Harry Morton was also Secretary-General-Designate of the British Council of Churches. It might not be altogether clear what the Methodist views on prelacy were, but we had a higher turnout of Methodist Chairs with Harry Morton there than ever before.

Bishopthorpe V was also to be a milestone in that it was the first year a woman church leader was welcomed to the consultation, in the person of Miss Joyce Blake of the Society of Friends. We may have lost the Pentecostals, but now we had gained the Quakers. Joyce Blake, headmistress of the Mount School, was a significant figure in educational and church circles in York. In addition, joining us for lunch we had the secretaries and chairs of the Local Co-ordinating Committees who had been invited to join the leadership.

The day promised to be a busy one: not only were there the details of Holy Week 1973 to discuss, but as a result of the 1972 consultation a report had been circulated to all leaders on the future of Call to the North itself. This Yellow Paper—"Call to the North: Its Future"—was the responsibility of Working Party 10, set up by the 1972 Bishopthorpe consultation, with Pamela Edis in the chair. The future of ecumenical mission in the Northern Province to the peoples of the North now hung on this document. It was radical; it cut bureaucracy, but clearly endorsed and provided for an ongoing northern movement of churches united in mission. The text had been presented to and accepted by the Central Co-ordinating Committee in January and was now forwarded to the consultation for approval. The atmosphere of the consultation was such as to suggest that the report would be adopted and commended to the churches.

The Yellow Paper sprang out of a genuine concern that the fruits of Call to the North should not be wasted through ineffective follow-up. The idea of mission had sometimes acquired a name for ineffectualness, as once a project of mission was over the local church often settled back into its customary pre-mission routine; the enthusiasm and sometimes even the new members then evaporated. The report therefore called for what amounted to a long-term programme of ongoing planning for mission in the North, which might culminate in 1980 with a further Holy Week project.

The paper's main recommendation was that the church leaders should continue to meet on an annual basis to oversee mission—the Call to the North. These meetings would steer a movement to influence the culture in which we lived and so enable the church people of the North to express their faith in categories meaningful to their contemporaries. However, in addition a number of practical suggestions were put forward. These included:

- a think tank on mission strategy for the North in co-operation with the Archbishops' Council on Evangelism;

- the production of a paperback on CTN which might convey more widely a vision of the churches of the North united for mission;[217]
- an immediate post-launch survey across the North to discover what impact the exercise had had;
- the development of study courses to assist lay house groups research the impact of CTN on the North.

In the Marsh Lounge

The session opened with the Bishop of Liverpool speaking to the subject "Mission today", with John Marsh in the chair. Our appreciation of the importance of the occasion had led to Stuart Blanch being put in to bat first. By the time we had all assembled, however, the buoyant and spiritual atmosphere of the previous day had strangely changed. George Andrew had been right about the importance of prayers together. Now the injection of newcomers, innocent of yesterday's prayer and fellowship, altered the chemistry of the gathering. From my seat close to Stuart Blanch I knew that he, the most sensitive of men, could feel the change. He was breathing deeply from sheer tension as the room waited expectantly, and the UDI bishop, newly arrived, then seated himself opposite the speaker.

We were not disappointed. Stuart Blanch spoke simply and brilliantly, taking his theme from the prophetic witness of Israel in the eighth/sixth century BC and calling the leaders of the Christian North to speak clearly and to be prepared to have a "strategy of mission" to which all the churches could address themselves. After introducing the idea of mission speaking to contemporary society, political and economic, he pointed out that the prophets engaged in the national politics of the day:

> ... having very pertinent, and as things turned out, wise things to say about the relationships between Israel and the other nations of the world, about treaties and trade pacts. They looked askance at the social life of their people and the commercial and economic structures of their day in which the rich became richer and the poor became poorer (Amos 6), in which profit was the

only standard of success (Amos 8:5), and in which inflation was rampant (Haggai 1:6).[218]

It was a limpid and thoughtful start for the day.

Next Dennis Corbishley, on behalf of the Central Co-ordinating Committee, reviewed the progress of CTN during the past year and spoke of the preparations for Holy Week that had been taking place. His account was robust and exciting; it left one in no doubt that the Roman Catholic Church endorsed this vision of united mission to the North. David Blunt followed, presenting the financial needs of the movement.

During the coffee break, it became clear that some new arrivals were not too pleased with how things were going. Although the differences that had raised such levels of anxiety at meetings in earlier years were less evident, the critics had not been silenced and their determination not to be deflected from their own traditions remained formidable. "I didn't come here to be lectured on the Old Testament," complained one, and then there were other complaints of insufficient time being allowed for debate and discussion. Fortunately the negative voices were outnumbered by the prevailing spirit of anticipation. Numbers attending, moreover, were higher than ever,[219] which led some to suggest that there may have been those who reasoned that if CTN could not be killed, then it had better be controlled by turning up for the business meetings. It was also clear, as year succeeded year, that the consultation was becoming a valued forum for discussion, fellowship, and mutual support for all church leaders. Nevertheless, the leadership made sure that the prime reason for our meeting remained mission and the launch of Call to the North.

After coffee the Archbishop of York took the chair, and it was my turn: first to outline the plans contained in Pam Edis's Yellow Paper, for follow-up to Easter 1973.[220] We could not afford to squander the hard-won fruits of unity and united mission in the months and years following Holy Week and Easter 1973. Therefore the proposed programme would ensure that the impetus of mission would continue to reinforce our new-found unity. Working together, the current leadership had seen the Christian culture of the North transformed from defensive maintenance to outward-looking growth for all our churches. We now hoped to sustain this growth for future years.

Then came the opportunity to set the proposals against the cultural background of social changes taking place within our society. The consultation was reminded of the widespread doubt expressed as to the value of any united presentation of a Christian apologia because "The world had heard it all before," or because "The churches had nothing to say," or else, "The world would not listen to what the Church had to say." These views were now to be challenged: the Church had much to say to contemporary society, and perhaps things it had not heard before. Our traditional gospel would be affirmed, but as Stuart Blanch had reminded us, although that gospel remained the same, experience taught us that our presentation of the gospel no longer resonated with those among whom we lived. We needed, as Jesus did in his teaching on the kingdom, to speak to the needs of contemporary society.

This had forced the Central Co-ordinating Committee back to scripture, to see what Jesus had to say. We discovered that his personal emphasis in all four Gospels was on his teaching on the kingdom. His emphasis in Mark 1:39, expounded in the synagogue at Nazareth, meant his word to us as the Church of the North was one of love, of righteousness, and of hope. The Committee had therefore asked:

> Could this possibly be something that our contemporaries might be able to hear and respond to? If so, how could this gospel of the kingdom be interpreted in our secular culture?

This led us to a dramatic change in our presentation of Jesus. He was indeed Saviour, and all churches were concerned to present the world with the challenge of Christ crucified, but Jesus himself told us that he came to change society through the preaching of the gospel of God (Mark 1:39). We might find that challenging, but the purpose of Jesus was to give faith that society might be changed. Such a faith involved acceptance of the kingdom, with its embrace of society as Jesus saw it: of justice and righteousness.

The ideas within the proposed study guide and manifesto were then outlined with references to Tawney, a situation that we as the Church needed to challenge. It was one of those occasions where the silence grows more intense as the speaker develops his theme, until it can almost be felt. Then, as I sat down, there was again silence, followed by the reaction.

No one commented on the importance of reaffirming the traditional gospel, but the idea that church leaders could speak to subjects such as work, unemployment, and inflation found little support. Such subjects, we were told, should be left to the economic experts. It was clear that the vision of the Church which had impelled Archbishop Davidson to intervene in economic and industrial matters in the 1920s was not going to be repeated.[221] Even William Temple's wise words on the social order made little impact.[222] Some decried the Committee's manifesto as an abandonment of "the gospel" they were called to proclaim. Others complained that "this does not represent the teaching of my church".

Then the report of Working Party 10 came under attack. The continuation of any united mission was the last thing some wanted to hear. There were complaints that its programme threatened their freedom of action for "mission in the future". These Provincial exercises, it was maintained, were both trying and unreal; they were a restriction on local liberty of action. Others suggested that the Church should in no way try to instruct the world what it ought to believe, but rather that the Church should be listening to what God was saying through the world. Even when enthusiastic and radical leaders like Bill Walker Lee warned the consultation that "if we just try to continue as we are we shall fizzle out; we must move forward together", ears proved profoundly deaf.[223]

These negative voices might have been strident but were a minority, as most church leaders present at Scargill affirmed that they had come to believe CTN to be a vehicle for expressing the mind of the Church of the North in its missionary vocation today. What we had achieved so far was too important to lose. Yet the opposition was sufficiently vocal as to deflect any serious attempt to build a consensus for future mission in the Northern Province.

The three "archbishops" held to their vision, and it was to their tenacity that the consultation owed its continued existence and that the launch took place. Where the leadership was united and committed, it appeared to carry the day. So it turned out, not only at Scargill but also in the major towns and even smaller communities of the North. Effective mission and ecumenism depended on the confidence and vision of the leadership involved. At Scargill, those who came for mission were augmented by those who came for the cause of unity. Both groups were supported by those who found themselves constrained by Vatican II and saw the movement fulfilling the ideals set by John XXIII. Indeed, it was the Roman Catholic voices that most strongly supported the belief that CTN should be continued, once 1973 had seen its launch.

The Archbishop of York concluded the morning with an exposition of the Easter Letter during which he dealt somewhat firmly and fairly with the critics. After Scargill, Harry Morton wrote to me concerning the attack on Working Party 10's report:

> I admire you for having a go. The topics were certainly on target but what you need is genuine authority behind you in order to carry most of the leadership in all the churches. It underlined for me a great area of weakness at the national level . . . and I will promote quickly a major study of ends and means in national life.[224]

Lunch came as something of a relief for the leadership. Objections had been aired and listened to. Once beyond the Marsh Lounge, a new sense of unity began to be apparent. After lunch the consultation reassembled to hear Gordon Wakefield, Chair of the Methodist Manchester and Stockport District, speak to a vision of the future. His was an irenic personality representing all that was best in Free Church leadership, and he was able to give to those listening a sense of their common bond. Harry Morton then spoke, as President of the Methodist Conference, commending the leadership of the North for coming together in this way and so shining a light for other Provinces:

> The holy impatience that the leaders themselves are showing about the missionary task is encouraging and puts all the rest of our ecumenical co-operation in a more realistic and hopeful framework.

Morton went on to suggest that a group of church leaders themselves should meet to arrange the agenda of future consultations; it would be composed of the leadership alone. This suggestion was enthusiastically endorsed and put into effect.

Next the leaders heard an inspiring series of short reports from each of the fourteen regions, given by representatives of the Local Co-ordinating Committees which had joined the consultation for lunch. These were impressive, spanning the entire North. However, as the regions believed themselves to be under-represented in the governance of the movement, the leaders decided to replace the Central Co-ordinating Committee with a new regionally based Central Consultative Committee (CCC). The compromise was useful, but no group ever again developed the same sense of purpose, unity, and fellowship within the movement as the Central Co-ordinating Committee.

The consultation finally concluded. Although uncertainty remained, and the debates had been critical, it was clear that the leaders had developed a sense of unity and genuinely did wish to meet the following year, even if only to look together at how things had gone in Holy Week 1973. We closed in prayer. John Marsh wrote to me afterwards: "I certainly came away from Scargill this year with better convictions. I am sure that the open discussion of Friday morning was most useful and had been much wanted by the rank and file."

I also had a note from Archbishop George Andrew:

> Thank you, John, for your inspiration and initiative, new ideas have a way of becoming accepted as time passes. I should like to congratulate you on the way everything turned out at Scargill.

CHAPTER 20

All Stations Go

York, the ancient capital of the Northern Province, with its medieval streets and venerable parish churches jostling with a wide variety of modern structures, provided a useful illustration of one community's response to Call to the North. Clifford Barker, Rural Dean of York, led the York Council of Churches in an enthusiastic and practical response to the Call.

Some twelve months earlier, following the Easter Letter, the Council of Churches had established a CTN committee to plan the work in York, with Clifford as chair. The committee first divided York into fifteen areas, each consisting of an ecumenical group of churches with a remit to work together in preparation for Holy Week 1973. Each area had its prayer support section, and each assisted financially to raise the £1,000 which was to be used for publicity and to stage the dramatic central features of the week. In addition, each area had its own series of lay ecumenical study groups to help its laity prepare for the week, using the study guide *Things People Say*. The groups were backed up by four major "Evangelistic Workshops" around the theme of Mark's Gospel—Birthmark, Hallmark, Earmark, and Question Mark—led by Michael Turnbull and David Watson.

Some 17,000 special CTN covers had been issued for local magazines to inform church people about CTN, while around 50,000 leaflets were distributed in a house-to-house visitation of the city to prepare the townspeople for the events of Holy Week. At the beginning of Lent, on Ash Wednesday 1973, teams visited the local schools, and Mark's Gospel was distributed to third-year children. At the same time an exhibition of children's work was held at St John's College, York, and a production of *Pilgrim's Progress* was staged by Theatre Roundabout. The hotels and guest houses of the city were also visited with material so that visitors to York over Easter might catch the flavour of this ecumenical enterprise. The *Yorkshire Post* had produced a CTN colour supplement for Holy Week, and 30,000 pre-publication copies had been ordered.[225] Clifford Barker wrote, "Two years ago there was apathy and cynicism: 'Call to the North' was regarded as 'Mission Impossible'; today it is encouraging to find tremendous enthusiasm." Periodic bulletins on Call to the North were designed to inform local people not only about CTN in York but also of the reach of Call to the North across the Province. The bulletins were one of the better attempts at local communication of the Provincial vision.

The city of Doncaster was another example of community response to Call to the North. The Doncaster churches had adopted the Call with enthusiasm, but fashioned it to meet the needs and opportunities provided by their town and district. They had made use of the Bishopthorpe material, selecting the parts they found relevant to Doncaster. Michael Jackson, the Vicar, wrote, "Call to the North provided a neutral title for people to do their own thing." The Council of Churches, of which Canon Jackson was Chair for the year, set to work to fashion a programme that would sweep the whole community into the work.

A five-star programme was devised, starting with a Bible Week and concluding with a Bible Exhibition. This included a town planning conference, a postal mission, and an ecumenical rally at the town's football ground. Here the Council of Churches had the visionary leadership of the Parish Priest of Doncaster, Canon Abberton. Thus Parish Priest and Vicar, working with their Free Church colleagues, effectively won the support of the whole church life of the area, which in turn generated the interest and participation of life outside the churches. "The Call to the North was successful," Jackson wrote, "because the leading clergy worked together and lent their support to the exercise."

The first of the CTN events was a Bible Week based on preparation in ecumenical house groups, using their own material. The clergy of the town had met to compose and agree the texts. After an autumn's work on the texts, the lay groups then united for a series of conferences led by Cheslyn Jones of Pusey House, Oxford.

The second event proposed by Doncaster Council was a conference on the future of the town itself. Local government reorganization was in the air, and Doncaster, astride the A1, as it snakes north through Yorkshire, has a famous Parish Church whose great tower dominates the industrial and commercial heart of the town. The Maude Report on planning had just been issued, and the Council of Churches took the initiative of inviting the Director of the Industrial Christian Fellowship, Nicholson Brown, to meet the leading citizens. From this came a series of pamphlets, *Portraits of Doncaster*. The aim was to help townspeople, churchgoing and secular, to understand the community in which they lived. Patrick Nuttgens of Leeds Polytechnic accepted an invitation to come to a further conference, presided over by the Mayor of Doncaster, to which leading citizens of the town had been invited together with members of the groups studying the pamphlets.

The third area of action lay in the houses of the people of the town using the services of the Post Office. A group of local Evangelicals together with the Council of Churches mounted a "Postal Mission". This was regarded as something of a triumph for the Council, as Evangelicals were reputed to have an unco-operative image whenever mission involved ecumenism. Large numbers of people were circulated with a postal coupon which allowed them to enquire about the Christian faith; those who replied were then attached to groups of local church folk in their neighbourhood.

All this led up to the launch of CTN in Holy Week 1973. On a glorious Palm Sunday the church people of the town, together with the leading citizens, gathered at Father Abberton's church, St Peter-in-Chains, which was filled for its consecration by the Cardinal Archbishop of Westminster, John C. Heenan. The consecration of the new church was the start of the week of CTN activity in the North. The great service of the morning was followed by a civic lunch in the Town Hall. Then a rally in Doncaster Rovers football ground provided the venue for a moving presentation of the Passion, followed by Cardinal Heenan's address. Finally, a number of crosses were blessed by the Cardinal, together with John Marsh and the Bishop of Sheffield, to be carried across the North. It was an exciting occasion for all concerned and a great act of Christian unity and witness. "Doncaster Rovers," Jackson commented dryly, "would be well pleased to get a crowd like that every week."

In Doncaster, CTN had become a movement rather than an event, and Doncaster had anticipated the thinking of the Bishopthorpe Committee by laying on, towards the end of the year, a Bible Exhibition to follow up the events of Holy Week and Easter. The choice of venue was imaginative, as the most suitable centre available was the new betting hall of Doncaster Racecourse. For a fortnight, streams of people came from Christian organizations together with schools, visitors, and townspeople.

On the other side of the Pennines, in a very different type of country on the Lancashire coast, the exercise took a different form. In the town of Formby local clergy took the lead, following the model programme of the Co-ordinating Committee. *Say Your Piece* was studied by ecumenical lay groups across the town. Having completed the study course, members of the groups set out to meet local organizations and to engage in house-to-house visiting. The process culminated on Good Friday 1973 with a gathering at the parish church of Holy Trinity in the town centre. Then a procession—far larger than anyone locally had thought possible—led by nine clergy from all the local denominations walked through the town to Our Lady's Roman Catholic Church. John Bickersteth, Suffragan Bishop of Warrington, preached to a church where people had to sit anywhere and everywhere, even on the chancel steps, while many crammed the aisles or stood jammed at the rear of the building. Easter Sunday following also drew great crowds, inspired by the events of the previous week.

Further up the coast at Blackpool, the main event took place in the Ice Dome of the Pleasure Beach on the Saturday. This was a "production" in true Blackpool style, set up by the Youth Committee of the Council of Blackpool Churches; Frank Morgan, Vicar of Cleveleys, was the director. The pageant centred around the story of the Fall and the redemptive act of Jesus on the cross. Some three hundred children were in the cast (plus a choir of fifty), and the whole, following the CTN emphasis, was set in the context of twentieth-century social and political problems as seen through Blackpool eyes. Racism, Third-World poverty, Western indulgence, holidaymakers getting away from it all, football crowds. It was a scintillating occasion, such as only Blackpool could sponsor.

Further north again, Lancaster provided what seemed to be the impossible, and probably still is impossible in most places—a united old-fashioned gospel mission with all the frills and everyone taking part. Geoffrey Tomlinson, Vicar of the Priory Church, had gathered together— through the Lancaster Council of Churches—representatives of all the churches in the town, including those who were not members of the Council. Here it was agreed to launch CTN with a Holy Week Evangelistic Mission and to invite Cuthbert Bardsley, Bishop of Coventry, or one of Billy Graham's evangelists to lead the mission.

Tomlinson wrote, "I phoned Cuthbert Coventry as soon as the meeting was over, and he agreed to come." Bardsley had been deeply interested in this movement of mission in the North since its inception. Moreover, his own father had been Vicar of Lancaster. He was delighted to receive the invitation, and the approach to Bishop Foley secured the full support of the Catholic community. The local Evangelicals decided early on that if they did not take action, a golden opportunity for evangelism in Lancaster might be missed. Yet they knew that only by involving the Roman Catholics could their evangelistic rallies be authentic as Call to the North activities. I was approached, and advised that they should talk with the Catholic Bishop Foley; in the event he proved generous and supportive.

The preparation was meticulous; more than twenty training sessions were held including four devoted to personal counselling. Fundraising events such as sponsored walks took place to cover costs, while publicity included cars touring the city with loudspeakers encouraging people to come to the Town Hall. As things turned out, Bishop Bardsley was faced with a health problem and had to ask his Missioner, Alan Warren, to stand in for him. The event, however, proved to be one of the more successful pieces of joint mission preaching to take place in Holy Week. Lawrence Jackson compèred each night in the Town Hall, the city's largest venue, in what can only be described as his racy, inimitable, and challenging way. Night by night the large auditorium was packed to the galleries, the churches working together as they had during the preparation. Together they provided the counsellors, bookstalls, choirs, and a wide variety of different mission activities. It was a triumphant refutation of those Catholics who feared indifferentism and of those Evangelicals who feared contamination from Rome. Undoubtedly the common sense of Bishop Foley and the leadership of the Vicar made it possible, so that church people exulted and the local populace was pleased and surprised. Years later Lancastrians remember Holy Week 1973 as "a bright spot in the life of all the churches".[226]

Further north again, participating in one of the more imaginative ideas to come out of Working Party 9, was Cumbria's cross-carrying marathon. The original suggestion, before the Bishopthorpe consultation, was the dedication of some fourteen large crosses by the church leaders at the Doncaster Palm Sunday Rally. These would then be carried by relays of church young people to a central point of each region. It was a measure of the opposition which still troubled the movement that the Scargill consultation was unable to endorse the plan. However, the more enthusiastic regions taking up the idea included Cumbria, the diocesan region of Carlisle, backed by Bishop Halsey. As the Working Party had forecast, this was one of those "dramatic shapes" that delight the media. Border Television took up the coverage with great enthusiasm as, day by day, viewers were shown the cross being carried over mountains by young ecumenical teams. Shots of the cross fording rivers or passing through towns and villages to its destination at the lovely cathedral at the centre of Carlisle entertained the county. Naturally, the papers were full of pictures of local young people taking part in the marathon, which provided support for the church committees and their witness in the areas through which the cross passed.

The public response to the opportunities for Christian witness took everyone by surprise. People turned out in force either to participate or to watch, helped by the gradual build-up over the previous year of preparation. Through the use of the press and local radio, together with the many hundreds of house groups, the CTN was brought home to the people of Cumbria. Kevin Logan's work was now paying dividends: *Songs of Praise* from Beverley Minster; two *Stars on Sunday* programmes dedicated to CTN and cleverly managed by Brandon Jackson; *Desert Island Discs*; "Thought for the Day", plus the vast coverage for months in the invaluable local press—*Lancaster Guardian, Blackpool Gazette, Liverpool Echo, Isle of Man Examiner, Sheffield Morning Telegraph, Hull Daily Mail, Burnley Evening Star, Crewe Chronicle, Wigan Observer, Formby Times*—the list seemed endless, but the overall impact was important and one that had been carefully planned. This coverage pulled out into the open many who would otherwise never have taken an interest in a religious event. Again, the mere fact that all denominations were taking part and that it involved the whole of the North meant that media people were interested.

Eric Treacy, Bishop of Wakefield, confessed that he had been lukewarm about the idea of a parade of witness through the city with all the church leaders taking part. "But when it came off," he said, "I was humbled and astonished at the vast march: it completely stopped the traffic. I've never seen anything like it." Of course there were others, equally certain, who did not take part. "You'll not get me marching," confessed one bishop grimly to me, "certainly not with my Chief Constable."

But marches there were, not only in the cities and towns, but even in the great commuter suburbs. One such was in Manchester's well-to-do suburb of Altrincham, which had as its vicar Michael Henshall. He had immediately seen the potential of Call to the North and had taken a full part in the preparatory work, planning and encouraging ecumenical groups. He then oversaw a massive visitation programme, to every home in the area, some 40,000 people with five Anglican and three Roman Catholic parishes as well as a variety of Free Churches. "On Wednesday, April 18th the two-year preparation period burst into full public gaze," he wrote, "with an enormous procession, over a mile long, led by Bishop Jack Brewer (the Catholic Auxiliary Bishop), Trevor Hubbard (the Baptist Superintendent), Gordon Wakefield (the Methodist Chair), and Francis House (an Anglican Archdeacon)." The parish church was crammed, but once inside the church a great feeling of common endeavour and unity took hold of the massive congregation. They listened with real concern to the four church leaders and dealt firmly with an enthusiastic heckler protesting against the presence of Rome. It was certainly an evening to remember.

"The essential outcome of the occasion," wrote Michael Henshall later, "was to give a real injection of life into the Altrincham and District Council of Churches." In a prosperous and church-going area, the Council of Churches was a fairly low-key affair. Call to the North thus united local Christians in a new way and gave an ongoing impetus to its work. Many were tempted to regard the Call as an isolated peg on the clothes line of time. But, Henshall added, "the long build-up was designed to give it an impetus far beyond the central events of 1973. The College of Christian Discipleship . . . in dispersion carried on the insights of the Call for many years."

A chronicle of events of this Holy Week period would make for tedious reading, even if the gathering of a full list were possible—the Festival on the Green at Scarborough, the great Pageant on the rugby ground at Wigan, the Ilkley March, the Festival Service at Mount Grace Carthusian Priory (which caused a traffic hold-up for miles), the "Bible Come to Life" exhibition at Southport, the Christian Commitment campaign for the villages of Elloughton and Brough, the colourful open-air "Drama of Forgiveness" played to the crowds at Crewe Market, the Monkwearmouth Festival celebrating the 1,300th anniversary of Bede's birth, the studies under the title *Who goes home?* on housing in the North East. The crowds pouring into Burnley football ground, queues at City Hall, Hull, so great that folk had to be turned away, the setting up of "Message" (a telephone service), the founding of the retirement home for the elderly at Wetherby, the Palm Sunday procession through Leeds after some 30,000 crosses had been distributed for window display in the city—these are some fragments from the rich variety of happenings that Holy Week.

Often local events captured the idea of involving the uncommitted. Kirkby Stephen was a case in point. This somewhat remote town of Cumbria had a lively branch of the United Nations Association. Its secretary, a convinced atheist, found himself pulled into a Passion Play in the vast cathedral-like Parish Church by the wife of the local vicar. "Mrs Rigg is a remarkable woman," he confessed to me later; "she had the whole town organized, and evidently she had an eye for casting, as I found myself playing the part of one of the Jews howling for the blood of Christ."

Great cities like Liverpool, on the other hand, presented obvious difficulties, and their contribution was often lower-key, with much of the action taking place in suburban parishes and district localities. The many theatres Liverpool boasts, however, were pressed into service by the local Co-ordinating Committee, inspired by Ian Ramsey's Festival idea, the Committee's strategy being to penetrate the regular clientele of the theatre and cultural centres with the Christian message. So encouraged, they laid on an "Arts Alive" programme involving plays with a particular Christian content for Holy Week, the general theme being "The Faces of Christ". The Royal Philharmonic Orchestra co-operated with a special

Call to the North performance of Bach's *Mass in B Minor*, together with readings by Canon Basil Naylor, Chancellor of the Cathedral. In addition, the Walker Art Gallery mounted a special exhibition, as did the Central Library. No attempt was made to augment audiences with church people, the object being to speak to non-churchgoers in their own milieu and in language they understood. The one "churchy" event that the Committee encouraged was a massive rally at the Pier Head on Good Friday afternoon with "The Gospel Story" presented by the talented Liverpool Irish Players in the presence of local church leaders and a large crowd from across the city.

The same thought of reaching the outsider lay behind the "pop festival" laid on by Chester Committee in their Cathedral. This was an exhilarating affair with large numbers of young people thronging the ancient building and spilling over into Abbey Square and the Cathedral Green. This event, attended by church leaders, bishops, Moderators, Chairs of District, and Superintendents, was designed to capture the ear of non-churchgoing youth and to introduce them not only to the Christian message, but to the personalities and buildings from which they had been estranged. Gerry Marsden of the "Pacemakers" (whose drummer lived in Altcar—silver disc on the wall) led the youngsters, three bishops, and a host of clergy in "You'll never walk alone". This was just as news came through that Liverpool were the new Football League champions. "It really lifted the roof of Chester Cathedral, it rivalled the Kop,"[227] Chester reported.

The Minster at York presented a somewhat different spectacle as the Christian people of the city were brought into a series of events designed to catch the ears and curiosity of non-churchgoers. Encouraged by the crowds, it was hoped that many would be drawn into the activities of the week. On the Monday and Tuesday, evangelistic rallies were held in the Minster, led by David Watson. These were followed on the Wednesday by a pop concert for young people and on the Thursday by a massive children's rally. On Good Friday, those who had been preparing over the previous eighteen months or more for Holy Week 1973 were asked to gather at the Four Bars of the city (a somewhat ambiguous term referring to the medieval gates of York). From here they converged in great processions on the Minster. Meanwhile the villages along the River Ouse had been asked to come to York in decorated barges surmounted by religious tableaux and join "the townspeople in the Minster". The great church reputedly seats 2,000 people, but when the 2,000-strong procession of those who had come by river reached the West Door of the Minster, they found 3,000 townspeople already standing inside. It was perhaps the greatest congregation the Minster had ever witnessed in modern times, as David Sheppard (by now Bishop of Woolwich) mounted the pulpit steps. "We were all thrilled with the preparatory work on the studies," one of those present admitted later; "the new vagrants' hostel the CTN was setting up was also an encouragement, but that rally was fantastic."

After an ecumenical prayer meeting in the Elim Pentecostal Church, the week culminated in a great Sunday service in the Minster when the Archbishop of York read "The Call". This letter, signed by the three church leaders, was addressed this time, not primarily to church people, but to the whole public of the North of England, affirming "our faith, our love, our hope, and our experience of wholeness, mediated to us in the Bible, the sacraments, and in the fellowship of our Church."

No effort was spared to get the message across. All the MPs of the North of England were sent personal copies from the church leaders with the message: "with your constituency at heart (we felt) you ought to hear from us as personally as possible." Eddie Neale and Michael Wright, the press officers, put in long hours making sure the message got through to all the media. All the major provincial papers carried special articles and news of the launch. Church leaders were urged to "think of ways in which we can come out from behind our barriers into the world without cheapening the gospel."

There was now an anxiety to get the working-class door open. "Someone suggested a Press Conference of church leaders in the Batley Working Men's Club," wrote Eddie Neale. The CTN had become a talking point for people everywhere, in working-class areas as well as middle-class parishes. Church people were found with their minds alive and active in conversation, able to speak about their faith, perhaps for the first time in their lives. The Bishop of Liverpool summed up the situation in his usual succinct manner when he commented, "It would be splendid if CTN were unnecessary, because we were all going forward together already."

PART 3

The New Brooms

CHAPTER 21

Looking Forward

So Call to the North was launched and made a considerable impact. The main effect was to change church relationships across the North permanently in a way quite unexpected by most; disparate churches had been brought together. There would now be no going back to sectarian suspicion and conflict.

In the decades ahead following the launch, the leadership hoped and planned to undertake a voyage of ecumenical mission. The launch had proved a quite splendid exercise. Everything across the North had gone to plan, and very few quirks had intervened to mar the exercise's impact. There were few who did not acclaim its achievement. Even many who had been doubtful expressed their surprise and acceptance, if not pleasure, at the success of this northern event. The central leadership, Donald Coggan, George Andrew Beck, and Stuart Blanch, with their Free Church colleagues, hoped now that the Northern Church's stance on ecumenism and mission would be permanently changed. Stuart Blanch wrote:

> The Call to the North was a tentative step in the right direction, which has, against all the odds, developed into a long-term practical campaign with considerable implications for the future.[228]

This was a brave vision; however, the leadership was well aware that it was something that would not be accepted easily. Their efforts to change the culture of the Northern Church to mission, even under the inspiration of the events of Holy Week/Easter 1973, would face obstacles. Many of the laity still innocently thought that the Easter launch was the end of the matter and that normality was now being restored to church life. For some church leaders, including many members of the clergy, what they had experienced during Holy Week had been an exercise out of keeping with their tradition or background. Despite its undoubted success, they were cautious of repeating the experience.

What can be said without contradiction is that the CTN had proved an exciting, demanding, and rewarding experience in unity and mission for clergy and laity alike. Its results would be lasting, not only in the lives of individuals but at the heart of congregations. Although Part 3 of this account records the failure of the three leaders to sustain their vision of ongoing unity in mission and church growth in the North, it was written—inspired by Stuart Blanch—in the hope that their example may stimulate others in the future to succeed.

The immediate results might be hard to assess, but they were easy to see and hear. Thus clergy, sometimes bishops, found themselves in shopping precincts and city streets being urged by members of the public to keep the movement going. Congregations were quoted as exchanging experiences of how CTN was being talked about in their factory or club. The laity had found a new confidence in talking about their faith to those who were non-churchgoers. The Liverpool Local Co-ordinating Committee heard of laity in Merseyside factories, Roman Catholics and Anglicans, talking about their CTN work openly and without fear, consulting one another, and of non-church people taking a sympathetic interest in the movement. Similarly a Carlisle layman confessed, "For the first time in my life it has been possible to speak to people at work about my faith."

The impact of Call to the North was certainly powerful; indeed, everyone in the North appeared to have been aware of this exercise by the Christian churches. But where pockets of doubt, uncertainty, apathy, indeed opposition remained, people might well have been puzzled that nothing had happened in their immediate locality.[229] In the event, everything had depended on local leadership. If the local clergy had the vision to back CTN, or if they could only allow the laity their heads, then things happened. It was therefore a misfortune that the 1973 Consultation at Scargill failed to accept the recommendation that an assessment of the exercise be made. We now had no record of the actual results of Holy Week and Easter. Still less were we able to make an assessment of the continuing numbers attending church, after an initial spurt following the Holy Week/Easter celebration. Certainly on the Lancashire coast numbers continued to climb throughout the 1970s in the Church of England.[230] Moreover, church attendances generally received a boost right across the North. The little rural parish of Altcar, which in the late 1960s had congregations of half a dozen, by the late 1970s had congregations which had risen into the sixties.

Fortunately the York CTN Committee held a review of the exercise some six months after the launch at Wydale Hall.[231] This was something the Central Co-ordinating Committee had been keen to see happen throughout the North, but which all too often failed to materialize. At Wydale, members believed that the impact on local congregations was observable and significant. We agreed that "we had discovered one another". Relationships between the churches had been transformed, and "Christians are beginning to get their nerve back."

One permanent change which was easier to observe and assess was the relationship between the Roman Catholic Church and the other Christian churches in the North. The sense of relief experienced by both Catholic and Protestant in areas where relationships had been tenuous or non-existent was palpable. This was true not only at the level of the pew, but in the official stance. Richard Hare, Bishop of Pontefract, wrote:

> Call to the North for me meant primarily that I was on Christian-name terms with Roman Catholic priests and Free Church ministers whom I might otherwise never have met except in the most formal circumstances.[232]

Similarly, Bishop Michael Henshall wrote:

> Most of all, Christians in the town had worked together in a new way and at a deeper level. That was the longer-term gain, for from that experience there was no turning back.

The other lasting benefit was the absorption into the life of the Church of the North of the structures set up by CTN for mutual consultation and support. An annual consultation for church leaders, now known as the Northern Consultation for Mission, still takes place year by year, as does the annual consultation for their executives. Again, the North West and the North East consultations continued to meet. "In addition many local regional committees had continued to meet but had changed their names into a local 'council of churches.'"²³³

But how much of the exciting new theology of mission survived is open to question. Much of its challenge was lost sight of as the local events moved back into gear, and traditional attitudes were reasserted. As with the National Mission of Repentance and Hope in 1916, the challenge to society went largely unheard and ancient expectations again imposed themselves on the new Provincial Consultation.

Although the same phenomena had also been observed elsewhere, the York Committee noted how difficult the exercise proved to get across to working-class areas. This led Michael Turnbull to suggest that the future work of CTN should involve stronger churches sending teams to work with the congregations of weaker churches, and Clifford Barker to hope for "a further provincial CTN exercise in 1976 or 7 with a preparatory programme beforehand". Looking back on the movement some years later, Clifford Barker, by then Bishop of Whitby, was to write, "the long term results are more difficult to isolate ... but there was a growing realization in all the churches that mission is a 'must' and that laity must be at the forefront of all this."

Despite enthusiasm in some major quarters, there were those for whom CTN had primarily been a call to return to the pew, proclaimed at Easter, over by Whitsuntide, and forgotten by Christmas. Bishop Lindsay wrote:

> The editor of the *Catholic Gazette* asked me earlier this year to write an article [for the *Gazette*] after Holy Week. He obviously thought he was inviting me to compose an epitaph, but I put him right.

CHAPTER 22

The Way Ahead

> Call to the North is basically an exercise in leadership designed to change attitudes and assumptions among church people so they might influence the culture and life of our society today.

These words summed up the hopes and purpose of the CTN leadership in general.[234] "We must continue to go forward," John Bickersteth (by now Bishop of Bath and Wells) commented. "All in all, CTN will always say to me that mission in unity is the only way forward." Bill Walker Lee put meat on these bones in his letter to the secretariat:

1. However much we have asserted that Easter 1973 is not the end of CTN, people will generally see it as the climax and so not expect more.
2. An impression may be given that the CTN organization is trying to perpetuate itself, because it has failed.
3. The time has come when our churches must take with complete seriousness the call to find unity in mission. This is not because we have failed to find unity and now seek self-preservation, but it is the world and its quite desperate condition that makes this demand upon us . . . there is no time to lose.
4. We therefore need a group at each level—Province, Diocese, District, Deanery, or Circuit—of men and women with the time, ability, and vision to:
    a. Think through new patterns of ecumenical experiment in mission.
    b. Advise and encourage those areas where little is being attempted.
    c. Be a bank for the collecting and collating of information.

The North is an ideal geographical unit for such a scheme.

This certainly resonated with Stuart Blanch's vision for changing the culture of the churches of the North from maintenance to mission. For the future, if these significant voices were to be listened to, a network or effective structure needed to be maintained, if not further developed.

A new structure for CTN

The Bishopthorpe Consultation meeting at Scargill did agree to a structure, although the one that had successfully served the movement in bringing CTN to fruition was abandoned. In its place, following Harry Morton's suggestion, a committee of nine church leaders was created to take control of the direction of the movement and to set the Bishopthorpe Consultation agendas. The Archbishop of York was asked to chair the group supported by two bishops; in addition, three Free Church leaders were chosen—a Methodist Chair, a United Reformed Church Moderator, and a Baptist Superintendent—together with three Roman Catholic bishops. This new "Committee of Nine" was given, as its primary task, the arranging of the Scargill agenda and acting as a "think tank" for missionary strategy in the North of England. These changes were agreed, with my role as Secretary reaffirmed.

Again, as the regions had lobbied for greater representation, the "Nine" would be supported by a new "Central Consultative Committee" representative of each region. This would be comprised of one member from each of the fourteen regions, chaired by Bishop Lindsay of Hexham and Newcastle, so representing the regions, supported by a secretariat of David Blunt, Dennis Corbishley, and me. This group would seek to stimulate local mission and act as a centre for the exchange of ideas. Donald Coggan, Archbishop of York, in joining the final meeting of the old Central Co-ordinating Committee, urged us to keep as many of the present committee on the new Central Consultative Committee as possible. "The conversion of CTN into an ongoing movement of mission with a future will take a lot of doing," he maintained; "your experience might well prove vital."[235] This proved to be a perceptive comment.

The Committee of Nine

Donald Coggan, establishing the new committee, asked the Bishops of Manchester and Liverpool to join him. The Archbishop of Liverpool then nominated Bishop Brewer (Auxiliary of Shrewsbury) and Dennis Corbishley to represent the Roman Catholic Church, together with Bishop Gerald Moverley (Auxiliary of Leeds). John Marsh suggested Bill Walker Lee (Methodist Chair of Leeds), John Williamson (the new Moderator of the Mersey Province of the United Reformed Church), and Trevor Hubbard (Baptist Superintendent of the North West) as the Free Church representatives. Harry Morton's contribution to the Scargill Consultation had emphasized the need for the leadership to take control of the agenda. This had been received with gratitude and thus had brought the Nine into being. The initial meeting of the Committee of Nine was at Bishopthorpe in 1973, at the invitation of the Archbishop of York. The atmosphere was warm, almost jocular, although not as tight or purposeful as the old Central Co-ordinating Committee. On the other hand, it was certainly more purposeful and committed than the somewhat strained and divided new Central Consultative Committee turned out to be. The church leaders took things fairly comfortably, riding the business, coming to know one another in an easy and familiar manner. As the 1973 Consultation had accepted the Yellow Paper's primary recommendation that the Consultation should continue to meet on an annual basis, the main item on the agenda was the next Consultation at Scargill (Bishopthorpe VI).

The composition of the Consultation was first considered. Traditionally this had been limited to the senior leadership of all the churches of the North—some forty-six members in all. These consisted of two Baptist Superintendents, one member of the Christian Brethren, fourteen Church of England diocesan bishops, fourteen Methodist Chairs of District, eight Roman Catholic residential bishops, one Salvationist, one member of the Society of Friends, and five United Reformed Church Moderators. However, the Nine now decided to invite a further eleven guests and observers. The observers would be representatives of significant central offices, such as the General Secretary of the BCC, and their acceptance of the invitations was to be a measure of how CTN had caught the attention and interest of churches across the country. Then there were those who had worked with the Consultation over the years, such as Archdeacon Fisher or Bishop Wickham, together with those members of the Committee of Nine who were not, as of right, members of the Consultation, including the Secretary, Treasurer, and Press Officer.

The Committee then turned to discuss the lessons of the launch. It was agreed that the main positive result lay in the great improvement in the relationships between the churches and their individual membership. From the leadership to the pew, Christians in the North had been challenged in their outlook to the world. Moreover, the general public of the North had been forced to take note of the churches in a new way. There was also a new awareness of the contribution that the churches made to society generally.

Secondly, York, Merseyside, and Chester all reported an increase in church attendance since Easter (although we had no means of accurately measuring the reported growth). Rex Kissack, Methodist Chair of Merseyside, did, however, provide one significant hard statistic. This showed that over the period when CTN was in preparation and during the launch, Methodism in the South of the country had continued to decline in membership, while in the northern districts of the Methodist Church the decline had been reversed and congregations had started to grow.[236] Further, it was generally accepted that all churches had received a boost in attendances as a result of CTN, although it was unclear as to whether this was due to the lapsed returning to their former loyalties or to a genuine outreach to the previously uncommitted.

The third issue addressed was the name "Call to the North". Patrick Rodger of Manchester probably put his finger on the pulse of the Consultation when he said that he was happy with planning for a further event in 1980, but unhappy with continuing to use the name CTN. The Bishop of Blackburn was even more direct when he said that the sight of the CTN symbol gave him a pain. It was an indication that we needed to change the name. However, Bishop Lindsay of the North East, who chaired the CCC, argued cogently against this, or allowing the movement to fade out. Speaking as a Roman Catholic, he reminded committee members that people had just become accustomed to working together under the banner of Call to the North; if we now allowed it to fade out, it would be assumed that this Christian exercise in unity had failed. If we changed the name, we would then have to raise new interest in something fresh all over again, just at the time when some were coming to terms with Call to the North. The Committee of Nine decided therefore, somewhat hesitantly, to recommend to the next Consultation that we keep the name. It was preferable to trying to get something going with a different title as a "follow-up". The Bishop of Liverpool had written:

> The time may come when it would be wiser to abandon the title Call to the North, but it would be sad to abandon the concept which is slowly developing out of it.
>
> The concept is nothing less than a "strategy for mission" no longer conducted by gifted individuals here or there, or by enthusiastic groups within this or that denomination, but a strategy which mobilizes the Church as a whole.
>
> So far Call to the North has been a series of engagements. Perhaps we have learned enough from them by now to be able to receive from God a "strategy for mission", which could influence the policy of the Church for a generation or more. The annual meeting of the leadership would then be seen not as a means of "keeping the Call to the North going" but as an integral part of the corporal life of our Churches organized for mission.

After considering the question of the name, the Nine then looked at a theme for our next meeting at Scargill. The decision was "Giving account for the hope that is in us", and I was asked to plan around the theme so that the agenda could be finalized at our meeting in December.

Members looked finally at more general matters. Firstly, the question of a vacuum of belief among younger people in the North, and Sir Keith Joseph's warning of increasing deprivation, particularly in the North. Then the shaken morale of the nation's leadership in 1973 was considered,[237] together with the role of our churches in the nation's healing, "providing" (Patrick, Bishop of Manchester, interposed) "it is not the healing of the hurt of my people lightly".[238]

Finance—its implications

David Blunt, our Treasurer, had written to draw the attention of the Nine to our financial situation, which was almost dire. Some church leaders, having entered into an agreement at Bishopthorpe to make an annual contribution to the work of the movement, had clearly failed to fulfil their commitment. Five of the fourteen dioceses of the Church of England had contributed to the work of Call to the North, three of the fourteen Methodist districts, and four of the eight Roman Catholic dioceses, together with the Congregationalist Church. This, he suggested, clearly questioned the real attitude of the church leaders and, indeed, their integrity, whatever they had said in public at Bishopthorpe.

We had always suspected that some church leaders went along with the flow at Scargill, not publically opposing the movement, but in reality not accepting the concept of a united and ongoing Province-wide movement of mission. They came to Bishopthorpe (or sent their representative), they were anxious to have their representatives on the central structures, as they needed to be in on the decision-making process, but their opposition was registered in their failure (perhaps silent refusal?) to finance the movement.

The Committee of Nine was uncomfortable with this challenge, but of course every leader in the North was a law unto himself. The Committee had neither power nor sanctions. The situation, however, was unfair; indeed, when Donald Coggan received a letter from one of his diocesan bishops explaining that the diocese could not afford the promised £50, he was deeply grieved. The message was clear: the annual Consultation was welcome, but the structure to support continuing mission was resented.

The financial viability of the movement therefore remained precarious. The Nine felt that any attempt by them as a group to right the matter might be further resented, and that our unity in mission was more important. Stuart Blanch doggedly insisted that to raise funds by voluntary means, such as the great charities or church societies employ, would be to disable commitment. The movement would no longer be a united movement of church leaders, but a voluntary society of those interested in mission. Yet David Blunt was embarrassed. He was aware just how much the Liverpool Diocesan Board of Finance was putting into the movement by way of secretarial support. I, too, felt embarrassed—given this shortage of funds—in submitting claims for travel to David. Yet I had no independent means. My stipend as a rural vicar at the time meant that I had to rely on weekly Social Security payments from the Post Office, so I had no alternative.

The Central Consultative Committee

The new Central Consultative Committee consisted of some fourteen members, one for each region (two for the North East Ecumenical Group). Some judicious negotiations secured the election of four Roman Catholics and three Free Churchmen. The Anglicans would have wished for five of each of the main traditions, but it was inevitable with the democratic processes operating that the Church of England would return the largest representation. However, Bishop Lindsay, the Roman Catholic auxiliary bishop of Hexham and Newcastle, was elected as Chair. Fortunately, both David Blunt and Dennis Corbishley agreed to serve on this new committee, and I was asked to continue as Secretary. Donald Coggan hoped that the new Central Consultative Committee representing the regions (soon to be nicknamed the CCC) might be able to work through the 1970s to the 1980s and so "provide the North of England with prophetic hope", as he put it. This was a brave vision which Donald no doubt would have hoped to lead, probably successfully, had he not soon been translated to Canterbury.

The Committee first met in May 1973, with David Blunt as Treasurer, and one of the first decisions made was to abandon the Bishopthorpe venue for its meetings and to use a series of different venues across the North. This had the attraction of helping to dispose of the image of a Bishopthorpe Committee handing down directives from on high; moreover, it enabled the leadership across the North to come to know and, we hoped, trust members of the CCC.

The mornings of the CCC's meetings were therefore spent on provincial business, while after lunch members met the local church leaders who apprised the Committee of the particular concerns of their locality. In this way members came to know church leaders across the

North and their primary concerns. The church leadership, in turn, was given some opportunity to influence the Committee and, it was hoped, so to help the leadership identify with and support its work. As CCC moved around the North, a series of fascinating venues were visited, none more so than the Castle of Bishop Auckland where John Habgood, the new Bishop of Durham, was host. He not only contributed most generously of his time, and indeed wisdom, to the debate, but led members in a striking and memorable Bible study in the inspiring chapel of the palace.

Bishop Lindsay set the Committee's agenda, as agreed by the Scargill Consultation, based on Working Party 10's Yellow Paper which gave the CCC its brief. The new Committee first reviewed the past of the CTN.

We had experienced three stages. The first had been one of exploration, from 1968 to 1971. This had been a period of vision but also of indecision, concern, and uncertainty. The period had been brought to a close by Bishopthorpe III deciding to commit the North to mission. The second had been a period of preparation, from 1971 to 1973. This had proved to be a new period of hope where the churches learned to draw together and establish ecumenical relations. It had proved to be a period for testing ideas and planning local projects, with a growth in trust and vision across the churches. This concluded with Easter 1973. We now faced a third period designed to establish the continuing presence of ecumenical mission for the North—the long haul from 1973 onwards.

The task, members accepted, would be difficult—continuous mission always was. The Committee was faced not only with the opposition of Catholics, who feared indifferentism and represented the more conservative Vatican of Paul VI, but also of Evangelicals who were still fearful of Rome. In addition, many people in all the churches were tempted to relax after the stress of the preparation for Holy Week and Easter and just return to the steady round of churchgoing, social action, and raising money. These were keen to suggest that, as CTN had now finished, mission should be left to the specialists. Thus the culture of the past threatened to return, to suffocate the leadership of the future.

The Yellow Paper had recommended that a Central Consultative Committee be established:

We think it is essential that (the present) commitment to, enthusiasm for and involvement in ventures of ecumenical mission should be fostered and encouraged by transforming the project into a "movement" . . .

The first task of the CCC, therefore, was to address the question of how to achieve the agreed vision of continuous mission by all the churches of the North. This item had a conspicuous place on the agenda of the early meetings. Practically speaking, it seemed that the most effective way would be to plan for an event towards which all the churches of the North could work. The most popular idea to emerge was that of Bishop Ramsey's *Kirchentag*. As a result a small group (Working Party 11) was commissioned to look at the possibility and to consult with those planning a similar ecumenical congress in the South West.

Despite this being the accepted will of the Annual Consultation as a whole, those who had never come to terms with the Holy Week/Easter event and thus feared another "northern event" had now both a platform and a veto. This was provided by the representative nature of the new Central Consultative Committee. Indeed, both Manchester and the North East made it quite clear that a further CTN event was something their own constituency could not and would not support.[239] This sent the Committee back to the drawing board, and as an alternative it was then proposed that a series of *Kirchentage* be devised. A group was elected (consisting of Geoffrey Lawn and Clifford Barker of York, Maurice Simmons of Durham, and Ralph Woodhall SJ of Liverpool) and was asked to investigate the possibility on behalf of the Consultative Committee and to report to the new Committee of Nine. The Nine, however, were still of the opinion that a united festival of some sort must be tried, and resolved later to take it forward.

The second item the Committee turned its attention to was the Yellow Paper's recommendation that the launch of CTN be written up in paperback form. Canon John Poulton had earlier written of "an experiment that could then be analysed and used as a basis for further action on a national scale".[240] The Bishopthorpe Consultation accepted that the Northern Province had indeed been engaged in a unique exercise in ecumenical mission which merited publication. Gavin Reid was approached to edit the work, with a number of contributors including Stuart Blanch, Ted Wickham, and myself.[241] A publisher was found—SPCK—and the work set in hand.[242]

Unfortunately, this approach eventually failed. In its place the Committee suggested that journalist Martyn Halsall be commissioned to research and write the book. Halsall had been a lively and vigorous member of one of the working parties, so knew CTN from the inside.[243] The Committee of Nine agreed to the proposal, and Lutterworth Press offered to undertake its publication. The publishers were thanked and Martyn Halsall commissioned.

Thirdly, the Committee went on to look into the possibility of helping the many hundreds, if not thousands, of ecumenical groups that had been set up as a result of CTN. This led Working Party 10 to suggest two possibilities:

1. A Lent Bible study and prayer booklet on the epistle of James;
2. A study booklet designed to assist people to understand their local community, its social make-up, traditions, and culture.

At the same time, Eddie Neale, the CTN Publicity Officer, suggested a series of imaginative broadsheets seeking to bring Christian insights to bear on issues of contemporary and local importance in the regions. These might be produced by the regions themselves and then widely used throughout the North. For example:

- Bradford could look at the immigration and racism issue;
- Carlisle, Cumbria at holiday evangelism;
- Liverpool at unemployment.

This idea was immediately taken up and the regions were asked to undertake the work in their Local Co-ordinating Committees.

Next, the Committee turned its attention to the recommendation, supported by the senior leadership, that an assessment of the impact of Call to the North be undertaken. This would involve the gathering of reports from lay groups, together with a questionnaire to all the churches of the North. The Committee realized that this might reveal nakedness as well as success, but at the same time it would present a clear picture which would be invaluable for future planning.

Stuart Blanch of Liverpool had circulated a questionnaire to all his parishes, designed to encourage forward thinking on mission. He sent a copy for the CCC to examine. The questionnaire consisted of twelve items for church councils to consider: whether their concerns were inward-looking and materialistic or outward-looking, concerned with the world and with mission. The Bishop had arranged for the Liverpool questionnaires to be distributed prior to his own annual visitation.

Nevertheless, the Committee was aware that at the Scargill Consultation a number of members had fiercely resisted any proposal for such an appraisal of CTN. An enquiry would clearly endorse the massive achievements of the CTN, but the Committee realized it might also unmask areas of under-achievement, an embarrassment to those involved. The Committee therefore had to set the potential value of any such appraisal against the opposition it would provoke. Thus it recommended that a survey should be undertaken in those regions which welcomed the idea. Despite these limitations, the results would prove invaluable to the authors of the CTN paperback; Ralph Woodhall was commissioned to collate the replies. Again, given the strong resistance by a vocal minority at Scargill, the Yellow Paper's further recommendations, important though they were, were simply not considered by the CCC. These had been:

1. confirming the emphasis on mission rather than on maintenance;
2. making Christians aware that they live in a missionary situation;
3. underlining the need for commitment to both God and our fellow people;
4. emphasizing that the concept of mission today should be seen not only in terms of personal evangelism but also as influencing the culture in which we live;
5. enabling church people to express their faith in terms meaningful to their contemporaries.

After noting that this would involve a programme of re-education, the Yellow Paper had suggested that "in Holy Week 1980 a further project might be considered". It also recommended that we should maintain the CTN title. However, there remained those who were determined that we should do neither of these things. Something of a tug-of-war developed, the one group calling for action and the other for the Committee to be primarily a meeting place for an exchange of ideas. This was a conflict between the "two Christianities", according to David Edwards, Dean of Norwich and Editor of the SCM Press, speaking at the Church Leaders Conference in Birmingham.

Despite the presence of David Blunt, Dennis Corbishley, and me, the new Committee—as Donald Coggan had shrewdly anticipated—had a very different view of itself from the old tightly knit Central Co-ordinating Committee. Unlike its predecessor, it did not take its brief from the Archbishops, but drew its authority from the regions. Thus it was far more representative of the various schools of thought within the churches. Mission was moved down the agenda.

Although—and perhaps because—the new Consultative Committee drew its *raison d'être* from the regions, it seemed to be even more resented by the church leadership at Scargill than its predecessor, the Central Co-ordinating Committee. The old Committee had operated with and under the authority of the "three archbishops", while the new Committee had no such limitation or authority. A further problem emerged as the Committee developed. Regional representatives on the CCC, if representing a diocesan area where their local church leaders did not support the movement, found their role precarious.

Whatever their origins, each church leader was king in his own castle, so this ecumenical Committee appeared to impose restraints on his freedom of action. The unique feature of the CTN movement was that it was indeed a gathering, in effect, of local sovereigns engaged in a common enterprise. Any such enterprise demands compromise, as the Bishopthorpe fathers discovered. However, if this new Committee was to fulfil the vision set by Bishopthorpe then its task must be so to equip and inspire church people that they in turn were able to inspire their fellow people to find faith.

Throughout the whole history of the CTN there was a tension between the independence the regions demanded and the leadership as represented by the Bishopthorpe/Scargill Consultations. There was a sense that, by dissolving the old Central Co-ordinating Committee, the regions had now gained control of the exercise. The Committee therefore flexed its muscles in suggesting decisions concerning the Scargill agenda. However, the church leadership was not prepared to accept such direction, and the new CCC had now to accept that it was primarily the executive arm of the Committee of Nine. The Bishopthorpe agenda remained the remit of the Nine alone.

The Festival—our new objective

The Nine met again in December to finalize arrangements for the 1974 Consultation and then to receive reports from the CCC. The first report of the Consultative Committee dealt with the "focus" of action in the future towards which the churches of the North might work in the intervening years. The CCC had examined the idea of a *Kirchentag* and had sent two members to Düsseldorf (1973). The Committee was prepared to recommend by a majority, that the churches of the North should undertake some similar exercise, perhaps in 1977. This would help the North continue to work together in the field of mission with a new target. However, the CCC made an important caveat: as the *Kirchentag* in Germany had grown out of a particular socio-political situation which could not be repeated in the United Kingdom, any exercise here should reflect our own cultural background in the North. Thus the CTN movement had to think in terms of a "Festival of Renewal".

The aim of the Festival would be "the renewal of the churches of the North with a spirit of confidence in the relevancy and power of the gospel". There would be five divisions to the Festival:

1. spiritual renewal;
2. listening to the Spirit of God in the world (this division was heavily influenced by the BCC's Liverpool Youth Festival, 1973);
3. thinking about, training for, and discussion of evangelism;
4. consideration of our socio-political structures;
5. a place for the Charismatic Movement.

Some 5,000 or more were expected to attend, so we needed to look for a university town as a venue, and then the paper went into details.

At the meeting of the Nine the Bishop of Liverpool spoke to the report. He pointed to the crucial need for vision in all our churches, in particular for new members joining us at this time. Such a movement would assist us to help them catch that vision. Moreover, he said, it was important that the leadership of the churches identified key areas of influence in trade unions, the mass media, and local government, which the Festival might well help us to do. We had the great advantage that the North had enough cohesion, identification, and goodwill towards the churches for a festival of this nature to pull into its life those without church commitment but with a concern for the health of society. We were also engaged in assisting our laity to penetrate society to share Christian insights. Finally, he suggested that the CTN would wither away as these objectives were naturalized within the life of the Church as a whole.

Patrick Rodger, Bishop of Manchester, then made the point that we must keep the church people of the North looking and thinking ahead and outward. He cited the World Council of Churches and its policy "to go for a jamboree every seven years". "Ought we," he asked, "really to be thinking of doing this in conjunction with the British Council of Churches? It would be a tremendous shot in the arm for them." This was a fascinating contribution by the Anglican leadership, considering that the Manchester member of the CCC had sought to veto any such move.

On the other hand John Williamson, Moderator of the Mersey Province of the United Reformed Church, represented the local vision:

> I do not like these organized events. They produce a sense of disillusionment once they are over; our task should be to discuss how and where we can work together towards unity. A Festival like this will take up all our energies and distract us from the task of unity. Moreover, those who go will form an elite and not really affect the churches.

Listening to the discussion it seemed that those in favour of the idea carried the day, although the Committee of Nine remained divided. The report would be received and presented to Scargill after more work had been done. As with the launch, nobody (as Maurice Simmons dryly observed) would be prepared to cast the first stone. Providing it was firmly based on solid preparations in the regions at the local level, providing it didn't involve expense, and providing the mass media took it up, we ought to be able to sell it to Bishopthorpe. In any event it was clear that the Archbishop was keen on the idea since he saw it as a means of maintaining the momentum and of avoiding the churches sinking back into maintenance mode.

Finally the Committee of Nine approved the revised programme for Bishopthorpe VI which would set the seal on the future.

CHAPTER 23

Vision, Impasse, and Decline: Bishopthorpe VI & VII

The need to speak a word from God to the people of the North was the primary objective of the senior leadership in the long debates that led up to the launch of CTN. This had now been accomplished; the light of the gospel had shone out across the North, and this had been a remarkable achievement. Now in 1974 the leaders met again at Scargill for Bishopthorpe VI to review the achievement.

At the time, there was undoubtedly a remarkable sense of thanksgiving and hope as they gathered again. The mere fact that Catholics and Protestants were worshipping together in that great chapel at Scargill was itself an inspiration. That they had been proclaiming the Word together was extraordinary, if not incredible. So it was an appreciation of the Holy Spirit's blessing on their common proclamation to the people of the North that filled many of those present with a sense of awe. The attendance was better than ever, the atmosphere warm, and the fellowship meaningful as they met together for prayer and contemplation.

However, for the business meeting on the second day, ominously—as on previous occasions—more leaders arrived. With the Archbishop in the chair, the Marsh Lounge quickly filled as leaders from across the North took their seats to listen to reports from the regions on how things had gone for them during Holy Week and Easter. The atmosphere was expectant and positive, the news outstanding. The leaders then broke for coffee and afterwards returned to business to look to the future. In the minds of the senior Bishopthorpe leadership, the ongoing and long-term objective of CTN was to engineer the transformation of the churches of the North from a focus on maintenance to that of mission. Bishop Howe was to remind the leadership that their success in uniting the churches of a whole Province in an exercise of mission had been unique.[244] Now it was clear that any attempt to maintain not only that unity, but also that focus on mission, was vital. Yet this objective was to test the resolve and, in particular, the leadership of the churches of the North to destruction.

In the minds of "the archbishops", Holy Week 1973 was always to be a springboard for the future. Thus for Donald Coggan, George Andrew, and John Marsh, not to mention Stuart Blanch, the maintenance of the momentum of mission was of prime importance. A strategy to unite the great Church of the North in its divine vocation thus lay behind the suggestion from Patrick Rodger of Manchester that the North—despite the Consultative Committee's experience—should adopt another "objective" to focus all our minds on mission. If this could be done, then the unity of the North-Country churches in their primary vocation of mission would be achieved over a period of the next seven years. The future of the unity of the North in mission appeared to lie within our grasp.

A group had therefore been commissioned to examine the possibility of a Festival for the North, based on the concept of the German *Kirchentag*, being such an objective. This concept was carefully researched and a plan of action prepared by the group. Their findings and recommendations were first presented to the Committee of Nine, which received the paper, appraised it, and gave it an enthusiastic endorsement. The paper was now excellently presented to the church leaders of Bishopthorpe VI by Geoffrey Lawn, Ecumenical Officer for York.

It soon became clear that the enthusiasm of the Committee of Nine and the vision of the senior leadership were not shared by all. The report on the Festival received a hostile reception from a vocal minority. On reflection, it appeared that what was being rejected was not Geoffrey Lawn's paper or recommendations, but the concept of the North being involved in yet another united exercise. The leaders concerned made it clear that they were anxious never again to engage in any united exercise in mission, however well prepared and presented. So although most church leaders present appeared to be clearly supportive of the Festival concept, they also understood these protestations; in face of them there was not the will to proceed. The fear of being involved in another co-operative exercise in mission meant that the senior leadership was now unable to move forward. The movement had indeed been replaced by a fellowship.

A lay voice

The 1974 Scargill Consultation then turned to consider its own composition. While the aim of the gathering had been to lead the North in mission, the essential ingredient of membership had been the executive leadership. Now that objective had changed, and its composition could be reviewed. Thus there was a suggestion that we should now have greater participation by the laity. This was made by the Methodist Chairs, who asked if it was not absurd for the churches of the North to meet solemnly together without a lay voice. This was a call that could not be denied, but it was in effect a sideways-move: away from the vision of a church leadership consulting as to how to promote mission, to that of a fellowship of churches talking about mission. Stuart Blanch's original endeavour to place the onus of mission on the church leadership had been lost. In the event, the matter was referred to the Committee of Nine.

A low profile

The leaders left Scargill with a sense of gratitude for all that had been achieved together and a clear determination to continue to meet. Nevertheless, in view of the fractious opposition to any form of united mission to the North, "I think it might be wise," Stuart Blanch observed to me afterwards, "if we kept a low profile for the time being." The low profile was—in effect—an admission of defeat, not of the concept of meeting, but of ecumenical mission; indeed there was never again any attempt to encourage a further exercise in united mission.[245] Despite this, I personally felt, as John Bickersteth commented, "What could be more interesting than unity and mission for the whole of the North?" As a Liverpudlian, by birth, the conversion of the North to a knowledge of Jesus was precious to me. Moreover, my own commitment to the working class, with whom I had identified in my factory life after leaving school, led me to continue to focus on CTN.

Meanwhile, news of the CTN's launch had been read in the church press across the country and also overseas. The result was that the leadership found itself being invited to speak on the subject of mission. The secretariat was also being called to answer questions on the concept and vision, both from home and overseas.

The Committee of Nine

The Committee of Nine had become a key body at the centre of the ongoing movement. Many of its meetings, now at Bishop's Lodge in Liverpool, were spent not only in prayer and planning the Scargill Consultations, but in thinking through what the concept of mission meant today. The prophetic nature of the Church was considered, with the need for the churches of the North at all levels to work this out. Bishop Patrick Rodger of Manchester and Bill Walker Lee emphasized that this must be done for circuit, association, deanery, and parish as well as at diocesan level.

The main focus then fell on the question of Christian integrity in the world of work. Lay members had drawn the attention of the group to the difficulty Christians found in living out their faith in the context of their working lives. This was one of the most important areas in the lives of many Catholics, who felt most alienated from their environment in the world of work, affirmed Bishop Jack Brewer. On the other hand, Patrick Rodger pressed the Committee to look at the polarization within the churches. This was something that had hampered the work of CTN. He commented on the conservative and the radical: "Those who adhere to the givenness of Christianity against those who make it up as they go along", quoting John Huxtable, the first Moderator of the newly founded United Reformed Church. Or those who believe that "Jesus Christ frees and unites, over against those who believe he restricts and divides". This concern was not restricted to CTN but had come to prominence at the BCC Church Leaders Conference in Birmingham in September 1972.

The issue was raised in a different guise by the Bishop of Newcastle, Ronald Oliver Bowlby, who called for "further study of what might be called both the evangelical/ecumenical divide and the conservative/radical divide". Indeed, this issue was genuinely and painfully experienced as the CCC struggled to fulfil its role. Bishop Bowlby therefore suggested "further and continuing attention to the theological roots which still prevent genuine communication and theological support for mission". These indeed were key to our future in mission and to the inability of the last Bishopthorpe to move forward. And so the theme that emerged for the 1975 Bishopthorpe was "Christian leadership in a society threatened by alienation".

In designing the shape of the 1975 Consultation, the Committee of Nine decided to allow more time for face-to-face discussion through the use of small groups. The decision involved inviting laity to participate in the groups, with time provided for discussion in open session. Again in response to the Bishopthorpe VI call for more lay participation, the Nine decided to recommend a meeting of the Nine plus nine laity, each member bringing a lay member, someone of Christian conviction and of some standing in his or her own field.

Lay involvement (Bishopthorpe VII)

Another year having passed, the Bishopthorpe Consultation met again at Scargill. March 1975 saw the first of a new-style Bishopthorpe. The original Consultation had to focus on the clerical leadership of the churches in order to achieve united action. Now this annual consultation opened its doors to the wider church and invited laypeople to address Bishopthorpe. Two notable speakers were the headmaster of Worksop College, C. H. D. Everett, who had been a distinguished diplomat, and Professor Graham Ashworth, who held the Chair of Environmental Studies at Salford University and was the President of the Royal Town Planning Institute from 1973 to 1974. Their subject was aspects of alienation in society.

Harry Morton, in a series of brilliant Bible studies in the chapel, looked at the alienation felt by Our Lord and asked the pertinent questions,

"What sort of Britain do we want?" and "What sort of people should we be?"[246] No decisions were asked of the conference, and plenty of time was given for both open debate and group discussion. After several years of experiencing some leaders only coming for the "business sessions", on this occasion the Nine had planned to overcome this division by arranging for the devotional and business sessions to be interspersed.

A tantalizing vision of "tomorrow" was then given by one of the more distinguished guests of the Consultation, Bishop John Howe, Secretary General of the Anglican Consultative Council from 1971, who was expected by some to follow Michael Ramsey at Canterbury. He addressed the Consultation in memorable words, telling the church leaders of the North that, to his knowledge, they were members of an assembly that was unique:

> Nowhere else in the world did all the leaders of a Province or of a country meet regularly in this way to consult together, let alone consult on questions of mission—the commission of our Lord.

Moreover, he suggested that in a recent visit to the West Indies he had found significant growth in mutual understanding. This had led him to feel that a way forward to unity might well be discovered in Provincial schemes, where churches had already come into a working relationship. Such was the North.

> You are leaders of the churches, engaged in something which may well be much greater than anything you have yet realized.

With his contribution, the annual consultation seemed to find its soul and unity. It never looked back or questioned its own existence again. It had become an annual gathering to which the church leaders of the North looked forward and for which they made time, and which national leaders—secular and lay, as we shall see—were prepared to attend and to address. It was a consultation where the future of the church of the North might be shaped, and in turn itself help to shape the nation.

Over the years the atmosphere at the Consultation had improved steadily, and 1975 was undoubtedly the best so far. It was outstanding, not only in the high level of attendance but also in its spirit. Bishop John Habgood, as he left the house for Durham, commented: "The future of the Consultation is no longer in doubt; it is far too valuable a support group for everyone."[247] Stuart Blanch summed up our feeling later in the year in referring to Call to the North:[248]

> We are in fact engaged in an enterprise unique in the history of the Church and of great significance for the Church as a whole. Only history will show whether or not we have been involved in something modest in its beginnings, often misunderstood, but of great significance for the Church and for the society we seek to serve.

This left me wondering if, as we had succeeded in establishing the Consultation, we could now have time left to succeed also with the network, something essential if we were to achieve the change in culture from maintenance to mission by reaching those in the pew and beyond.

However, as the leaders left Scargill, they were not to know that we were about to enter a period of dramatic and significant changes of personnel in the North, during which these dreams and hopes would finally evaporate.

CHAPTER 24

Structures

The Scargill meeting of church leaders was the one indispensable part of the CTN movement. Stuart Blanch, in a perceptive comment, had made it clear that he believed he knew his fellow church leaders well enough to see that our present structures might prove unsustainable. "Our task," he said to me, "was to discern the signs of the times; we have no blueprint for people to conform to." This, in effect, meant the Committee of Nine had to focus on the annual Bishopthorpe meeting and in doing so had a clear field in its thinking and planning for CTN. Stuart's comment also led the new Central Consultative Committee to stimulate the greatest freedom for the regions to develop varieties of action, but at the same time to be an instrument to hold together the diverse amalgam of interests, beliefs, and theologies represented on the Committee.

The CCC was fortunate in its Chair. Bishop Hugh Lindsay brought serenity and dry humour to the meetings. In this arena, with their experience of the old Central Co-ordinating Committee, the Chair, the Secretary, and the Treasurer also worked together to keep the new committee on course. It had been created to encourage ecumenical mission to continue in the localities, so rather than using administrative nomenclature, the term "network" was another neutral word coined by Stuart Blanch to calm the fears of those leaders suspicious of structures. The Central Consultative Committee went on to produce a number of publications for ecumenical study groups, for which there was a steady and increasing demand. It was also a servicing agency for keeping the vision of mission in unity alive in the North at the local level, by supporting and representing the Local Co-ordinating Committees. The house magazine *ROOTS*, a broadsheet designed for this end, was the brainchild of Eddie Neale.

Although the creation of the new CCC had been Bishopthorpe's response to regional demands for better representation in the decision-making process, it had the unforeseen effect of confirming the suspicions of those leaders who resented any infringement of their status by attempts to run the Bishopthorpe Consultation from below. The Committee thus fell between a number of stools. It was representative not only of the fourteen regions but also of rival schools of theological thought, in addition to rival denominational loyalties. These made for internal dissent. Again, there were members of the CCC with a vision to unite the North in some prime activity of Christian witness, but others, equally vocal, who were determined not to countenance any such thing. They saw the CCC as primarily an arena for the exchange of information and ideas.

David Blunt was the first to recognize that attempts by CTN to create an organization that did justice to regional aspirations for recognition was not working. "When a body such as the CCC gets into the state it is at present," he wrote in 1975, "I think the time has come when it should dissolve itself without any loss to the movement."

New church leaders

Despite the hopes, and indeed efforts of the leadership, the newly-found local enthusiasm for mission engendered by the launch gradually began to fade. Geoffrey Tomlinson of Lancaster wrote, "It was the changes of personnel among ministers and clergy that caused evaporation of enthusiasm." It was not that the new people, coming in from other parts of the country, did not believe in ecumenism or mission; it was the absence of a shared experience that changed a culture of intimacy and enthusiasm back to formal, if decent, relationships. As Ronald Bowlby, Bishop of Newcastle, had said of his own coming to the North, "It is very difficult to convey the idea of Call to the North in words. It has to be experienced."

Thus despite the leadership of Stuart Liverpool and the backing of archbishops and of Free Church leaders like Bill Walker Lee, a number of those newly appointed to church leadership in the North found the ecumenical movement they had inherited both unexpected and constraining. Many just did not see the need for Province-wide ecumenical mission. Some new leaders had heard negative comments when in other parts of the country before their appointment to the North, and on their arrival declared their objective was to "kill off CTN". There was an unspoken assumption that the South was sophisticated and so knew how things should be done; the North was clearly ready to be helped. With the best of intentions, incoming leaders believed they had to correct this northern aberration. As one put it, there could be no "Treaty of Rome". CTN, therefore, was viewed as compromising their own particular church's stance or discipline; moreover, the Provincial dimension was proving a distraction from more important local things in the field of social witness. Some believed that the theology of the movement was deficient; others suggested that it was a form of spiritual blackmail, indulging the emotions of the faithful while lecturing the world.

The Bishopthorpe leadership, however, believed that experiencing CTN in its ongoing action, along with hearing the case for ecumenical witness, would prove conclusive. Encouraged by the "archbishops", therefore, Dennis Corbishley and I visited every new church leader appointed to the North. We were encouraged to discover that they all appeared anxious to be invited to Scargill. However, it was also clear that many newcomers viewed the supportive "network" with suspicion, as it appeared to them to compromise their local autonomy.

Arthur Liston was newly appointed from Bristol as the Baptist Superintendent for the North East; he had an outgoing personality and made me most welcome. He confessed that he had heard splendid reports of the Scargill gathering, but had reservations as to the rest of the organization.[249] This view was reinforced by Ralph Fennell, the new Chair of the Methodist West Yorkshire District. Fennell had replaced Tom Morrow, whose sudden and unexpected death robbed Northern Methodism of one of its most imaginative leaders. Another voice was that of Alasdair Walker, who had come to Leeds as United Reformed Church Moderator in place of Norman Beard, who had been a member of our original Central Co-ordinating Committee. Having previously worked in York, Walker—speaking in October 1975—confessed that the pressure of the conventional view that "mission is something that is undertaken and then finished" had proved too much for CTN, even in

York. He was not surprised that in Leeds he again found CTN regarded as something over and done with. It was good to hear, however, that the annual consultation was evidently becoming generally accepted, and the meeting with Alasdair Walker gave hope that a further period of time would result in the network becoming accepted as well.

The Central Consultative Committee was, despite its internal traumas, the vehicle that really linked the leadership with the pew. Without the active witness of the pew, the leadership remained only an elite fellowship of leaders and a means of mutual support. It was the lay people of all the churches who could leaven society in the North with the Christian faith. The CTN vision was to inspire the laity through the network; it was they who could then reach the hearts and minds of their non-churchgoing neighbours. Moreover, the network was the only organization that could instantly be activated, if a Scargill Consultation of the future were to decide on another northern-wide exercise. This was where the real coming together was taking place in the fields of mission and unity: in the localities. It could not be abandoned. The call for abandonment of the network was being made in the interests of the personal independence of individual leaders, but at the expense of the people of the North.

Of course, the failure to get the new kingdom theology of the movement, as expressed in the Manifesto, generally accepted by the leadership meant that CTN, for many, was still seen in terms of "an old-fashioned evangelistic effort". As vividly expressed by Walker Lee, this was "supposed only to last for a week". The new voices also included some powerful Church of England diocesan bishops, who sought to close down their Local Co-ordinating Committees. This was a disaster; it broke the link between the Central Consultative Committee and the local areas serviced by the secretariat. These new leaders brought with them from their previous spheres conventional concepts of evangelism and these proved to be the beginning of the end for Call to the North as a movement united and able to reach the grass roots throughout the North in mission.

The future of the structure

"There were no structures in the early Church," one leader grumbled to me. In the end, the Bishopthorpe leadership was forced to ask if we needed to reassess the situation. It had to be confessed that there was not the will within the churches to keep CTN alive. Its local presence was withering, and new aims and structures were needed. Maybe the way forward would have to lie in a movement designed to support the professionals and the leadership rather than to influence the secular North through the voice of the pew. This led to a reassessment of the name and the existing structure, and to a fundamental change of direction within the movement. For the present, it was clear that the existence of the "network" represented a threat to leaders. Bishop Hugh Lindsay wrote:

> You will find it increasingly difficult to keep CTN on the same lines as before. At one end of the scale people will be saying that they know it, you are really only telling them what they are already supposed to be doing. Towards the other end of the scale we will be saying that without some sort of organization, reminder, whatever, most people will do nothing.

Some of us hoped that, with time, the spectre of a "threatening" network would disappear and the potential of a useful piece of ecumenical machinery be revealed. This was not to be. The spectre was continually conjured up by those coming into the Province from elsewhere and meeting CTN for the first time, bringing with them presuppositions based on what they had heard of gospel campaigns. Often they supposed they would find themselves resisting some highly-organized pressure group or centrally directed enterprise. "I'm not going to submit my diocesan plans for mission to be vetted by anyone," one new bishop told the Committee of Nine somewhat belligerently in 1976. He seemed taken aback when he discovered that no one expected him to do so.

The night of old assumptions on campaigns of mission was too dark for the light of the new tomorrow to be perceived.

CHAPTER 25

The New Brooms

The reluctant archbishop

Within twelve months of the 1975 Consultation, Arthur Michael Ramsey had announced his retirement from Canterbury. This was destined to lead to a period of turbulence for CTN and to end its role as an active force for mission. Speculation immediately centred on Donald Coggan as Ramsey's successor.

Thus it was no surprise to discover that, despite his age, Donald Coggan had indeed been invited to become the 101st Primate of All England. What was perhaps more surprising was that he took so long to decide whether to accept the move. He had already bought his retirement home in the North.[250] Four days went by while the Archbishop said his prayers, saw his doctor, consulted, and talked with his family. In the end, his enthronement at Canterbury was a splendid occasion. It took place on the Feast of the Conversion of St Paul in 1975 and, perhaps for the first time, was fully ecumenical. Princes and Moderators, Heads of State and Cardinals were all in attendance. Moreover, trouble had been taken to invite representatives from many walks of life, except (curiously and perhaps unfortunately) anyone from the trade unions.

In the under-croft after the service, Donald Coggan and his wife moved among their many guests, and speculation then switched to York. Archdeacon Linsley was gloomy: "There are those who already say that now Coggan has gone, CTN must be wound up." It is obvious that there were those who, if they came to York, would close CTN down, including the annual Consultation.[251] Later Linsley wrote to me: "The appointment to York is vital," he said; "much prayer will have to be made, so many people outside the Church see the point of CTN . . . if, however, your bishop comes to York you will have a friend at court, and you will certainly need one."

Curiously, I had no such anxieties; I had worked over the years seeing divine providence overrule, and further recent experiences at the Scargill Consultations made me feel the movement was secure. Even when Stuart Blanch asked me about my future, I replied with confidence. However, Stanley Linsley had a better overview than I did, and I came to realize that he knew the scene. Indeed, such was his anxiety that he enquired, as he was shortly to retire, if I would be prepared to follow him as archdeacon. This took me by surprise—I had never thought of it, and it didn't happen.

Then it was announced, to our delight, that Stuart Blanch had been invited to move to York—at least we could be assured that the annual Consultation would continue and that the vision of mission and unity for the North was secure. But I was sad, for I was losing my bishop with his wise words and gentle guidance. In the same period, sadly, we also lost George Andrew Beck, who retired to live at Upholland. He had been a godly and true friend, whose vision and inspiration had carried the Roman Catholic Church throughout the whole period of the CTN exercise. Though he was now far from well, he continued his ministry of encouragement in retirement, reading the first draft of this book, chapter by chapter, as it was written. This loss of two of the three moving spirits of the movement was to mark the effective end of the endeavour to transform the Northern Province into a united, continuing, and powerful movement for mission.

A further delight for us all, although it was to weaken our Committee of Nine, was the announcement in Rome on 12 December 1974 that Bishop Hugh Lindsay, Chair of the CCC, had been appointed Bishop of Hexham and Newcastle. In consequence, we lost his active participation in our work, and Stuart Blanch asked me to represent him at the subsequent enthronement. I travelled up to Newcastle and discovered just how deep Hugh Lindsay's roots were in the North East. He had been christened in St Mary's Catholic Cathedral, confirmed, made deacon, priested, consecrated, and was now to be enthroned there. He took as his text, "The scribes sit in Moses' seat", using it to illustrate the teaching office of the bishop. It was a moving and inspiring occasion. During his address at the reception, in welcoming me he paid a most gracious tribute to Call to the North. Lindsay's place as Chair of the Consultative Committee was taken by Dennis Corbishley.

A further change took place when John Marsh wrote to say that he would no longer be able to fulfil his role as the third "archbishop"; indeed, he was already retired from active ministry when he agreed to represent the Free Churches. A measure of the success of CTN was then seen in the new spirit of unity among the Free Churches of the North. Instead of looking to London for a successor, as had happened before, Bill Walker Lee called a meeting of Free Church leaders, who elected Trevor Hubbard, a Baptist, as the "third archbishop" to represent them at the Bishopthorpe Consultations.

Then, again to our delight, the news was released that Bishop David Sheppard was to be translated to Liverpool from Woolwich. Thus the future of evangelism in the North seemed secure. But to our great surprise and dismay, it was a very different Sheppard from the one we had known at the Mayflower Family Centre in Canning Town; on his arrival, he made it clear that his first purpose was to close down CTN.[252] He had clearly thought deeply about this Province-wide initiative, of which he had heard so much in Woolwich. He was quite open with me that he was not prepared to allow this Provincial initiative to hinder his own plans for Liverpool. It had to go.

I did not doubt his sincerity or ability in this chosen aim, but hoped—and indeed prayed—that after he had been to Scargill and had experienced something of the mission of CTN, the commitment to evangelism I had known him to have in the past would lead him to support CTN, or at least to modify his opposition. I had seen so many new leaders arrive from the South, Free Church and Anglican, clearly ready to try and close down this northern mission, that I believed the experience of its vision would lead to a change of mind.

David Sheppard's splendid enthronement in Liverpool cathedral, resplendent in episcopal robes and, unusually for Liverpool, a bishop's mitre, did not bode well for the province-wide vision of his predecessor. My hope was that he would come to Scargill, perhaps become involved in our committee work, and so catch a vision of all the churches of the North working together for the kingdom. His support for the movement would then be invaluable. An opportunity was afforded at the time, with two vacancies occurring on the Committee of Nine: Donald Coggan's move to Canterbury provided one place, and the other was created by Patrick Manchester letting me know that he was writing to the Archbishop to say that he felt it was good to have a change.[253] So it was that Stuart Blanch decided Denis Wakeling, Bishop of Southwell, together with David Sheppard, should be invited to fill the vacancies.[254]

Bishopthorpe VII (1975) had undoubtedly been a great success. The Committee of Nine, meeting at the home of Trevor Hubbard (now the "third archbishop"), was also full of confidence for the future. It had been the first consultation to be chaired by Stuart Blanch, with his gentle, easy, and relaxed style, leading Trevor Hubbard to comment, "In the past there was a feeling that Scargill was trying to dragoon people into a particular way of mission; now it is trying to equip church people in the task of mission." In the same vein, Catholic Bishop Jack Brewer mused, "Scargill might well become a meditation on mission rather than a policy-making discussion of methods."

The Committee of Nine might well feel gratified by its work. The CCC, on the other hand, was still in some confusion following the rejection of its work in 1974. There was some suggestion that it might be placed under the umbrella of the British Council of Churches, a move which would solve our structural problems and provide it with adequate secretarial back-up from London. The idea of linking us with the BCC was canvassed at a meeting of the Committee of Nine, although nothing was done. Meanwhile, Dennis Corbishley wrote of the future:

> I think there is great value in having a committee of "second eleven" status (people like Eric Chard, Maurice Simmons, myself) with regional responsibilities who would come together three or four times a year to share thinking and experience. I think such a committee could work with the "approval" of the church leaders.

This was a wise suggestion as, at the cost of geographic representation, it removed the endemic conflict between "authorities".

Then the debate on the name of the movement again emerged. "We can't just continue to Ca-a-a-a-a-a-ll," Eddie Neale said in exasperation at a meeting of the CCC. However, fears that the whole edifice might collapse if we tried to change the name had now died down, so we needed a new name to maintain the momentum of the movement. The suggestion "Northern Consultation for Mission" presented itself. Such a name would continue to focus our minds on mission, the fundamental purpose of the original Consultation. Being a "consultation", it would not be threatening to the church leaders. Moreover, the word "Northern" would help us maintain our corporate solidarity and focus on the North. This was discussed with Dennis Corbishley, who was asked to write a paper setting forward the new look for the movement. The new structure would retain the existing Bishopthorpe Consultation and Committee of Nine. The contentious Central Consultative Committee, however, would be replaced by Dennis Corbishley's suggestion of a second-strings Consultation based on the four super-regional groups that had originally been suggested in 1969.

The annual consultation

The 1975 Scargill Consultation, in its final plenary session, had discovered an interest in the phrase "the other side of society". The Methodist Chairs had made the running and called us to "listen to men like Clive Jenkins and Joe Gormley".[255] The Bishop of Durham dryly suggested that perhaps instead of listening, we might well have a consultation on the fact that "we both belong to institutions with very large non-functioning memberships".

Following this debate, the Committee of Nine, preparing for the next Scargill, decided to try and explore and understand the role of the factory classes of the North, a section of society in so many ways estranged from the churches. My own background in the trade union world prompted me to suggest that we should invite Len Murray, General Secretary of the Trades Union Congress, to address Bishopthorpe VIII. Murray proved delighted to be invited, and readily agreed (correspondence with him revealed that "Len" stood for Lionel). The small groups would have their discussions angled to this area, and each would be joined by a trade union official.

It was decided to invite Dom Basil Hume, Abbot of Ampleforth, to lead our thinking and praying in chapel. The Committee suggested that his theme might focus on Harry Morton's striking question to the Scargill Consultation, "What sort of society do we want? The contribution of Christian leadership". It was a challenge, but the Abbot gladly accepted our invitation.

Then came the announcement from Rome, in February 1976, that Derek Worlock (Bishop of Portsmouth) had been preferred to Liverpool; this met local expectations and caused little comment. I therefore wrote to congratulate the new Archbishop and to welcome him on behalf of CTN. In return, he invited me to visit Bishop's House. I was happy to respond and went, ready to look to him—as indeed I had to George Andrew—for guidance and co-operation in working with Roman Catholics across the North.

However, in the new Archbishop I met a very different prelate from his predecessor and was reminded of my visit to Rome. Worlock was courteous, but did not appear very interested in ecumenical mission. Indeed, in a friendly way he regaled me with stories of how he had been insulted and demeaned by Michael Ramsey when at Canterbury. This left me baffled; it was so out of character with the Ramsey I had known for years that it was hard to credit. However, given my experience of Rome and Middlesbrough, I could see that we might now face an uphill struggle in assisting CTN to survive. Worlock, although not a *Venerabilist*, had been secretary to three Archbishops of Westminster in turn and was very much at home in Rome. He might be post-conciliar in time, but did not appear to be so in thought.

I reported my contact to David Sheppard, who was interested but indicated that he did not expect me to explore relations with the Catholic Church in Liverpool any further. He himself would be in touch with Derek Worlock. In the event, Sheppard so charmed the new Archbishop that their partnership became a legend and did much to cement the earlier work of the Stuart Blanch/George Andrew alliance. The latter, which had transformed relationships between Protestants and Catholics in the North, then became a distant memory.

Next came the announcement from Rome of the appointment of Dom Basil Hume to be Archbishop of Westminster. This not only surprised many in the Roman Catholic community, but unfortunately also robbed us of Basil Hume's potential contribution to Scargill.[256] Adrian Hastings notes that Worlock and Hume complemented each other, both being children of Anglicans who had converted to Rome.[257] Now it seemed that Worlock noted the way the Westminster wind was blowing and changed course. The authoritarian prelate melted into Sheppard's congenial companion, although that was to cause some consternation in the Liverpool Roman Catholic camp.

Bishopthorpe VIII

Given the new interest shown at Scargill in "the other side of society", the Committee of Nine now looked afresh at the Salvation Army's role in the life of the Church. The Army specialized in reaching out to the working classes and the poor. Although the Army had always been represented at Bishopthorpe, unlike the other mainstream churches an invitation had not been extended to all the leaders of their seven main divisions in the North.

The Committee of Nine therefore asked me to explore the matter in London with the Army's General. This led to a visit to the HQ of the Salvation Army, which I found very helpful. Moreover, General Clarence Wiseman turned out to be receptive and indeed interested to hear first-hand of this northern initiative. As a result, all the Divisional Commanders in the North received an invitation to the following Consultation. They were to make a significant contribution, although some voices were heard questioning if the Consultation was now becoming too big.

The Consultation met at Scargill in the spring of 1976 on 13 March—it was our eighth Bishopthorpe. The attendance level remained very high, and most of the church leaders in the North were present. I met Len Murray off the train at Leeds and drove him to Scargill. In his address to the leadership, he stressed the responsibility of the Christian Church for those who formed the major part of any society: the artisan, the working class, and the poor. He was blunt. Their status, he challenged the leaders, was often unrecognized by the churches. Murray's subtle mixture of humour, Christian understanding, and plain speaking captivated his audience. In the debate that followed he readily dealt with some sharp questions.

After lunch and the plenary session, Murray had to leave, to the clear disappointment of the church leaders, for a further speaking engagement at Ruskin College, Oxford. The obvious regret of the leaders suggested a cultural change in the churches of the North. The leadership had become aware in a new way of the importance of the working class, the trade union movement, and its influence in the life of the nation. This was something Murray had insisted must be taken into account in any serious thinking on our strategy of mission.

The Committee of Nine had this in mind when preparing for Bishopthorpe IX in 1977. There would clearly be much to be said for asking someone to speak who could provide for our leaders a window onto the national scene. This might allow them to assess the pressures that formed and moulded people in the North. Only thus could the Committee help the Scargill leaders in planning an adequate strategy for speaking to the nation.

The spiritual needs of the North, if not the nation, had been at the forefront of Stuart Blanch's mind. Len Murray may have captivated Bishopthorpe VIII, but Stuart himself had taken the whole assembly by the ears in a superb address on the "Theologies of the Kingdom". The Archbishop drew the attention of the Consultation to the section of Mark 6:1–8:2, which he felt reflected Israel's obligation to the nations of the world. Drawing his argument from Jonah, Deutero-Isaiah, and Genesis, Blanch recalled the churches of the North to their concern for the spiritual needs of the people of the North. It was this biblical thinking, he maintained, that sustained the burden of CTN and indeed provided the justification for Donald Coggan's initiative of the autumn of 1975, his "Call to the Nation".

The Archbishop of York's address had sought to recover the original direction of the Call to the North and to inspire the northern leaders with a new vision for a united strategy of mission. Michael Turnbull, now Bishop of Durham, was inspired by this powerful exposition, and indeed experience of Christian unity, when he later attended a meeting of the Northern Convocation in York. At a combined session of both houses, he therefore introduced a motion commending Call to the North.

Further, he called for renewed thinking on "our strategy of mission in the Church of England". This was warmly received, although then an apparently pious amendment was introduced. This replaced the word "strategy" by "prayer", a manoeuvre which successfully deflected the force of Durham's proposition away from mission.

The Archbishop of Canterbury's "Call to the Nation" meanwhile, had coincided with the publication of the CTN study guide, "What sort of nation do we want?" This caught the imagination of the public, and thousands of copies were ordered from the CTN office, so placing an enormous strain on the voluntary groups concerned with printing, binding, packing, and posting. Dennis Corbishley commented to the following Bishopthorpe Consultation, "We thought of ourselves as a 'five-a-side' football team, then suddenly we seemed to be on 'Match of the Day.'"

The movement towards integrating the structures of CTN with the developing ecumenical structures of the churches had been moving quietly forward. The Blackburn Regional Committee emerged in a new form as the Lancashire Ecumenical Committee with Eric Chard as its Secretary. In Liverpool the Regional Committee became the Mission Committee of the Merseyside Churches Ecumenical Council, with the Methodist Norman Denny as its Chair. Manchester, Sheffield, and the North East continued to be part of the local ecumenical structure.

Unfortunately, this was not so across the whole of the North. As local church leaders withdrew support, many strategic parts of the network just quietly disappeared. This development made Dennis Corbishley's paper setting out new structures for the Northern Consultation for Mission all the more important. Meanwhile, David Sheppard's attendance at Scargill—as I had hoped—gave him new insights into the movement. He wrote to me:

> May I say how impressed I was with this year's day and a bit; I thought the time was extremely well used . . . it was a feather in the cap of the organization.

Although privately acknowledging the effectiveness of the Province-wide ecumenical mission that he encountered in coming north, I found—in trying to exploit this experience with my bishop—that it did not deflect David Sheppard from his primary vision to make Liverpool, rather than the Northern Province, an outstanding example of Protestant–Catholic unity. Building on the Blanch–Beck foundation, his achievement was impressive in the national publicity it achieved. Sadly, however, it narrowed the impact of a Province-wide initiative down to a single diocese. At the same time it made both bishops household names, which had a profound and positive effect on the public appreciation of church unity, not only in the North but throughout the country.

Meanwhile, the CTN leaders had been asked for their opinion on the future. The replies were enthusiastic concerning the Annual Consultation. "This year's Scargill," wrote Gordon Wakefield, "was perhaps the best ever; it has become one of the events to which I look forward with increasing pleasure." There was, however, uncertainty concerning the organization by which the Annual Consultation influenced the wider church. It seemed clear that the existence of the Committee of Nine, the Central Consultative Committee, and their supporting secretariat was felt, not only by David Sheppard but by leaders of other denominations, to threaten their independence of action.

From the Free Church perspective, John Marsh had written of the Consultative Co-ordinating Committee, "It would be wise and economic to reduce our committee structure." Similarly Frank Amery, the Methodist Chair of Sheffield, put a question mark against the continuation of the secretariat, "with its burden on the churches". However, Stuart Blanch summed up the general mind when he wrote, "I am quite sure that the Consultation must go on; this year's attendance shows that this view is more widely held than it was two or three years ago." Again, this focus on the meeting of the leaders proved to be perceptive.[258]

The question of structures, therefore, was now seriously considered by the Committee of Nine. With the plethora of replies before its members, I was asked to prepare a paper on the theology and methodology of our work. The Nine were meeting, on this occasion, in my cottage near Liverpool.[259] The prime purpose of this session was to plan the next "Bishopthorpe", due to meet again at Scargill in 1977.

The Nine first agreed to consider the structural change advocated by Corbishley, then the replies from the church leaders led Gordon Wakefield to propose that we consider "the need to occupy ourselves with questions relative to the churches and the nation". This led Derek Worlock to point to the importance of educational questions, and in this he was supported by a letter from Charles Oxley of the Christian Brethren. The Committee of Nine therefore decided to take the first subject (on questions relative to the nation) in 1977 and the second (education) in 1978. There was little appetite, however, for exploring the theological questions that lay at the root of mission, so Gordon Wakefield suggested as a title for 1977, "The Christian's Role in Public Affairs".

Following the success of Len Murray's contribution in 1976, the Nine took a deep breath and decided to invite the Prime Minister, Harold Wilson, to address us. Wilson was a clear thinker with a Christian understanding of society. His was a mind that most of our leaders would find challenging, if not fascinating. His insight into Britain's economic woes had been shown in 1969 by his Government's White Paper *In Place of Strife*; moreover, his party's traditional commitment to peace meant he had kept Britain clear of the Vietnam War. Wilson immediately agreed to the Archbishop's invitation, and I found, somewhat to my surprise, when dealing with his briefing and detailed arrangements, that he was always readily available at the end of a telephone in 10 Downing Street.[260]

For our initial day, it was decided to ask Jack Brewer, Auxiliary Bishop of Shrewsbury, to lead our devotions.

More structural change

The Committee of Nine turned to Dennis Corbishley's paper on our structures and agreed to replace the Consultative Co-ordinating Committee with a meeting of suffragan and auxiliary bishops, diocesan missioners, and ecumenical officers from across the Northern Province. This new body would give the leaders a valuable support group throughout the North. At the same time, the Committee of Nine supported the suggestion that the time had come to change the name of CTN to the "Northern Consultation for Mission".[261] The secretariat, meanwhile, was translated to Bishopthorpe itself, under the direction of David Blunt.

Bishopthorpe IX

Another year having passed, Bishopthorpe IX (1977) took place at Scargill and saw a full attendance of church leaders with a real spirit of unity and purposefulness, while Bishop Jack Brewer's Bible studies were masterly.

However, Sir Harold Wilson surprised me—when I met him off his train at Leeds—by saying he had decided not to speak, apart from an introduction, but would engage instead in a question-and-answer session.[262] The leadership was disappointed, although the subsequent debate was frank and vigorous.

In the business session, the new structure was readily adopted and the new name accepted. With it, the annual consultation changed its direction; no longer was it primarily concerned with discovering its own unity, nor was it preparing for a common exercise in mission, it had become a fellowship of church leaders, deciding on its own agenda. "We have become," commented Bishop Moverley, the Auxiliary of Leeds, "an In-service Training Unit for Bishops."

A new body

The Consultation agreed to disband the Central Consultative Committee and set up the new meeting of suffragan bishops and ecumenical officers. The role of this group was to implement the decisions of the Committee of Nine and oversee the practicalities of organizing future Bishopthorpe Conferences held at Scargill.

Time to move on

My bishop, however, now made it clear that he believed it was best for me to move on, so it was with some thankfulness that I was able to look back to what had been achieved. "The relics of yesterday" had been abandoned, with their fear of Rome, superiority of Canterbury, and splintering of the Free Churches. Instead we were seeing "the beginning of tomorrow", with the Christian churches of the North growing in unity and recovering their strength. Sadly for me, I then discovered that Dennis Corbishley was also to be translated out of the Northern Province and, finally, that the central word "mission" had been dropped from the title of the annual meeting of the church leaders of the North.

It is now nearly fifty years since Call to the North was conceived. As this account is revised, the churches (generally speaking) are all reduced in numbers, apart from some Pentecostal or Independent Evangelical congregations. But Christians themselves are much more united and aware of the largely "non-religious" and multi-faith world they now inhabit and to which they now witness.

Postscript

The annual consultation meeting of church leaders has survived, as indeed foreseen by Stuart Blanch. Its popularity as an annual event for the North appears to be undimmed. In 1985, on becoming Bishop of Wakefield, David Hope commented on how surprised he was to find a regular meeting of all the church leaders of the North just before Holy Week. "Its great value," he said, "was to be a sort of ecumenical retreat. We gave papers to one another."[263] Then after serving as Bishop of London and on returning north as Archbishop of York, he again spoke of the annual consultation, saying that its "value lay in our interpersonal relationships, something not experienced in the Southern Province". Free Church leaders expressed similar sentiments. Under the leadership of York, the churches of the North had discovered a new purpose and unity.

In March 1967 the *SS Torrey Canyon* sank off the coast of Cornwall. Reports at the time suggested that the sheer size and weight of the vessel prevented the ship from answering the helm, and so avoiding the Seven Stones Reef. The churches of the Northern Province in the early 1970s presented a similar problem, although carrying a cargo infinitely more precious than the tanker; so despite a unique project of evangelism inspired by a remarkable and visionary leadership, once that leadership had moved on, the churches largely resumed their former ways.

In the end, only the annual consultation remained, itself a valuable witness and legacy of Call to the North. But in the process the North itself had changed, if not into churches united and dedicated to mission, then to churches with a vision to recognize and live in harmony together. This was the Tomorrow of which Call to the North was the Beginning.

In the name of God: Amen.

John Gaunt Hunter
2016

Glossary of Names

Amery, Frank M.	Chair of the Sheffield Methodist District (1969–1978)
Ashdown, Hugh E.	Bishop of Newcastle (1957–1972)
Bardsley, Cuthbert	Bishop of Coventry (1956–1976)
Beck, George Andrew	Archbishop of Liverpool (1964–1976)
Bickersteth, John	Bishop of Warrington (1970–1975); Bishop of Bath and Wells (1975–1987)
Bishop, Mark	Secretary to Bradford Council of Churches
Blake, Joyce	Headmistress and Quaker Representative to CTN
Blanch, Stuart Y.	Bishop of Liverpool (1966–1975); Archbishop of York (1975–1983)
Blunt, David	Lay Chaplain to Donald Coggan as Archbishop of York
Bowlby, Ronald Oliver	Bishop of Newcastle (1973–1980)
Bowles, Cyril	Bishop of Derby (1969–1987)
Brewer, John (Jack)	Auxiliary Bishop of Shrewsbury (1971–1983); Coadjutor Bishop of Lancaster (1983–1985); Bishop of Lancaster (1985–2000)
Brunner, George	Bishop of Middlesbrough (1955–1969)
Buckley, Michael	English representative to the Vatican Secretariat for Christian Unity
Chard, Eric	Vicar of St Bartholomew's Ewood (1960–1972); Vicar of Downham (1972–1988)
Clark, Sydney	Baptist Superintendent of the North East Area
Claxton, Charles	Bishop of Blackburn (1960–1971)

GLOSSARY OF NAMES

Coggan, Donald	Archbishop of York (1961–1974); Archbishop of Canterbury (1974–1980)
Collie, John N.	Vicar of Ecclesall (1968–1990)
Corbishley, Dennis	Parish Priest of Ambleside
Cross, Stewart	BBC Northern Religious Adviser (1968–1976); Bishop of Doncaster (1976–1982); Bishop of Blackburn (1982–1989)
Cryer, Neville B.	General Secretary of the British and Foreign Bible Society (1970–1986)
Cunningham, Séamus	Bishop of Hexham and Newcastle (2009–2019)
Davison, Leslie	President of the Methodist Conference (1962); first President of the Methodist Conference to be received in audience at the Vatican (by Pope John XXIII, 1963)
Denny, Norman	Chair of the Liverpool Methodist District
Downey, Richard	Archbishop of Liverpool (1928–1953)
Edis, Pamela	Secretary to the Bishop of Liverpool, Leader of Working Party 5
Ellis, Edward	Bishop of Nottingham (1944–1974)
Ellison, Gerald A.	Bishop of Chester (1955–1973); Bishop of London (1973–1981)
Fenwick, William	Divisional Commander of the Northern Division of the Salvation Army (1969–1971); Moderator of the North West Province (1956–1970)
Fisher, Leslie G.	Archdeacon of Chester and Canon Residentiary (1965–1975); Chair of the Church Information Board, formerly Home Secretary of the Church Missionary Society
Foley, Brian Charles	Bishop of Lancaster (1962–1985)
Foley, Graham	Vicar of Leeds (1971–1982); Bishop of Reading (1982–1989)
Foskett, Reginald	Bishop of Penrith (1967–1970)

Galliford, D. George	Canon and Prebendary, later Canon Treasurer of York Minster (1969–1975); Bishop of Hulme (1975–1984)
Goyder, George	Industrialist, significant Anglican layman, member of the Standing Committee of General Synod
Gray, Joseph	Auxiliary Bishop of Liverpool (1969–1980); Bishop of Shrewsbury (1980–1995)
Greer, William D. L.	Bishop of Manchester (1947–1970)
Habgood, John	Bishop of Durham (1973–1983); Archbishop of York (1983–1995)
Hallsall, Martyn	Journalist at the *Southport Visiter*
Halsey, H. David	Bishop of Carlisle (1972–1989)
Heenan, John Carmel	Archbishop of Westminster (1963–1975), Cardinal from 1965
Henshall, Michael	Vicar of Altrincham (1963–1976); Bishop of Warrington (1976–1996)
Holland, Thomas	Coadjutor Bishop of Portsmouth (1960–1964); Bishop of Salford (1964–1983)
Howe, John	Bishop of St Andrews (1955–1969); Executive Officer of the Anglican Communion (1969–1971); Secretary General of the Anglican Consultative Council (1971–1982)
Hubbard, Trevor	Baptist Superintendent of the North West Area
Huddleston, E. U. Trevor	Bishop of Masasi (1960–1968); Bishop of Stepney (1968–1978)
Huxtable, John	Congregational minister and Principal of New College, London (1953–1964); first Moderator of the United Reformed Church (1972–1973)
Jackson, Brandon D.	Vicar of St Peter's Shipley (1965–1977); Provost of Bradford (1977–1989); Dean of Lincoln (1989–1997)

Jackson, Keith	Economist and Head of the Social Studies Division of Liverpool University
Jackson, Lawrence	Vicar of Holy Trinity, Coventry (1965–1973); Provost of Blackburn (1973–1992)
Jackson, Michael J.	Vicar of Doncaster (1969–1973)
Jarvis, Arthur Cecil	Elim District Superintendent of the North West and Minister of Elim Barnsley Pentecostal Church
Jeffery, Robert	Secretary of the British Council of Churches' Department of Mission and Unity (1968–1971)
Johnston, William	Archdeacon and Diocesan Missioner of Bradford (1965–1977)
Jones, Ivor	Lecturer at Hartley Victoria College, Manchester; Methodist theologian and biblical scholar
Jones, Norman B.	General Superintendent of the Lancashire and Cheshire Association of Baptist Churches (1961–1971)
Jones, Richard C.	Methodist tutor, later Principal of Hartley Victoria College, Manchester
Kissack, Reginald (Rex)	Chair of the Liverpool Methodist District (1965–1975)
Lawn, Geoffrey	Rector of Newton Kyne, York (1970–1974); York Diocesan Ecumenical Adviser, later Vicar of Doncaster (1974–1982)
Lawrence, L. Roy	Vicar of Hyde (1968–1975); Vicar of Prenton (1975–1996)
Lee, Bill Walker	Chair of the Leeds Methodist District
Lindsay, Hugh	Coadjutor Bishop of Hexham and Newcastle (1969–1974); Bishop of Hexham and Newcastle (1974–1992)
Linsley, Stanley Frederick	Archdeacon of Cleveland (1965–1974)
Logan, Kevin	Journalist and CTN Press Officer
Macmillan, Harold	Conservative Prime Minister (1957–1963)

Marsh, John	Congregationalist scholar, first Professor of Christian Theology at Nottingham University, later Principal of Mansfield College, Oxford. Moderator of the Free Church Federal Council (1970–1971)
Martin, Clifford A.	Bishop of Liverpool (1944–1966)
Minshull, E. Lincoln	Chair of the Darlington Methodist District (1968–1979)
Montague, William John	Anglo-Catholic Residentiary Canon of Wakefield Cathedral (1962–1972)
Moorman, John R. H.	Bishop of Ripon (1959–1975); Moorman had led the Anglican delegation to Vatican II (1962)
Morgan, Frank C.	Vicar of St Andrew Cleveleys (1965–1981)
Morrow, Thomas M.	Chair of the West Yorkshire Methodist District
Morton, Harry O.	President of the Methodist Conference (1972), later Secretary General of the British Council of Churches
Moverley, Gerald	Auxiliary Bishop of Leeds (1967–1980); Bishop of Hallam (1980–1996)
Murray, Lionel (Len)	Baron Murray of Epping Forest, OBE, PC, a Methodist by conviction
Neill, Ivan	Provost of Sheffield (1966–1974)
Oxley, Charles	Representative of the Christian (Open) Brethren
Parker, C. George St M.	Bishop of Bradford (1961–1971)
Patey, Edward H.	Dean of Liverpool (1964–1982)
Pollock, John C.	Clergyman of the Church of England, official biographer of Billy Graham
Poulton, John	Research and Development Officer, later Executive Secretary of the Archbishops' Council on Evangelism (Canterbury)
Ramsey, Arthur Michael	Archbishop of Canterbury (1961–1974)
Ramsey, Ian T.	Bishop of Durham (1966–1972)
Raynor, Herbert	Chair of the Preston Methodist District

Reid, Gavin H.	Publications Secretary, Church Pastoral Aid Society (1966– 1971); Education Secretary, United Society for Christian Literature (1971–1974)
Rodger, Patrick C.	Bishop of Manchester (1970–1978)
Savage, G. David	Secretary of the Merseyside District of the Baptist Church
Snow, George D.	Bishop of Whitby (1961–1971)
Springbett, Harold	Presbyterian minister at Allerton (1957–1970), Moderator for the Presbytery of Liverpool (1969–1970)
Strutt, R. Gordon	Bishop of Stockport (1965–1983)
Taylor, F. John	Bishop of Sheffield (1962–1971)
Taylor, Michael	Principal of Northern Baptist College, Manchester; later Director of Christian Aid
Todhunter, John	Roman Catholic educationalist from Norfolk
Treacy, Eric	Bishop of Wakefield (1968–1976)
Turnbull, Michael	Chaplain to the Archbishop of York, Donald Coggan (1965–1969); later Chief Secretary of the Church Army (1976–1984); Bishop of Rochester (1988–1994); Bishop of Durham (1994–2003)
Vine, Aubrey R.	Congregationalist minister; Professor at Yorkshire United Theological College, Bradford; General Secretary of the Free Church Federal Council
Wakefield, Gordon	Chair of the Manchester and Stockport Methodist District (1971–1979)
Watson, David C. K.	Evangelical author, Rector of St Michael-le-Belfrey, York (1973–1982)
Watson, Richard	Bishop of Burnley (1970–1987)
Weights, Kenneth	Chair of the Newcastle-upon-Tyne Methodist District (1966–1974); President of the Methodist Conference (1971)

Wheeler, Gordon   Bishop of Leeds (1959–1975)
Wickham, Edward R. (Ted) Bishop of Middleton (1959–1982)
Willebrands, Johannes   Cardinal and Secretary of the Vatican's Secretariat for Promoting Christian Unity
Williams, Richard (Dick) Rector of Woolton, Liverpool (1968–1979)
Woodhall, Ralph   Jesuit and Parish Priest of St Francis Xavier, Liverpool
Worlock, Derek   Archbishop of Liverpool (1976–1996)
Wright, Frank S.   Canon Residentiary, later Sub-Dean of Manchester Cathedral (1966–1974)
Young, Canon C. Edwyn Rector of Liverpool (1964–1972)

Bibliography

Primary

Manuscript sources

First set
Folders containing papers based on chronological years: 1969, 1970, 1971, 1972, 1973, 1976, 1977

Second set
Folders containing papers based on activities:
Folder 1 Meetings of Call to the North Executives
Folder 2 Meetings of the Central Co-ordinating Committee
Folder 3 Meetings of the Committee of Nine
Folder 4 Meetings of the Central Consultative Committee
Folder 5 Correspondence with partner churches
Folder 6 Correspondence with the Archbishops' Council and with Billy Graham, John Pollock, CMS, Dennis Corbishley, Joe Gray *et al.*
Folder 7 Prayer card, logo, correspondence with Rural Deans and cathedrals

Third set
Folders on working parties:
Folder 1 WP one, two, three, and four
Folder 2 WP five
Folder 3 WP six, seven, eight, nine, and ten

Fourth set
Talks and addresses

Printed sources

Bernard, J. F. (ed.), *The Works of Bishop Butler*, vol. 1, pp. 287–288, "A Charge delivered to the Clergy at the Primary Visitation of the Diocese of Durham" (1751, reprinted 1900).

Booth, Charles, *Life and Labour of the People in London* (third series, 1902).

Gore, Charles (ed.), *Lux Mundi: A Series of Studies in the Religion of the Incarnation* (1889).

Herbert, Charles, *Twenty-Five Years as Archbishop of Canterbury* (Wells: Gardner, Darton & Co, 1929).

Hobson, Richard, *What God Hath Wrought: An Autobiography* (London: fourth edition, Thynne, 1913).

Hume, Dr Abraham, *Missions at Home; or a Clergyman's Account of a Portion of the Town of Liverpool* (1848).

Mass Observation, *Puzzled People* (London: Gollancz, 1947).

Pius XI, *Quadragesimo anno* (1931)

Schweitzer, Albert (tr. William Montgomery), *The Quest of the Historical Jesus* (1910).

Reports

Catholics and Christian Unity: Ecumenical Commission of England and Wales (Catholic Information Office, 1969).

Facts and Figures about the Church of England (Church Information Office, 1962)

Paul, Leslie, *The Deployment and Payment of the Clergy* (Church Information Office for the Central Advisory Council for the Ministry, 1964), a report to the Church Assembly on C of E staff apportionment.

"State of Trade" (House of Commons Debate; Hansard, 24 May 1928), from Hansard 1803–2005, available online.

"Television and Religion" (Gallup Poll; University of London Press, 1964).

Secondary

Books

Bonhoeffer, Dietrich (ed. Eberhard Bethge), *Letters and Papers from Prison* (SCM Press, 1971).

Boulard, F. (tr. M. J. Jackson), *An Introduction to Religious Sociology* (London: Darton, Longman & Todd, 1960).

Brown, Callum G., *The Death of Christian Britain* (London: Routledge, 2001).

Chadwick, Henry, and Evans, G. R. (eds), *Atlas of the Christian Church* (London: Macmillan, 1987).

Cox, Harvey, *The Secular City: Secularization and Urbanization in Theological Perspective* (London: SCM Press, 1965).

Gilbert, Alan D., *The Making of Post-Christian Britain: A History of the Secularization of Modern Society* (London: Longman, 1980).

Gill, Robin, *The Myth of the Empty Church* (London: SPCK, 1993).

Goodhew, David (ed.), *Church Growth in Britain: 1980 to the Present* (Farnham: Ashgate, 2012).

Hastings, Adrian, *A History of English Christianity 1920–1985* (London: Collins, 1986).

Heenan, John C., *The People's Priest* (London: Sheed & Ward, 1951).

Hoskyns, Sir Edwyn and Davey, Francis Noel, *The Riddle of the New Testament* (London: Faber & Faber, 1931).

Küng, Hans, *The Council and Reunion* (London: Sheed & Ward, 1962).

McLeod, Hugh, *The Religious Crisis of the 1960s* (Oxford: Oxford University Press, 2007).

Pawley, Margaret, *Donald Coggan, Servant of Christ* (London: SPCK, 1987).

Pollock, John, *Billy Graham: The Authorized Biography* (London: Hodder & Stoughton, 1966).

Robinson, John A. T., *Honest to God* (London: SCM Press, 1963).

Schumacher, E. F., *Small Is Beautiful: Economics as if People Mattered* (Abacus edn. 3rd repr. Sphere Books Ltd, 1976).

Tawney, R. H., *Religion and the Rise of Capitalism* (London: Penguin Books, 1922; Pelican reprint, 1948).

Temple, William, *Christianity and Social Order* (London: Penguin, 1942).

Thomas, A. C., *Christianity in Roman Britain to* AD *500* (Batesford, 1985).
Thomas, J. Heywood, *Paul Tillich: An Appraisal* (London: Lutterworth Press, 1965).
Tillich, Paul, *Systematic Theology*, part vi, vol. III, "Life and the Spirit, History and the Kingdom of God" (Chicago: University of Chicago Press, 1964).
Ward, Maisie, *France Pagan? The Mission of Abbé Godin* (London: Sheed & Ward, 1949).
Wickham, E. R., *Church and People in an Industrial City* (Cambridge: Lutterworth Press, 1957).
Williams, Dick, *Stuart Blanch: A Life* (London: SPCK, 2001).
Williams, H. A., *The True Wilderness* (London: Penguin Books Ltd, 1978).
Williams, Shirley, *Climbing the Bookshelves* (London: Virago, 2009).

Journals
Hilliard, David, "The Religious Crisis of the 1960s: the experience of the Australian Churches", *Journal of Religious History* 21:2 (1997), pp. 209–227.

Pamphlets
Barley, Lynda, *Time to Listen: Christian Roots, Contemporary Spirituality* (London: Church House Publishing, 2006).
Liverpool Diocesan News (Liverpool Diocesan Board of Finance, Church House, Liverpool), June 1966–December 1978.

Thesis
Hunter, J. G., "From Heaven to Fame: Monument Inscriptions in North West England 1550–1850", unpublished MPhil thesis (Lancaster University, 2008)

Notes

1. The Bishop of Liverpool, in addressing the second Bishopthorpe Consultation on 2 May 1970, spoke plainly about "the need to associate church leadership with mission rather than maintenance". At that time, this represented a distinct shift in the general culture of most church traditions.
2. Speaking to the leadership of the northern churches at Bishopthorpe VII, 1975. Bishop Howe made this judgment in the light of his recent visit to the Americas.
3. David Goodhew (ed.), *Church Growth in Britain: 1980 to the Present* (Ashgate, 2012); Lynda Barley, *Time to Listen: Christian Roots, Contemporary Spirituality* (Church House Publishing, 2006), pp. 3–9.
4. Hugh McLeod, *The Religious Crisis of the 1960s* (Oxford University Press, 2007), p. 1.
5. The Provisional Irish Republican Army (IRA) was formed from the old Irish Republican Army between 1969 and 1971.
6. Maynooth: a university town in County Kildare, Ireland, and the home to Ireland's main Roman Catholic seminary, St Patrick's College. It is also the Pontifical University and confers canonical degrees in Canon Law.
7. Letter to the author from John Pollock, 28 March 1969. "The idea of John Todhunter and mine was that Billy Graham should be invited as missioner (Perhaps from a central point in Liverpool with TV relays)."
8. Letter to Stuart Blanch, 1968.
9. Concerning mission Stuart Blanch had written, "Tomorrow Donald, Cuthbert and I are having lunch with two others to discuss the possibility of a nation-wide mission." Dick Williams, *Stuart Blanch: A Life* (London: SPCK, 2001), p. 101.
10. As reported to me by John Pollock. Billy Graham had conducted a three-month Greater London Crusade in February 1956 at the invitation of the Evangelical Alliance, an ecumenical, broadly conservative Protestant body.

11. This was true particularly of France and had been the case over many decades. Maisie Ward, *France Pagan? The Mission of Abbé Godin* (London: Sheed & Ward, 1949).
12. *Facts and Figures about the Church of England* (London: Church Information Office, 1962).
13. The city produced a string of comics including Tommy Handley, Ken Dodd, Jimmy Tarbuck, Arthur Askey, Derek Nimmo, Ted Ray, Freddie Starr, and Rob Wilton, who had the nation in tucks.
14. Designated European Capital of Culture in 2008.
15. The mitre was the official headdress worn by civil servants in the Byzantine Empire. In the twelfth century, Pope Leo XI adopted the mitre for bishops of the Catholic Church; the Eastern Churches, however, never adopted the mitre. At the English Reformation, the headdress was replaced by the Canterbury cap; later, under the Stuarts, the mitre was adopted again, but has remained controversial. Archbishop Michael Ramsey wore the traditional English Canterbury cap in 1966 on his visit to Pope Paul VI.
16. Conferring the right to appoint clergy to parishes.
17. Dr Abraham Hume, *Missions at Home; or a Clergyman's Account of a Portion of the Town of Liverpool* (1848).
18. Church people were uneasily aware of a decline in churchgoing, although the situation was magnified by the late nineteenth-century commitment to providing church seating for the whole population, leading to empty pews in the twentieth century. Robin Gill, *The Myth of the Empty Church* (London: SPCK, 1993).
19. At the subsequent meeting of Convocation Stuart Blanch was able to make a positive report and on 15 January 1969 Stuart Blanch's diary read, "The commissioning of the twelve was not episcope but evangelism—suitable portent for the meeting of the Upper House today." Williams, *Stuart Blanch*, p. 102.
20. The battle was fought between the troops of William III of Orange and the army of James I at the crossing of the River Boyne in 1690.
21. In 1911, 58.4 per cent of the Catholic population of England and Wales lived in the ecclesiastical province of Liverpool; Adrian Hastings, *A History of English Christianity 1920–1985* (London: Collins, 1986), p. 473.
22. Richard Downey speaking in the Picton Hall, Liverpool, in 1938 of his vision for the future of Roman Catholicism on Merseyside.

23 Hastings, *History*, p. 489.
24 "Elliott and his 'Hollow Men', Camus, Beckett, Golding and Gide expose the situation."
25 "The effective presentation of Christ, not as an historical figure but as a living Saviour, able to relate man to his highest destiny, unity with his creator, God the Father."
26 Experience of work in a factory on leaving school had convinced me that for my fellow workers, the "gospel of the kingdom" was more relevant as a Christian message than the "gospel of salvation". The latter appeared irrelevant to those who had lost any real concern for an afterlife.
27 Leslie Davison, *Sender and Sent: A Study of Mission* (Epworth Press, 1969).
28 Holy Week would have the advantage of capturing the attention of the secular media and so bringing our message before the general public.
29 Having split with Constantinople in 1054, Roman Catholics believed themselves now to be the only "true church". Thus to meet with a Protestant body would be to afford Protestants some measure of recognition. This recognition was never even contemplated until John XXIII.
30 Coggan, so we were to learn later, was right to be impressed, as Beck's ecumenism was in stark contrast to his own Roman Catholic contemporaries— Middlesbrough was deeply conservative and cautious concerning Vatican II's implications regarding Protestants.
31 Donald Coggan's CICCU background, from his Cambridge days, led him to be cautious of ecumenical mission; Margaret Pawley, *Donald Coggan, Servant of Christ* (SPCK, 1987), p. 33.
32 Donald Coggan himself had had a sheltered upbringing, but he faced reality when it came to house-to-house visiting during his first assistant curacy, at St Mary's Islington. He wrote, "One does not realize the dense heathenism of London till one gets to grips with it, visiting the homes of the people." Pawley, *Donald Coggan*, p. 43.
33 Before the meeting the Archbishop asked if I would be prepared to help him with the project. I agreed, as I knew my bishop would have been consulted. However, I commented that this would mean he would go to Canterbury. Donald Coggan looked taken aback, but replied, "We all know who is likely to follow Michael; what makes you say that?" "Since being accepted for the ministry," I explained, "all those I've served have moved to higher responsibilities." So it was to prove with Coggan also.

34 Bishop E. R. Wickham, speaking to the North West group in March 1971 at Whalley Abbey, expressed his belief that long-term mission should be structured on the concept of the 'zone humane'".

35 Being the CTN Secretary involved visiting the church leaders across the region. Subsequent travels gave me ample opportunity to talk with the people of the towns I visited. This led to the discovery that, irrespective of official or civic boundaries, people "felt themselves" to be northerners or Midlanders. The southern boundary of the North might well be drawn on the basis of felt loyalties through North Lincolnshire, mid-Nottinghamshire, and Derbyshire, perhaps even Shropshire. Thus Nottingham city, although in the Northern Province, felt itself to be in the Midlands.

36 Dick Williams comments in *Stuart Blanch*, "For John Hunter, 30 years later it was to be remembered as 'the most striking meeting I've been to in my life.'" (p. 103).

37 Ramsey was perceptive. The vision of the churches of the North united in an ongoing mission to the world was ultimately to founder on this tension between local and provincial.

38 Dick Williams notes that in January 1969 Stuart was already using the initials "CTN" in his diary; Williams, *Stuart Blanch*, p. 102.

39 Williams reveals Stuart Blanch's inner thoughts, confided to his diary: "The strongest impression was of the poverty and confusion of the Church, but the most enduring impression may well be of the strange, secret triumph of God's will over ours, Alleluia." *Stuart Blanch*, p. 105.

40 One of the striking and unexpected lessons of this exercise for Anglicans was that all the other denominations, when it came to the crunch, looked to the Church of England both for leadership and also for financial support; the latter was not always appreciated by some Anglican bishops.

41 In order to give me some standing across the range of northern church leaders, it seemed right now to accept a canonry. I felt ambivalent, our Lord's words "seek the lower place" ringing in my ears. I was reassured when a colleague pointed out it was merely an Honorary, not a Residentiary Canonry!

42 Some Anglicans felt that financial differentials were indefensible for Christian clergy. Donald Coggan gave away a large proportion of his salary; Pawley, *Coggan*, p. 168.

43 John C. Heenan's *The People's Priest* (Sheed & Ward, 1951) was unusual in advising the priest to visit everyone in his parish, including Protestants. The

Catholic Missionary Society, in contrast, set itself the task of recovering the lapsed; Hastings, *History*, p. 480.

[44] See the "triumphant ultramontanism" of Cardinal Merry de Val; Hastings, *History*, p. 147.

[45] Bishop Lindsay, Coadjutor Bishop of Hexham and Newcastle, although charming, expressed deep unease at the thought of admitting other Christian bodies to be "legitimate churches".

[46] "When the Church is obedient to Christ in the matter of evangelism, He of the greatness of His heart throws in as a kind of bonus a growth in unity." Donald Coggan contributing to the General Synod debate in November 1974; Pawley, *Coggan*, pp. 160–161. Even so, uniting for mission remained a step too far not only for some Conservative Evangelicals and Pentecostals, but for some Catholics also.

[47] One of the subsequent examples of mission was Donald Coggan's "Call to the Nation" of 1975, which was a purely Anglican initiative. He called a group together at Lambeth, in 1974, to prepare. It was clear that Coggan saw he had but a limited time as Archbishop before retirement. This meant he could not afford the lengthy preparatory negotiations experienced by Call to the North. "The Archbishop decided to move swiftly, and . . . alone." Pawley, *Donald Coggan*, p. 198.

[48] The Society for the Propagation of the Gospel in Foreign Parts (Church of England), 1701; The White Fathers (Roman Catholic), 1868; The London Missionary Society (Anglican and Congregationalist), 1795; The Church Missionary Society (Church of England), 1799. Even earlier, the Society of Jesus (Roman Catholic), 1534.

[49] Most of the founders of the Church Missionary Society were members of the Clapham Sect, a group of activist evangelical Christians. Ignatius Loyola's *Rules for Thinking with the Church* declared, "That we may be altogether of the same mind" (Rule 13).

[50] The differences were apparent in the 1954 Billy Graham London Crusade. Although supported by the then Archbishop, Geoffrey Fisher, a senior canon of Southwark could write of Graham's preaching, "It is not the Gospel at all. It never speaks of anything other than a sentimental relationship between the individual and God." John Pollock, *Billy Graham* (London: Hodder & Stoughton, 1966), p. 6.

[51] "The intention was to make evangelism a leadership exercise, not to try and sell to church leaders a plan developed by a group of enthusiastic Evangelicals." Pawley, *Donald Coggan*, p. 164.

[52] This indeed was the essence of Billy Graham's preaching: "sin, righteousness and judgment". Pollock, *Graham*, p. 340.

[53] J. G. Hunter, "From Heaven to Fame: Monument Inscriptions in North West England 1550–1850" unpublished MPhil thesis (Lancaster University, 2008).

[54] This point was stressed by the Manchester executives in January 1972.

[55] David Hilliard, "The Religious Crisis of the 1960s: the Experience of the Australian Churches", *Journal of Religious History* 21:2 (1997), pp. 209–227.

[56] *Honest to God* (London: SCM Press, 1963) was written by the then Bishop of Woolwich, John A. T. Robinson. It criticized a conventional image of God as an "old man in the sky" and aroused a storm of controversy on its publication, not least because it was a bishop of the established Church who was writing this. *The Secular City: Secularization and Urbanization in Theological Perspective* (SCM Press, 1965), by the North American religion scholar Harvey Cox, reflects the optimism of the Kennedy era and confidence in the potential of human achievement, proclaiming a future world in which human beings will live in modern cities where religion will no longer be part of their lives. Both Cox and Robinson draw on Dietrich Bonhoeffer's idea of "religionless Christianity", though interestingly Cox later recanted.

[57] Report to the Church Assembly on Church of England staff apportionment by Leslie Paul, *The Deployment and Payment of the Clergy* (Church Information Office, 1964). It related staffing to the established Church's responsibility for the spiritual welfare of everyone in the parish and introduced the concept of Team Ministries, with a Rector and Team Vicars.

[58] The lyrics by Tim Rice, set to music by Andrew Lloyd Webber, were based roughly on the biblical account of the last week of our Lord's life. The rock opera begins with the preparation for the arrival of Jesus and his disciples in Jerusalem and ends with the crucifixion. Contemporary attitudes and sensibilities, as well as slang, pervade the lyrics, with ironic allusions to modern life through the depiction of political events.

[59] Arthur Michael Ramsey, Archbishop of Canterbury, pointed to the theological shortcomings of *Jesus Christ Superstar*.

60   John Profumo, Secretary of State for War in the 1963 Macmillan government, had an adulterous relationship with a London "call girl", Christine Keeler. This he denied to the House of Commons, which led to his resignation.
61   *Small Is Beautiful: Economics as if People Mattered* is a collection of essays by British economist E. F. Schumacher (Blond & Briggs, 1973). The phrase "Small Is Beautiful" came from a phrase by his teacher, Leopold Kohr. It is often used to champion small, appropriate technologies that are believed to empower people more, in contrast with phrases such as "bigger is better".
62   "A Charge delivered to the Clergy at the Primary Visitation of the Diocese of Durham" (1751) 1; reprinted in J. H. Bernard (ed.), *The Works of Bishop Butler* (London: 1900), vol. i, pp. 287–288.
63   He was wise: although the Free Churches of the North East were ready, the Roman Catholic Diocese of Hexham and Newcastle certainly was not.
64   In working earlier with the Billy Graham Manchester Crusade team, I was astonished when an American member expressed his amazement at the influence and cultural penetration of the Church of England. It presumably contrasted with his experience of the weakness of the Episcopal Church in the United States.
65   Pollock, in analysing the Billy Graham Manchester Crusade of 1961, appears to suggest that the organization might have been wiser to have opted for Liverpool as its venue for a crusade in the North West; Pollock, *Graham*, p. 296. Certainly my impression when observing the event was that more coaches were rolling into the Maine Road football stadium from Liverpool than from Manchester itself.
66   These annual walks, held on the Friday following Whit Sunday (Pentecost), were especially popular with the Free Churches, although both Church of England and Roman Catholic churches also took part. They originated in a procession celebrating the coronation of George IV (1821), but developed over the years into a walk of witness particularly by Sunday school children, but supported by the clergy and congregations of the churches concerned. The processions were often led by brass bands and enormous banners.
67   A biennial Christian congress of 150,000 people, which takes place in late May in a German city. It was founded by the German Evangelical Church in 1949, and in the years between the Protestant *Kirchentage* the Roman Catholic Church organizes a similar event, the *Katholikentag*. Since 2003

there have also been a number of ecumenical *Kirchentage* jointly organized by Protestants and Catholics.

68 David Blunt had been a schoolmaster before accepting the role of Lay Chaplain. He was an able administrator and well versed in Church of England affairs, being the son of Alfred W. F. Blunt, Bishop of Bradford (1931–1955). The latter's forthright Diocesan Conference address initiated the 1936 abdication crisis.

69 The constraints church leaders were under was illustrated by Wakefield. The Bishop himself was very supportive of a northern initiative from the outset, but found himself constrained by the tradition of his diocese and opposition from his diocesan officials. They were, moreover, backed by some of the other local churches in Wakefield.

70 Some seven years later this meeting was still taking place, to the surprise of a newly-arrived diocesan bishop, who confided its existence to me.

71 Writing at this time, Schumacher said, "The modern economy is propelled by a frenzy of greed and indulges in an orgy of envy." *Small Is Beautiful*, p. 30.

72 See Mass Observation, *Puzzled People* (Gollancz, 1947) and Charles Booth, *Life and Labour of the People of London* (third series, 1902). Despite this evidence, it was commonly believed by the artisan class that the Church depended on the ignorance of the poor for its major support.

73 The prime exception here was the Roman Catholic Irish working class. Until Irish independence and membership of the European Union, Irish nationalism resisted English Protestant imperialism by using its firm allegiance to Rome as a bulwark. Once Irish independence and prosperity were achieved, this motivation was no longer felt by the Irish working class.

74 Richard Hobson, *What Hath God Wrought: An Autobiography* (Thynne, 1913, fourth edition), p. 86.

75 This was illustrated by the example in France of Brittany farmers, who attended mass regularly whilst at home, but never went to church when working near Paris; F. Boulard, *An Introduction to Religious Sociology* (Darton, Longman & Todd, 1960).

76 E. R. Wickham, *Church and People in an Industrial City* (London: Lutterworth Press, 1957), pp. 42, 44.

77 Wickham, *Church and People*, pp. 70–71. Robert Peel, when Prime Minster, was acutely conscious of the spiritual needs of new inner-city parishes resulting from the Industrial Revolution and set up the Ecclesiastical

Commissioners to fund the building of churches and payment of clergy in the poor inner areas of the industrial cities. This fund for the urban poor then matched that provided by the pious and godly Queen Anne, whose "Bounty" was designed to augment the stipends of poor rural clergy. These two massive financial funds, designed to redress the balance of the Church's care for the poor, were merged in 1948 to become the Church Commissioners.

78 *Ibid.*, p. 16.

79 Although this issue was discussed by the panel in the 1960s, later scholarly comment may be found in Hugh McLeod, *Religious Crisis*, p. 9.

80 Whalley Abbey, the Retreat House for the Diocese of Blackburn. The house had been a country manor, originally built by a Catholic family using the stone of the adjoining Cistercian abbey. The ruins of the abbey now lie in the grounds of the house and have been designated Grade 1 listed. William Temple, when he was Bishop of Manchester, bought the house for the Church.

81 Bishops of the Church of England at this time still wore the eighteenth-century dress of the short cassock and gaitered leg, suitable for riding on horseback around churches within the diocese.

82 "[A] life-long capacity to stand against the tide for conscience sake" was how his biographer put this characteristic of Donald Coggan; Pawley, *Coggan*, p. 29.

83 "Patterns of secularization, just like patterns of revival, are not terminal but cyclical." Hastings, *History*, pp. 33–34.

84 This phenomenon was addressed at the third of four lectures given to the clergy recess at Lee Abbey in 1970 by J. G. Hunter. Historically, there have been high points in religious practice in the twelfth, sixteenth, and nineteenth centuries, interspersed with low points in the fourteenth, eighteenth, and twentieth.

85 There was irony in this, as Blanch had originally laughed at the idea of allowing the contemporary world to influence the presentation of the traditional gospel. Now it was his intellectual weight and spirituality that carried the day.

86 Kenneth Weights transformed the Central Mission in Newcastle before being elected Chair of District. In 1970, when he found himself to be President Designate of Conference, he exclaimed in astonishment to his friend Rex Kissack, "Just think of it; me! Damn silly, I do not know what my father would say."

87 This had been declared by Pope Leo XIII in his encyclical *Apostolicae curae* (1896).
88 In Bootle, Lancashire, as vicar I visited young people who had been baptized in the Church of England fourteen years earlier. This was to remind them of their baptism and to invite them to a Confirmation training class. I was surprised to discover that whole families had been re-baptized by the local Roman Catholic priest, who had required this before he could give their close relative, a lapsed Roman Catholic, a Catholic burial. This particular discipline ceased with Vatican II.
89 Father Fitzpatrick, parish priest of St Monica's Bootle, made this clear to me when I was vicar of St Matthew's Bootle (1956–1962).
90 Cardinal Heenan, when challenged at the 1972 British Council of Churches conference in Birmingham, did accept that there might be a case for Roman Catholics to join with "non-Catholics" in prayer, indeed, even Communion, but only, he stressed, in exceptional circumstances such as concentration camps. But he made it clear, this was taking as given the unique position of the Roman Catholic Church as the only true faith, never otherwise. Canon Pawley (who inadvertently had failed to switch off his microphone) was heard to murmur, "Let us pray for more concentration camps."
91 Such as G. K. Chesterton, author and poet (1874–1936), and Alec Guinness, actor (1914–2000).
92 "[S]egregating Catholics, so far as possible, from the dangerous influences of other churches"; Hastings, *History*, p. 149.
93 A massacre that successfully wiped out Protestantism in France. "Throughout Europe, it 'printed on Protestant minds the indelible conviction that Catholicism was a bloody and treacherous religion.'" Henry Chadwick and G. R. Evans (eds), *Atlas of the Christian Church* (London: Macmillan, 1987), p. 113.
94 "Always the same".
95 One of the most striking images engraved on my memory of this time is of the Archbishop of Liverpool, in response to an invitation from Stuart Blanch, attending a service in Liverpool Anglican Cathedral. George Andrew presented a tall, solitary figure at the head of the southeast transept below the lectern, dressed as a bishop of the Roman Catholic Church. Never before had such an event—a Roman Catholic archbishop visiting Liverpool's Protestant

cathedral—occurred. His courage, humility, and generosity of spirit moved us all.

96   In the 1960s, a Roman Catholic priest in Liverpool was weeping as he walked up Park Lane near the centre of the city. I inquired, "What is the matter, Father?" He answered, "I used to have a parish where my church was full for mass, now only a few come; I do not know what I have done wrong." It led me to comfort him, assuring him that this was not personal failure. He had done nothing wrong. Today we all faced the cultural impact of secularism. The Protestant churches had experienced this over many decades, although for the Catholic community it was sudden and quite new.

97   Heenan, *The People's Priest*, p. 218.

98   Hans Küng, *The Council and Reunion* (London: Sheed & Ward, 1962).

99   Preaching before the University of Cambridge in 1946 Geoffrey Fisher, Archbishop of Canterbury, proposed an "innovative step forward". In order to stimulate church relations in post-war Britain, he suggested that the Non-Conformist denominations take episcopacy into their system. His initiative gave inter-church relations a boost, and a result was the Anglican-Methodist reunion scheme of the 1960s. This imaginative step forward, however, failed to achieve a large enough majority vote when it came before the Church of England's Church Assembly in July 1969. Its failure then cast a shadow over inter-church relations. During the ecumenical heyday of the 1960s and early 1970s, evangelicals within Methodism and Anglicanism played a major part in helping to defeat the proposed Anglican–Methodist reunion scheme.

100 This organization was launched in the Methodist Central Hall, Westminster, under the leadership of Leslie Brown in October 1974.

101 These churches in many cases evinced both church growth, and a distinct distrust of Roman Catholicism.

102 Except in areas where church leaders had made it clear that they did not want the embarrassment of local councils knowing about the initiative before the official instructions had been sent out by the denomination concerned.

103 Aide-memoire of the Central Co-ordinating Committee, 19 November 1971.

104 See Chapter 2.

105 Graham had told John Pollock, in referring to Call to the North, "This does sound rather encouraging." (Letter from John Pollock, 19 July 1970.) It probably led to the Graham organization later supporting CTN despite the doubts of fellow Evangelicals.

106 This suggestion came from Thomas M. Morrow, Methodist Chair of West Yorkshire.
107 In particular, Archdeacon and Diocesan Missioner William Johnston, and Mark Bishop, Secretary to the Bradford Council of Churches.
108 Letter from the Bishop of Liverpool to participants, February 1971.
109 In personal conversations it became clear that most Christian laity in their daily work, not wishing to be regarded as "Bible punchers" or "psalm singers", just kept their heads down, tried to live a Christian life, but reserved their active Christian witness for church events, normally at the weekends.
110 The conference was made up of nine Free Church leaders—four Baptists, three Presbyterians, a Methodist, and a Salvationist—nine members of the Church of England, five Roman Catholics, and a member of the Orthodox Church.
111 One important aspect of lay witness which emerged, but which was not fully addressed, was the common saying, "You cannot mix religion and business" or "Religion and politics don't mix." These suggested that there were "no-go" areas for faith which were tacitly accepted by Christian laity. See R. H. Tawney, *Religion and the Rise of Capitalism* (Penguin, 1922; Pelican reprint 1948), p. 18.
112 *Unitatis redintegratio* (Decree on Ecumenism) 822.
113 *Catholics and Christian Unity: Ecumenical Commission of England and Wales* (Catholic Information Office, 1969), p. 3.
114 When I first met the Archbishop of Liverpool, I enquired of His Grace how he would like to be addressed. He smiled and replied, "I think by my baptismal names, George Andrew."
115 Hastings notes that once Vatican II was over it soon became clear that "the attitudes of the Roman Curia had not changed much" . . . the curial staff were "recovering much of their old predominance"; *History*, pp. 528–529.
116 Hastings's comment that Heenan and his fellow Catholic bishops "cultivated a polite disdain for Anglicans" (*History*, p. 479) summed up my experience on this occasion. I came later to wonder if this was a defensive mechanism adopted to cope with an over-mighty Church of England.
117 Hastings writes of Heenan's dual personality: "Theologically he was a pure conservative ultramontane . . . His reformism could be vigorous." *History*, p. 564. Clearly I had encountered his conservative ultramontane side.

[118] Heenan had been George Andrew's predecessor at Liverpool and creator of the reduced and more realistic (yet still inspiring) Roman Catholic Cathedral, commonly known as "Paddy's Wigwam".
[119] Hugh McLeod comments on "the failure of Pope Paul VI to carry through the reforms to which the Council was pointing"; *Religious Crisis*, p. 12.
[120] The Archbishop of Liverpool, over tea a month earlier at Archbishop's House, had warned me of the time needed for "the slow process of reshaping mental attitudes". "After all," he had said, "it has taken many meetings for us to have grown together." It was only later that I realized he had the Bishop of Middlesbrough in mind.
[121] Letter, 1 November 1971.
[122] Experience of clergy working among working-class men in particular, whether in public houses, in factory visits, or open-air work, provided evidence that it was the words and life of Jesus that they knew and quoted. This justified the Call to the North's emphasis on the kingdom, which was the primary gospel of Jesus himself.
[123] Margaret Pawley comments on the ability of Donald Coggan to be firm and clear in such situations in describing his presidency of the Northern Convocation, *Coggan*, p. 151.
[124] John Marsh's home was at Cockermouth in Cumbria. He was generally best known to the Christian public for his *St John* in the Pelican Gospel Commentaries (1968).
[125] Father Dennis Corbishley, parish priest of Ambleside, a nephew of the theologian Father Thomas Corbishley SJ who, in 1966, was the first Roman Catholic since the Reformation to preach in Westminster Abbey.
[126] Letter from the Archbishops' Council on Evangelism. The letter contained details of a December 1970 Methodist Consultation in Frankfurt which proposed a "world-wide Mission and Evangelism offensive" to be put to the World Methodist Council in August 1971, meeting in Denver, Colorado.
[127] Michael Parker, author of the inspirational "The Consideration", had retired, his place taken by a new bishop, Ross Hook. The debate seemed at times to be an endorsement of H. A. Williams's chapter on fear, "A Kingdom Divided", in his *The True Wilderness* (Constable & Co, 1965; Penguin, 1968), p. 66.
[128] This was to be the last meeting of CTN which Lt-Col Fenwick was to attend, as his position was then taken by Lt-Col Frederick Buist.

129 Ted Wickham had been steadfastly opposed to "evangelism" in the traditional sense (Pollock, *Graham*, p. 297), hence this unexpected support was likened to a "conversion" (letter to John Poulton, 24 May 1971).
130 Everyone from the North West was still aware of the 1961 Billy Graham mission at the Manchester City FC ground. Although successful in that many responded to the three-week event, it left Manchester largely unmoved; Pollock, *Graham*, p. 296.
131 It was left to the local church leadership of each area (based on the Anglican dioceses) to decide on the composition of their local co-ordinating committee. There was no attempt at any central direction, except to suggest an equality of membership for each tradition: Anglican, Free Church, and Roman Catholic.
132 The network consisted of a series of local ecumenical committees, linked to a diocesan committee itself linked to the Central Co-ordinating Committee.
133 In retrospect, the appointment of Hugh Lindsay was shrewd, as the Diocese of Hexham and Newcastle was very conservative and made little effort to accommodate CTN.
134 Reported from a meeting of diocesan missioners and ecumenical officers.
135 In 1959, the Catholic Church of England and Wales had called the first Heythrop Conference on Christian Unity. Since that time, although this development was spasmodic, priests had begun to join local Councils of Churches.
136 This was clearly the view of the Catholic Church: *Catholics and Christian Unity: Ecumenical Commission of England and Wales* (Pinner: Catholic Information Office, 1969), p. 2.
137 Letter to J. B. Leake of the British Council of Churches Department of Mission and Unity, 17 July 1972.
138 "Television and Religion" (Gallup Poll, University of London, 1964).
139 Callum G. Brown, *The Death of Christian Britain* (Routledge, 2001), p. 2.
140 Daniel Cohn-Bendit, a German political leader active during the student unrest of 1968 on the Continent.
141 Although not positively drawing their inspiration from Dietrich Bonhoeffer, theirs was akin to his thinking. Bonhoeffer saw a time coming in which religion would prove to be fundamentally irrelevant. "We are moving towards a completely religionless time; people as they are now simply cannot be religious anymore. Even those who honestly describe themselves as 'religious' do not in the least act up to it, and so they presumably mean something quite

different by 'religious.'" Letter to Eberhard Bethge [Tegel], 30 April 1944, in Dietrich Bonhoeffer (ed. Eberhard Bethge), *Letters and Papers from Prison* (London: SCM Press, 1971), p. 279.

[142] The various modern versions of the Holy Communion service in use in this period prior to the publication of an authorized modern liturgy, the 1980 *Alternative Service Book*.

[143] Williams, *True Wilderness*, p. 10.

[144] Letter from Bishop Joseph Gray to the Secretary, 13 April 1973.

[145] Nottinghamshire. Sometimes it appeared that leadership met with local reluctance. In the case of Southwell (Nottinghamshire), half the diocese looked to the Midlands. The Roman Catholic Diocese of Nottingham was in the Catholic Province of Westminster. Thus the Christians of Nottingham, both Catholics and Protestants, considered themselves Midlanders, so not committed to CTN. However, Christians living in the north of Derby Diocese (in the Anglican Province of Canterbury) did look to York and CTN.

[146] See aide-memoire of the Central Co-ordinating Committee, 21 April 1972.

[147] Letter to the author from Leslie Fisher, 18 April 1972.

[148] *Lux Mundi: A Series of Studies in the Religion of the Incarnation*. A collection of twelve essays from liberal Anglo-Catholic theologians, edited by Charles Gore (1889).

[149] However, the first issue of the "Action North East" newsletter in the autumn of 1972 stated, "ACTION NORTH EAST is a project by all the Churches of the North East to implement 'Call to the North' in ways that are meaningful to our own Region."

[150] Those engaged in open-air preaching in this period were aware that from the crowd came questions about the lifestyle of church leaders and about bishops' salaries, contrasting them with Jesus's lifestyle. The Church Commissioners' publications of the 1950s openly boasted of the wealth of the Church of England. This was not lost on its working-class critics, often to the embarrassment of the speakers.

[151] At the time, often mocked by the non-churchgoer as proclaiming "pie in the sky when you die". Almost every sociological analysis referred to the Church or to religion as an institution whose primary purpose was to prepare people for death. This we knew had been developed as the main apologia of the Church by "Paul's gospel" as expounded in Romans 5.

152 Although the *Conservative* party still represented many of the rich and powerful, the *Labour* party was heavily committed to the poor in society and representatives of the working class and the trades union; this factor was later acknowledged by McLeod (*Religious Crisis*, p. 195).

153 A. C. Thomas, *Christianity in Roman Britain to* AD *500* (London: Batesford, 1985).

154 This position had been addressed by the German–American theologian Paul Tillich.

155 "A man whose teaching still had the power to thrill"; Williams, *True Wilderness*, p. 53.

156 First Secretary of the Communist Party of the Soviet Union from 1953 to 1964 and Chair of the Council of Ministers, or Premier, from 1958 to 1964. Khrushchev famously commented that Yuri Gagarin, the first man in space, "had not found any God".

157 Albert Schweitzer, tr. William Montgomery, *The Quest of the Historical Jesus: A Critical Study of Its Progress from Reimarus to Wrede*, (London: Adam & Charles Black, 1945), p. 70.

158 In a lecture at Leicester University to a conference on "Group Dynamics" (1967).

159 Paul Tillich deals with this issue in the third volume of his *Systematic Theology*, part vi, *History and the Kingdom of God* (London: James Nisbet & Co, 1964).

160 J. G. Hunter, "From Heaven to Fame: Monument Inscriptions in North West England 1550–1850", unpublished MPhil thesis (University of Lancaster, 2008).

161 As early as the late seventeenth century Archbishop John Tillotson was warning against disbelief in hell, predicting the result would be an increase in social unrest and crime among the lower orders.

162 Speaking to the author in 1959 of the Vestey Tower of Liverpool Cathedral.

163 See Newton's "T'was grace that taught my heart to fear" or Wesley's "No condemnation now I dread", or any seventeenth-century Puritan diary.

164 7 September 1972.

165 It was very clear that local regional committees were concerned about the need to convince "reluctant clergy" about the worth-whileness of Call to the North—see aide-memoire for Carlisle Regional Committee, 19 October 1971.

166 William Temple replied to his critics who regarded answered prayer as no more than coincidence, "When I pray, coincidences happen; when I don't,

they don't." Quoted in David Watson, *Called & Committed: World-Changing Discipleship* (Wheaton, IL: Harold Shaw Publishers, 1982), p. 83.

[167] Leslie Fisher, writing to the author on 18 April 1972, stressed, "We are very conscious here that Lent and Easter '73 will be only in a very partial sense a 'climax', because we are already looking into the future and want to make it quite clear that after Lent 1973 there will still be a need for continuing mission."

[168] Letter from E. R. Wickham, 4 February 1972.

[169] These tensions within the Catholic community came as a surprise to me: having formed so warm an appreciation of the spirituality of George Andrew Beck, I assumed he was typical of the Catholic hierarchy. However, Adrian Hastings is perfectly clear that Beck was one on his own, as "Godfrey had transformed the English hierarchy into a Roman clique ... Almost the only non-*Venerabile* (*sc.* alumnus of the Venerable English College in Rome) bishop of any weight in these years was George Andrew Beck." *History*, p. 479.

[170] Although officially a Free Church appointment, their difficulties with funding led the CIO to agree to fund the post, on condition that the Free Churches provided office facilities. *Cf.* letter to Dennis Corbishley, 28 February 1972.

[171] Quoted in J. Heywood Thomas, *Paul Tillich: An Appraisal* (London: Lutterworth Press, 1965), p. 5.

[172] "Donald Soper and George McLeod had been Graham's loudest British critics ... together with Bishop Ted Wickham." Pollock, *Graham*, pp. 276–277. These three represented significant voices in Methodist, Presbyterian, and Anglican circles.

[173] Thomas, *Tillich*, p. 6.

[174] *The Six Gospels*.

[175] Harold Springbett had made this clear in our early days.

[176] Letter, 3 November 1971.

[177] This attitude was not new: Lord Melbourne, Queen Victoria's first Prime Minister, was heard to remark with some indignation, "Things have come to a pretty pass if religion is going to interfere with private life." Tawney, *Religion and the Rise of Capitalism*, p. 18. Further, Adrian Hastings was later to write, "[T]he principal intellectual ... orthodoxy of England in the 1920s was no longer Protestantism, nor was it Catholicism or any other form of Christianity. It was a confident agnosticism." *History*, p. 221. By the 1960s, that agnosticism was shared by many in the working class.

178 N.B. the public and political reaction to the Church of England's report, *Faith in the City: A Call to Action by Church and Nation* (Church House Publishing, 1985).

179 In the twenty-first century, a variety of the practices were introduced under the euphemism "quantitative easing" to offset the worst effects of the financial crisis.

180 David Ricardo, British economist (1772–1823), author of *The High Price of Bullion* (1810).

181 The "fiduciary issue", annually voted upon, replaced the "Gold Standard" as the control mechanism for money supply.

182 "The condition of the workers is the question of the hour. It will be answered one way or another, rationally or irrationally, and which way it goes is of the greatest importance to the state." Pope Leo XIII, *Rerum novarum* (1891).

183 "Working the welt" was the name given to the widespread practice among Liverpool dockers, whereby each gang would split in two—half would work on the ship, while the other half played cards behind the packing cases. Different industries had different methods of avoiding work.

184 In 1859 Samuel Smiles published his famous work, *Self-Help*.

185 Shirley Williams, *Climbing the Bookshelves* (London: Virago, 2009), p. 92. Williams vividly describes her experience of intimidation exercised by fellow-workers on those believed to be hardworking.

186 Montesquieu, *Notes sur l'Angleterre* (1748).

187 Tawney, *Religion and the Rise of Capitalism*, p. 284.

188 The treatment of the miners at the time of the General Strike of 1926 had not been forgotten by the working class.

189 Pius XI, *Quadragesimo anno* (1931), 134.

190 Mrs Gaskell, *North and South* (1855), clearly refers to the incipient beginnings of this war in her novel, where she has an employer proclaim, "This is a war, a war which the masters must win."

191 William Temple, *Christianity and Social Order* (London: Penguin, 1942).

192 Significantly, E. F. Schumacher, author of the acclaimed *Small Is Beautiful*, was Economic Advisor with the British Control Commission in Germany from 1946 to 1950. His views were clearly reflected in the new German industrial structure.

193 Aide-memoire of the Central Co-ordinating Committee, 6 September 1972.

194 Letter, 18 November 1972.

195 At Canterbury, Coggan used these arguments for his "Call to the Nation"; Pawley, *Coggan*.
196 See the January 1973 aide-memoire of the Central Co-ordinating Committee.
197 Writing in November 1971, the Bishop of Liverpool, Stuart Blanch, had commented to me, "There will certainly be clergy who will not read the letter in public, and there may well be bishops who do not encourage it to be read."
198 It was sometimes said of the church laity that, like the St Lawrence River in Canada, when it came to Christian witness they were "frozen at the mouth".
199 It appeared curious to the Committee that many in the South appeared to be so opposed to this Northern attempt to unite in mission.
200 John 3:11. Williams, *True Wilderness*, p. 13.
201 The friendship generated by a meal together was central to the later *Alpha* movement.
202 Report to Major-General Adam Block, 13 July 1972.
203 Middlesbrough's Catholicism was very conservative. The Bishop and the blessed Virgin were carried annually shoulder-high through the streets in procession, preceded by children scattering rose petals. His experience appeared to be heavily influenced by pre-Vatican II concerns.
204 Unilateral Declaration of Independence—based on Ian Smith's rejection of London's wish for Rhodesia to move towards African rule.
205 This was a measure of the "voluntary" nature of the exercise, which was entirely dependent on winning the hearts and minds of church leaders.
206 David Blunt, reporting on the financial situation to the executive's meeting in January 1972, noted that out of the fourteen Anglican dioceses, five had sent their contribution, three out of the twelve Methodist districts, three of the eight Roman Catholic dioceses, together with a contribution from the Congregationalist Church. Further contributions may have been made subsequently, but this report lends substance to David Blunt's concern.
207 Frank Amery, Chair of the Sheffield District of the Methodist Church, wrote on 5 December 1972, "I have already informed you of my disagreement with the proposed appeal to local churches . . . I shall inform the superintendents of this District that I have not authorized an appeal."
208 Aide-memoire of the January 1973 meeting of the Central Co-ordinating Committee.
209 Letter from the Central Co-ordinating Committee, August 1972.

210 The Secretariat felt surprised, given the deep evangelical commitment of both Stuart Blanch and Donald Coggan. However, fear of Rome was still widespread in England, as the story told by Baroness Williams of her encounter with prejudice on the farm illustrates; Williams, *Climbing the Bookshelves*, p. 73.

211 Coggan, the leader of CTN, had impeccable Evangelical credentials, yet Hastings can write, " . . . as a bishop and a scholar, he was a little too liberal to retain the full confidence of Evangelicals but too Evangelical to be quite on the wavelength of either liberals or Anglo-Catholics." *History*, p. 556.

212 Hastings comments, "in strict Evangelical eyes an Evangelical who accepts a bishopric . . . even Donald Coggan, is almost bound to be judged . . . as something of a sell-out." *History*, pp. 456–457.

213 At the time it appeared baffling that the most significant evangelistic outreach the North had experienced should be unmentionable to a conference of Evangelicals. However, Donald Coggan's biographer writes of the Archbishop of York, "[H]e had begun to be regarded with something near suspicion by the Evangelical wing of the Church of England, as having embraced some liberal tendencies." Pawley, *Donald Coggan*, p. 161.

214 Kevin Logan went on to offer for the Anglican ministry, being accepted by the Bishop of Blackburn, who well knew his background. He subsequently became a very valued incumbent. One of the startling facts of late twentieth-century ecumenism was the number of ex-Roman Catholic laity now to be found, often serving as Church Wardens, in Anglican parishes.

215 A saying attributed to Jesus, not found in the Gospels.

216 The atmosphere was reminiscent of the occasion in May 1941 when Roman Catholic organization The Sword of the Spirit organized a great ecumenical conference in London, and Cardinal Hinsley—at the request of Bishop Bell of Chichester—led the assembly in the Lord's Prayer. Hinsley was rebuked for this by his fellow bishops, though interestingly, as Hastings notes, not by Rome itself; Hastings, *History*, p. 395.

217 John Poulton, Research and Development Officer of the Archbishops' Council, writing from Canterbury to the Archbishop of York in May 1971, had suggested that "some account can be written up of the particular lessons in ecumenical mission which clearly are already emerging". The January 1973 Central Co-ordinating Committee meeting worked out in detail the shape of the publication.

218 R. H. L. (Dick) Williams, "A study of the interactivity of personal faith and cultural context in Stuart Blanch's eight books about the Bible and society", unpublished PhD thesis (Liverpool University, 2013), pp. 87, 88.

219 Invited had been fourteen Anglican diocesan bishops, fourteen Methodist Chairs, seven Roman Catholic diocesan bishops, five Moderators of the United Reformed Church, and two Baptist Superintendents—all the senior leaders of the great churches of the North. In addition, representatives of the Pentecostal church, the Christian Brethren, the Society of Friends, and the Salvation Army had been invited as full members. Then, as observers, Leslie Fisher, Neville Cryer (British & Foreign Bible Society), John Pollock, John Poulton, and J. Taylor.

220 The report of Working Party 10.

221 Davidson, after consultations with the Free Church leaders, issued an appeal designed to bring an end to the General Strike and ensure industrial peace; Charles Herbert, *Twenty-Five Years as Archbishop of Canterbury* (Wells, Gardner Darton & Co, 1929), p. 107.

222 See Temple's 1942 book *Christianity and Social Order* (London: Penguin, 1942).

223 Notes of the Central Co-ordinating Committee, 22 November 1972.

224 "Britain Today and Tomorrow" programme.

225 See the Central Co-ordinating Committee's aide-memoire, January 1973.

226 Letter to the author from Mrs Jill Dart of Lancaster, 2013.

227 Forty years later, the Bishop of Bradford, Nick Baines, on a visit to war-torn Sudan, found his car stopped by the military at a checkpoint by night. He was questioned about his purpose and where he was from. When he answered "originally Liverpool", the Sudanese soldier smiled and said, "You'll never walk alone."

228 *Liverpool Diocesan News*, No. 55, July 1973.

229 The Bishop of Southwell wrote to me on 13 January 1972, "I am afraid we are not as yet committed to this project in the diocese." Despite this caution, he attended Bishopthorpe and sent representatives to CTN meetings. The Roman Catholic Diocese of Middlesbrough took little part, apart from sending the Cathedral Administrator to a meeting in Durham. Some Free Church leaders remained unconvinced of the wisdom of co-operating with Rome.

230 According to reports from Formby and Lancaster in particular.

231 York Diocesan Retreat and Conference Centre, Scarborough.
232 Writing this account some forty years later, the author encountered spontaneous comments from members of the public. These were to the effect that they remembered the occasion, and the impact it had made on their local church relationships. Meetings then started were sustained today. Bishop David Hope spoke warmly of the annual gathering of church leaders which still met, but now at the Roman Catholic venue of Hinsley House, the headquarters of the Roman Catholic Diocese of Leeds.
233 Writing in the late 1970s.
234 Part of the author's address given to the clergy of the Diocese of Birmingham at the invitation of the Bishop of Birmingham, Laurie Brown, following Easter 1973.
235 In his enthronement sermon at Canterbury, Coggan spoke of "a period in which a loss of nerve had been a prevailing attitude [in the Church]" and pleaded for "those fruits of the spirit of confidence and joy"; Pawley, *Coggan*, p. 183.
236 It was at this time that Rex Kissack, himself a Manxman, asked me if there was any chance of me being the next Bishop of Sodor and Man. I was pleased by this confidence, but it was not in my hands and I still felt committed to CTN.
237 The country had an inflation rate of over eight per cent, which had led to escalating prices and demonstrations, some with over a million protestors; at the same time OPEC restricted oil to Britain in response to the UK's support of Israel, resulting in Prime Minister Ted Heath imposing a three-day working week.
238 He was quoting Jeremiah 6:14, "the healing of my people lightly saying 'Peace, peace,' where there is no peace". Patrick Rodger was anxious that root causes should be addressed.
239 Stuart Blanch's original insistence on the CTN exercise being decided by agreement among church leaders had avoided this problem; an exercise in leadership, he called it. The new structure, however, was destined to prevent any further attempts to act together in mission.
240 Letter from the Archbishops' Council on Evangelism, 15 January 1970.
241 See letter from Pam Edis, 29 December 1972.
242 Largely due to the good offices of Stuart Blanch.

[243] After some twelve months, Martyn Halsall told the Committee that he felt unable to research the project adequately and was withdrawing. In response Stuart Blanch approached others, including the Publicity Officer; when these approaches failed, Blanch asked me to write up CTN, as someone with a good knowledge of the project. I felt quite inadequate and made it clear. Blanch, however, maintained a steady pressure on me to write, which led to the first draft of this book.

[244] Secretary General, Anglican Consultative Council.

[245] When, as Archbishop of York, Stuart Blanch suffered a relapse, it may have had its roots in this failure of a vision.

[246] These two questions were to form the basis of the National Initiative in Evangelism, following the Archbishop's Call to the Nation. The CCC, with some prophetic insight, had prepared a study guide under the editorship of Ralph Woodhall SJ.

[247] The CTN Consultation had become significant enough for the Vatican to take notice. Archbishop Bruno Heim, the Apostolic Delegate, had signified his intention of attending; however, fog at London Airport prevented his joining the consultation. The Bishop of Leeds waited in vain at Leeds Bradford Airport, on our behalf, to welcome him.

[248] Addressing his first Diocesan Synod at York.

[249] All too soon he was to die prematurely, after only twelve months in office.

[250] Pawley, *Coggan*, p. 173.

[251] As Coggan had been an Evangelical, it was generally assumed that the new appointment to York was likely to be an Anglo-Catholic.

[252] One of our local clergy, Canon Neville Black, who had been in touch with Bishop Sheppard at Woolwich, warned me that Sheppard's episcopal experience in Southwark had changed his churchmanship fundamentally. He was now very different from the committed Evangelical I had known earlier.

[253] At the time Pat Manchester's withdrawal was a great disappointment, but with hindsight I wondered if he had come to the conclusion that the pursuit of mission for the North as a Province was a lost cause, so now he had other things to do. Similarly, I was surprised when Donald Coggan, then at Canterbury, began to offer me significant parochial livings in the South, expressing surprise that I was still engaged in this northern enterprise. Again, the same factor led me to wonder if the demise of what had been

Stuart's glorious vision for the whole Christian North engaged in mission had something to do with his later temporary breakdown while at York.

254 I had personally hoped that John Habgood of Durham would have been invited to join the Nine.

255 Leading trade union figures of the period; Association of Scientific, Technical and Managerial Staffs and the National Union of Miners.

256 His place at Scargill was taken by Father Thomas Cullinen OSB, also of Ampleforth.

257 Hastings, *History*, p. 642.

258 The annual meeting was still active in 2014 and deeply appreciated by successive archbishops, as expressed to the author by John Sentamu. This was now long after the founders of CTN had passed from the scene.

259 On accepting Lord Sefton's offer of the living in 1965, I found I had inherited a fine seven-bedroom Georgian vicarage set in its own grounds, with coach house and kitchen garden. I just could not afford to live there, so moved to a farm-worker's two-bedroom cottage instead.

260 Harold Wilson announced his retirement on 5 April 1976, before he actually came to Scargill.

261 There was a clear determination to keep the Consultation's focus primarily on mission.

262 Sir Harold surprised me by relating how he had been determined to appoint David Sheppard to Liverpool (his own constituency was Liverpool, Huyton), although this had been against the advice of both Archbishops and his own ecclesiastical secretary, who had wanted Sheppard for a future vacancy in the Southern Province.

263 Speaking to the author in the autumn of 2012.

EU GPSR Authorized Representative:

LOGOS EUROPE, 9 rue Nicolas Poussin, 17000 La Rochelle, France

contact@logoseurope.eu

www.ingramcontent.com/pod-product-compliance
Lightning Source LLC
Chambersburg PA
CBHW071700160426
43195CB00012B/1534